PROFESSIONAL
KILLERS

PROFESSIONAL KILLERS

by
GORDON KERR

Futura

A *Futura* Book

First published by Futura in 2008

Copyright © Omnipress 2008

ISBN: 978-0-7088-0364-6

Produced by Omnipress Limited, UK

Printed in the EU

Futura
An imprint of
Little, Brown Book Group
100 Victoria Embankment
London EC4Y 0DY

Photo credits: Getty Images

CONTENTS

INTRODUCTION

Killing for a living is a very specialised profession. If you were to run an ad in a newspaper for a hitman, there are some specific qualities you should be looking for.

Firstly, and probably, most importantly, you would be looking for someone without a vestige of conscience or emotion. He or she kills coolly and calculatedly without stopping to think. It's just a job, after all. The moment a contract killer stops to consider the implications of a hit, or thinks too hard about his victim, his career is effectively over.

The most successful professional killers are people who kill without compunction – men like Bugsy Siegel, leading light in the Bugs and Meyer Gang that terrorised New York in the 1920s. Bugsy was a sociopath and probably also a psychopath. He was part of the infamous Murder Inc., an independent killing machine operating under the umbrella of the Mob. Mobsters could keep their hands clean by employing Bugsy or one of the other killers that made up Murder Inc. – calculating murderers such as Abner 'Longie' Zwillman, Lepke Buchalter and Dutch Schultz. Or Roy DeMeo and his Gemini Crew of hoodlums and lowlife who would kill anyone who had become an irritant and deal with the body with a ruthless efficiency a butcher would be proud of. They would dispatch the victim in a room above their 'head office' – the Gemini Lounge in Brooklyn, New York – drain the blood from it and dissect it before dumping the body parts. To do that, you could not have a conscience or any fear of the consequences of your act.

Philadelphia 'Little Nick' Scarfo had absolutely no qualms about killing. In fact, like Bugsy Siegel, he rather enjoyed it. So much so that even when he was boss he liked nothing better than to accompany his soldiers on hits. On one memorable occasion he and some of his men went after Vincent Falcone. He thought that Falcone, a partner in one of his businesses, was ripping him off. Falcone was invited to dinner at a gang hideaway where he was shot in the head, before being finished off with a bullet in the heart. In the midst of the killing, an excited Scarfo gushed to one of his henchmen, Phil Leonetti: 'I love this!'

Of course, the Mafia once had a policy of only killing their own and many Mafia hitmen held fast to the philosophy that if somebody was to be killed, he probably deserved it. Hitman Jimmy 'The Weasel' Frattiano once said: 'I didn't have much feeling. I never killed nobody that was innocent. They were all gangsters. They were killers themselves. It might bother me if I killed an innocent person, somebody that didn't deserve it. Guys that I fooled with, they were out to kill us. I couldn't kill a woman, innocent people, kids. I couldn't do that.'

Also on the list of pre-requisites in your job ad would be a capacity for relentless thoroughness and an eye for the smallest detail. The really good hitman does his homework, making a complete study of his victim, his habits, his friends and associates, the places he goes for a drink or to buy his morning paper. He will follow him for days and sometimes weeks, ascertaining what the victim's routine is, searching out potential locations for the hit, and, of course, ensuring that there is an escape route to get him away from the scene of the killing as swiftly and as calmly as possible.

Bugsy Siegel, lording it on the West Coast in the late 1930s and establishing the Mob's hold on the film and gambling businesses out there, was handed the contract to kill Harry 'Big Greenie' Greenberg, who had gone on the run from New York, firstly to Montreal in Canada and then to California. Murder Inc.'s Albert 'Tick-Tock' Tannenbaum was brought in to carry out the hit and Whitey Krakow, Bugsy's brother-in-law, and West Coast fight promoter, Frankie Carbo, were enlisted to help. They began to carefully track Big Greenie's movements, soon establishing that every evening, at exactly the same time, Greenberg would go out in his car, drive to a nearby store and buy a newspaper. The trap was set and, one evening, as he was heading for his car at exactly the same time as always, Tick-Tock was waiting for him, gun in hand. As Greenberg fell to the ground, blood oozing from several bullet holes, Tick-Tock was already on his way back to the East Coast, 2,500 miles away.

Method is critical and should be high on your list. Obviously, stab wounds or gunshot wounds make it pretty obvious that a premeditated killing has taken place. Arranged accidents are, without doubt, the best ways to dispose of someone without being caught. A preferred method of several professional killers involved that handy but deadly implement, the ice-pick. Normally used to break up ice, it is a simple tool, somewhat like a sharpened screwdriver. Used effectively – plunged into the victim's ear and deep into the brain, for example – it can kill someone instantly and fairly bloodlessly. The other benefit of the ice-pick was that it was difficult to identify the means of death. Murder Inc. operatives such as Abe 'Kid Twist' Reles and Harry 'Pittsburgh Phil' Strauss made it their dispatching tool of choice and Reles became so adept with it that his victims' cause of death was often wrongly attributed to a cerebral haemorrhage rather than an ice-pick in the ear. Fortunately, post-mortem techniques have vastly improved from the early decades of the 20th century or the ice-pick would probably be selling in greater quantities!

One last point for your ad for a killer to do your dirty work: it helps greatly if the perpetrator is not connected with you in any way. The Mafia were particularly good at this and even the St Valentine's Day Massacre – probably the most famous hit of all – was carried out by a team mainly made up of hired guns from outside Chicago. Using hitmen unconnected to you can bamboozle the authorities and will confuse anyone who wants to exact revenge on you for the hit. They are sure you did it, but, then again, why was Joe Schmo from that city 300 miles away involved? Did the victim have something else going on of which they were unaware? And while they puzzle, you walk away scot-free.

So, you have advertised for your professional killer. But, who is going to come knocking on your door in reponse to your ad?

There are a number of different types. Your applicants are more often than not going to be male. There have not been many female pros. Colombian cocaine queen, Griselda Blanco, undoubtedly the most ruthless female criminal in history, was an exception, an extraordinary woman who ruled an empire of drugs and death. The Indian bandit, Phoolan Devi, was another, but she was a killer taking revenge on society for the horrific abuses she had suffered. Britain's only female contract killer to date, Te Rangimaria Ngarimu, was a rank amateur, killing a villain for the money to return to her native New Zealand. But the amateur is a category of professional killer to be avoided at all costs. More often than not, he will already be involved in criminality, probably of a low-level kind. This, in itself, presents several problems, making the likelihood of being caught all the more probable. Firstly, he is likely to be already known to the police for his other activities. With DNA and the other forensic techniques available these days, one small error, one tiny detail will be enough to bring the law down on him and, eventually, you. And that is the second point – mistakes. The amateur, by his nature, is not going to carry out the action with the cold efficiency of the professional and he is usually caught.

So, only hire the consummate professional. You will not have to do more than brief him, give him his money and wait. Within the time required to get it right, he will make his move, carry out his action and fade into the scenery as quickly as he emerged from it. He will be gone. Job done.

PART ONE

KILLERS
FOR
THE MOB

AL CAPONE

Sometimes it is hard to remember that Al Capone really did exist and was not the work of a crime writer, so all-pervasive is he in the public consciousness. With his smooth suits, silk ties, fedora and gruesomely scarred face, he was the embodiment of the American gangster.

His beginnings were slightly different to those of many of the children of Italian immigrants. His father, Gabriele, arrived in America in 1894, from the village of Castellmare di Stabia, 16 miles south of Naples. Gabriele was a barber who could read and write Italian and he was accompanied by his pregnant, 27-year-old wife, Teresa, two-year-old son, Vincenzo and baby son, Raffaele. His ambition in the new world was to earn enough money to open his own barbershop.

The family started out in an apartment in a slum area of Brooklyn, near the Brooklyn Navy Yard, but Gabriele's ability to read and write got him a job in a grocery store, while Teresa took in sewing work. Her third son, Salvatore, was born in 1895 and her fourth on 17 January 1899. He was named Alphonse Gabriel Capone.

When Gabriele eventually opened his barbershop, in Park Avenue in Brooklyn, he moved the family in above it. This area was more cosmopolitan than the one in which they had previously been staying and young Al, as he called himself, mixed with Irish, Germans, Swedes and Chinese, an international experience that benefited him later in life when he ran his crime empire.

Al went to school from the age of five, but at the age of 14 he was hit by a woman teacher and retaliated. He was expelled, bringing his formal education to an abrupt end. Crucially, around this time, the family moved to Garfield Place where Capone would meet some formative influences – his wife, an Irishwoman called Mae, and the mobster, Johnny Torrio.

Torrio was a new breed of hoodlum; something of a criminal visionary, and Capone noted carefully how he ran his affairs – numbers racketeering, brothels and prostitution – like a business enterprise. It was Torrio who would invent the concept of the National Crime Syndicate in the 1930s. He was a role model for local boys, including Capone who earned pocket money by running errands for him. He won Torrio's trust and was given more to do. Meanwhile, Capone learned the art of appearing, like Torrio, respectable to the outside world while being involved in the world of organised criminality.

When Torrio moved to Chicago in 1909, other forces began to influence the ten-year-old Capone. He started running with street gangs, the South Brooklyn Rippers, the Forty Thieves Juniors and the Five Point Juniors, but there was no real sign yet of the criminal mastermind he would turn into in years to come. He lived at home and worked diligently to help the family, first in a munitions factory and then as a paper cutter. He was a quiet boy who did not stand out.

When he met Frankie Yale, a young man of Calabrian origin, Capone really began to change. Frankie was a tough nut who saw violence as the only way to get ahead in life. He had opened a bar on Coney Island and, on Johnny Torrio's advice, took Capone on as a bartender.

Yale was ambitious and had his eyes on the Chicago criminal empire run by old-time gangster, 'Big' Jim Colosimo. In May 1920, he made his move, shooting Colosimo dead in his restaurant, but he failed to get his hands on the business and Johnny Torrio, who had been working for 'Big' Jim, took it for himself. Prohibition was adding a huge boost to criminal earnings and Torrio could add income from speakeasies to what he was already earning from thousands of brothels and gambling joints.

Torrio introduced the 22-year-old Al Capone to this world and, before long, he was his partner rather than his employee. He ran the Four Deuces, a combination speakeasy, gambling joint and whorehouse, and his brother Ralph arrived to work with him. Meanwhile, Al made friends with Jack Guzik who would become a lifelong friend. From a Jewish Orthodox family that earned its living through prostitution, Guzik was like a big brother to Al.

Married now to Mae, with a son called Sonny, he was going up in the world and bought a house for his family in a respectable neighbourhood. To his neighbours, he was a second-hand furniture dealer.

But things changed when Chicago's corrupt mayor, 'Big Bill' Thompson, was succeeded by the earnest reformer, William E. Dever. Graft became more difficult, forcing Torrio to decide that they should move their operations out of Chicago. The suburb of Cicero seemed ideal. There they could easily buy up the entire city government and police department. Capone was put in charge of establishing the operation in Cicero and managed it with little opposition. His older brother Frank (Salvatore) handled the city government, Ralph managed the opening of a working-class brothel called the Stockade and Al put his energies into the gambling side of the business, investing in a new gambling joint, the Ship. At the same time he took control of Hawthorne Race Track.

On municipal election day in 1924, Capone's men did what they could to stop opposition candidates having any chance of success, kidnapping workers, stealing ballot boxes and threatening voters with violence. News spread of their activities and the Chicago Police Chief decided to intervene. He sent 79 armed police officers in plain clothes and driving unmarked cars to Cicero. This convoy approached Frank Capone as he walked down the street. They recognised him and opened fire on him, riddling his body with bullets. They called it self-defence since Frank pulled a gun when he saw the cops approach carrying guns.

Al was furious but, in spite of the best efforts of the authorities, the day was won and Cicero was his. He threw the most lavish funeral ever seen in the town for his brother. The flowers alone cost $20,000.

For five weeks, Capone exercised restraint, but after Joe Howard, a small-time thug, assaulted his friend Jack Guzik when Guzik refused him a loan, Capone tracked Howard down in a bar. Howard was stupid enough to call Al a 'dago pimp' and Al, in a rage, shot him dead. William H. McSwiggin, known as 'the hanging prosecutor', went after Capone for the murder but witnesses seemed to develop memory loss as soon as the name Capone was mentioned. He got away with it, but the case gave him notoriety very different to the discreet anonymity sought by Johnny Torrio and his ilk.

Al Capone was now 25 and a powerful and wealthy man. He was also acutely aware that he was in the sights not just of the law, but also of rival mobsters who wanted a piece of his action.

Dion O'Banion was one such. He had a growing florist and bootlegging business but was a dangerously unstable individual who killed on a whim. Torrio and Capone often had to make peace amongst rival gangs who were their allies and when O'Banion went to war with the Genna brothers, O'Banion provided Torrio with a solution. He said he would retire if Torrio would buy his brewery from him. Knowing that there was going to be a raid at the brewery, O'Banion arranged a meeting there with Torrio. During the raid, Torrio was arrested and O'Banion refused to give back the money Torrio had paid him. A big mistake.

Not long after Torrio's arrest, a large funeral was taking place for the head of the Unione Siciliana in Chicago, Mike Merlo. When three gangsters walked into his florist shop, O'Banion thought they had merely come to collect a wreath. He reached out his hand to shake theirs and one of the men, knowing that the florist always kept one hand free to grab one of the guns he kept in three special pockets tailored into his suits, grabbed his free arm. Six gunshots later, O'Banion lay on the floor in a pool of blood. No one was ever charged with his murder.

However, a couple of O'Banion's associates, 'Hymie' Weiss and 'Bugs' Moran, were convinced they knew who was ultimately responsible and from then on, Johnny Torrio and Al Capone had to take careful precautions. Torrio even left Chicago for a while which was not a bad idea as, during the next two years, there were a dozen attempts on Capone's life, in spite of the two bodyguards who accompanied him everywhere he went and the fact that he travelled only at night.

When Torrio returned to the city in January 1925, Moran and Weiss struck. As he left his car to walk to the door of his apartment building they attacked, shooting him in the chest, neck, right arm and groin. Moran then put his gun to Torrio's head and pulled the trigger to finish him off. But the gun was empty and all Torrio heard was the click of the hammer. He was rushed to hospital where Capone organised security for him, even sleeping on a cot in his room to ensure his old friend was safe.

The incident understandably made a deep impression on Torrio and he was never the same man again.

While serving a nine-month sentence for the brewery arrest, he made the decision to get out of organised crime. He called Capone to the prison and handed over all his assets – brothels, nightclubs, gambling joints, breweries and speakeasies.

Capone was now a force to be reckoned with and a very wealthy one at that. He moved his headquarters into a suite at the Metropole Hotel at a cost of $1,500 a day and suddenly he was famous. He was advised by newspaper editor, Harry Read, to cultivate political connections and become more visible. He was seen at the opera, he attended sporting events and charitable functions. He became almost respectable. After all, he was only a bootlegger and everybody drank.

He was still no angel, though. In December 1925, Frankie Yale invited him to a Christmas Day party at one of his speakeasies, the Adonis Club. He told Capone that he had learned that a rival, Richard 'Peg-Leg' Lonergan, planned to gatecrash the party with his men and suggested cancelling. Capone told him to let the party go ahead and organised a surprise Christmas present for Lonergan. When the gate-crashers burst into the club at around 3 a.m., Capone calmly gave a signal and Lonergan's men did not even have time to pull their guns out before being peppered with bullets.

By early 1926, Capone was on top of his game. In

the New Yorker magazine, he had been described as 'the greatest gang leader in history' and he had done a deal with Yale that would completely change the interstate transportation of bootleg whisky. In April of that year, however, he made his first mistake. He heard that a rival bootlegger, Jim Doherty, was drinking in Cicero. This represented a territorial insult to Capone. What he did not know, however, was that Doherty was in the company of 'the hanging prosecutor', Billy McSwiggin.

Capone and his men waited for Doherty outside the bar in which he was carousing and when he staggered out in the company of others, they opened fire with machine guns. Doherty and McSwiggin were killed, creating a huge outcry against gangster violence and especially against Al Capone who, it was widely believed, had been behind the killings. But there was no evidence to implicate Capone and officials and police were embarrassed by the fact that he still walked the streets. The police took revenge, launching a series of raids on his establishments and forcing Capone into hiding while detectives scoured the country and beyond for him, their searches stretching as far as Canada and Italy. All the time, he was with friends in Michigan, reconsidering his life, thinking of giving up his criminal activities, of using his fortune to pursue legitimate business enterprises.

As a first step, he negotiated his surrender to Chicago police, returning in July 1926 to Chicago to face the murder charges that were stacked up against him. Amazingly, the authorities failed to establish enough evidence to bring him to trial and they had to set him free. Back in business, Al sought to make his peace with Hymie Weiss who was still smarting over Dion O'Banion's demise. Capone offered him a favourable business deal, but Weiss turned it down. The following day Hymie Weiss was gunned down.

As people became more and more disgusted by the violence on their streets, Capone held a bizarre, highly publicised press conference, at which he appealed to fellow bootleggers to end the violence. 'There is enough business for all of us without killing each other like animals in the streets. I don't want to die in the street punctured by machine-gun fire,' he said. An amnesty was negotiated whereby it was agreed there would be no further murders or beatings and for two months it held. Then, in January 1927, a friend of Capone, Theodore 'Tony the Greek' Anton, was killed and they were back where they started.

May 1927 saw the return to power of the corrupt 'Big Bill' Thompson but a decision in the Supreme Court put new pressure on bootleggers and especially on Capone. It stated that income tax should be paid even on illegally-derived revenues. This meant that the

Internal Revenue Service (IRS) was now in a position to pursue Al Capone and his money. Capone was unconcerned, however, and carried on much as before, becoming a jazz impresario with the opening of his famous Cotton Club. He seemed to have no prejudices, either racial or social, and helped the careers of many black musicians, including Louis Armstrong.

But they were closing in on him, and wherever he went the police were not far away. When he travelled, he found police at every station en route. They surrounded his house and repeatedly arrested him for the smallest things. He was hounded. Meanwhile, the IRS was making a detailed investigation of his income and expenditure, no easy task as all his business was conducted through third parties and every transaction he made was conducted with cash.

Frankie Yale was becoming a problem to Capone. Their whisky deal was not working as envisaged and there were numerous hijackings, for which Capone thought Yale was probably responsible. On Sunday, 1 July 1928, Yale was drinking in a Brooklyn speakeasy when he was called to the telephone. Whatever he was told on the phone sent him running out to his car. He drove off, but minutes later, as he drove along Forty-fourth Street, he was pushed to the kerb by a black sedan and sprayed by a hail of bullets from several different types of gun – revolvers, sawn-off shotguns and machine guns. Problem solved.

Capone moved from the Metropole to a special suite with its own kitchen at the Lexington Hotel. He had secret doors installed, in case he needed to make a swift exit. Now, seeing the end of Prohibition approaching, he was beginning to invest in other rackets such as unions and protection.

However, Bugs Moran was still a blot on Capone's landscape. He had twice tried to kill a friend of Capone's, Jack 'Machine Gun' McGurn. Capone agreed that Moran should be assassinated and gave the task to McGurn who put together a crew consisting of some top out-of-town mobsters, Fred 'Killer' Burke, James Ray, John Scalise, Albert Anselmi, Joseph Lolordo and, from Detroit's Purple Gang, Harry and Phil Keywell. They would take part in the most famous incident in gangster history.

The date for the hit was to be Thursday, 14 February, Valentine's Day. Moran and his henchmen were to be lured to a garage to buy whisky. Four of McGurn's men would be waiting for them there, dressed in stolen police uniforms and trench coats in order to look as if they were raiding the place.

A man who resembled Moran was spotted by the Keywells and four of the phoney cops went into the garage where they found seven men. They took the men's guns and lined them up against the wall. They then opened fire with two machine guns. All were killed apart from Frank Gutenberg who was still breathing.

Two of the killers were then marched at gunpoint out of the garage in their trench coats as if they had been arrested by the other two. They got into a stolen police car and drove off.

There was one small problem. Bugs Moran was not one of the dead men. He had been late for the meeting and, seeing the stolen police car outside the garage, had driven past the scene. When police arrived, they found Frank Gutenberg still alive and asked him who had shot him. He replied: 'No one. Nobody shot me.' He died shortly afterwards.

Everyone knew that Moran had been the intended target and that Capone was behind it, but there was nothing to connect him to the killings. He had been in Florida, after all. The Valentine's Day Massacre received massive publicity on a national scale and Capone became the subject of countless books and newspaper articles. He loved the notoriety, employing noted journalist and short story writer, Damon Runyan, as his press agent. President Herbert Hoover announced that the federal agencies were focusing all their efforts on Capone and his associates.

But, Capone had other fish to fry. Three men, Albert

Anselmi, Giuseppe 'Joseph Hop Toad' Giunta and John Scalise, were causing him problems. So he arranged a meeting with them over a lavish dinner. They ate and drank until midnight, but when Capone pushed his chair away from the table, they realised, as he began to speak of their disloyalty, that they were in big trouble. They had forgotten the old Sicilian tradition of hospitality before execution and, worst of all, they had stupidly left their guns in the cloakroom.

Capone's bodyguards jumped on them, tying them to their chairs with wire and gagging them. Capone picked up a baseball bat, walked the length of the table and stood behind one of the men. He swung the bat, smashing the man's shoulders, arms and chest. He then did the same to each of his other guests, reducing them to a pulp. One of his bodyguards then shot each of the three in the back of the head.

The Valentine's Day Massacre and the subsequent publicity forced the US government to launch a plan to attack Capone on two fronts -- firstly, through Treasury agents searching for evidence of tax evasion and secondly, to gather evidence of breaches of the Prohibition laws. Prohibition Agent Eliot Ness, was the man charged with the second task and he put together a team of young agents to carry it out known as 'the Untouchables' because they were impervious to bribery.

Meanwhile, at a conference in Atlantic City in May 1929, the Mob was reorganising in an effort to stop the territorial battles that had become the norm. As part of this, Capone was ordered to hand over his interests to Johnny Torrio to divide up. Capone, of course, had no intention of doing anything of the kind.

After the conference he went to a movie but, on leaving the cinema, he was approached by two detectives who arrested him for carrying a concealed weapon. He was convicted and sent to prison where he remained until the following March. On his release, he was enraged to find that he had been made Public Enemy Number One on a new list compiled by the Chicago Crime Commission, adapted by J. Edgar Hoover, head of the FBI, as a list of the Most Wanted criminals.

Things began to get increasingly difficult. His brother, Ralph, was convicted on tax evasion charges in October 1930, and Ness and his 'Untouchables' began raiding and closing down Capone breweries at will.

By now, the government had succeeded in infiltrating Capone's organisation and one agent discovered that when one of his establishments had been raided years previously, a ledger had been taken that contained information that could bring Capone's empire tumbling down. Miraculously, Capone had not killed the two bookkeepers responsible for the ledgers after the raid had taken place and the man on the inside learned their names. When they were tracked down, both men agreed to cooperate.

Ness, for his part, was out to humiliate Capone. During their raids on Capone's breweries, the Untouchables had captured dozens of Capone's trucks which were to be auctioned. Ness called the Lexington and managed to be put through to Capone. 'Well, Snorkey,' he sneered, using a nickname only the gangster's close friends dared use, 'I just wanted to tell you that if you look out your front windows down onto Michigan Avenue at exactly 11 o'clock you'll see something that should interest you.' Capone was puzzled and slammed the phone down, but was horrified when at 11, all his trucks slowly drove past the hotel in convoy. He was incandescent with rage.

In spring 1931, the US government started to move. An indictment was returned against Capone for a tax liability of $32,488.81. In June, a second indictment was returned on 22 counts of tax evasion totalling over $200,000. A third arrived a week later. Ness and his team provided evidence that charged Capone and 68 of his gang with 5,000 separate violations of the Volstead Act, the law that had introduced Prohibition. On the day the trial started, the judge was full of surprises. Realising that there had been efforts to bribe jurors, he arrived in court and ordered that the jury that was to deliberate on the Capone case should be swapped with a jury in another courtroom. Capone was horrified. Worse still, he had pleaded guilty, believing he and his lawyers had a deal with the authorities that would get him a light sentence but the judge was having none of it. Instead of the two-year sentence he had been expecting, he was sentenced to 11 years, fined $50,000 and ordered to pay costs of $30,000. To add insult to injury, as he left the court, an IRS official slapped papers on him announcing that the government was seizing property belonging to him, in lieu of tax. Capone tried to attack him but was restrained.

He went to Atlanta Prison, a tough federal facility, where he enjoyed special privileges. But, in August 1934, he was sent to the new Alcatraz Prison in San Francisco Bay where his privileges ended. He seemed to bear up well, but his health did not. He had contracted syphilis as a young man and it developed into neurosyphilis. By 1938 dementia had set in and the man who had once commanded a huge crime empire went into serious decline.

He was released in November 1939, spending his first six months of freedom in hospital. His health slowly got worse and he was cared for by his wife,

Mae. Finally, Al Capone, the most famous gangster of all, died of cardiac arrest, aged 48, on 25 January 1947 with his family at his bedside.

BUGSY SIEGEL

The eyeball rolled like a blue marble across the room, coming to a halt 15 feet from the socket in which it had spent the past 42 years, staring back eerily at the scene of carnage. It was the first shot that had done it, hitting him in that handsome head of his as he lolled on Virginia's chintz sofa, reading the newspaper. Another four bullets slammed into his body one after the other, smashing his ribs and destroying his lungs. Three bullets went wide of the target, but the five that hit him were more than enough. At 42 years of age, Benjamin 'Bugsy Siegel' Siegelbaum was as dead as they come.

The hit signalled the end of a career that stretched from the crime-ridden slums of Brooklyn to ownership of a 35-room Hollywood mansion and the company of film stars and celebrities. A lot of blood had flowed during that time – much of it caused by Bugsy – but, out in the Nevada desert, stands his memorial, a shimmering complex of hotels and casinos, a Mecca for gamblers, the city of Las Vegas.

The trouble with Bugsy was also what made him a guy you wanted to have around. If a sociopath is a person who has no sense of responsibility, lacks moral sense and guilt and displays no change in behaviour after punishment, then Bugsy was a sociopath. He used people, believed that is what they were there for. Robbery, rape, murder – it did not matter to him. But, as his partner in crime Meyer Lansky once said: 'When we were in a fight, Benny would never hesitate. He was even quicker to take action than those hot-blooded Sicilians, the first to start punching and shooting. Nobody reacted faster than Benny.'

And that's how he earned the nickname 'Bugsy', a term used by gangsters for men who show no fear or who are willing to do jobs that others balk at. Nonetheless, Bugsy hated the name, although it was a term of endearment, and it would not have been wise to use it to his face. Probably best to stick to plain 'Mister Siegel'.

Just under six feet tall, black-haired and blue-eyed, Bugsy Siegel was the prototype racketeer and when his friend George Raft played gangster roles in films, it was hard to tell whether he was copying Bugsy or whether Benny, in his life, was copying Raft.

Growing up in Brooklyn's Williamsburg area was tough in the early 1900s. Irish, Jewish and Italian émigrés huddled together in dire conditions of poverty and disease, desperately trying to make a go of life in the land of the free. It was there that Benjamin

Siegelbaum was born, in 1902, to poor immigrant Russian parents. He did not intend to stay poor for long and by his early teens he had devised his first racket, charging protection money from street vendors.

Around this time, the young Benny bumped into the man who would not only change his life, he would also be instrumental in ending it – the teenage Meyer Lansky, a Polish Jew who would join Bugsy in assembling a notorious gang of ruthless thugs and killers, known as the Bugs and Meyer Mob.

There are various stories of how the two met. One says that Lansky rescued Bugsy from a beating by an equally young Charles 'Lucky' Luciano after Bugsy had been caught having a fling with a prostitute who worked for Luciano. Another says that Lansky stopped Siegel from shooting someone at a pavement craps game just as the police were about to arrive, saving him from arrest.

However they met, Lansky was a bright kid, later known as 'the Brain', who recognised that Jewish boys on the make needed to organise themselves in the same way that the Irish and Italian kids had. So, he formed a gang and its first member was Benny Siegel. 'I told little Benny that he could be my number two,' Lansky recalled years later. 'He was young but very brave. His big problem was that he was always ready to rush in first and shoot – to act without thinking.'

Another gang member, Doc Stather, remembers: 'Bugsy never hesitated when danger threatened. While we tried to figure out what the best move was, Bugsy was already shooting. When it came to action there was no one better. I've never known a man who had more guts.'

The gang contained men who would later become some of America's most notorious gangsters – Abner 'Longie' Zwillman, Lepke Buchalter, future head of the infamous Murder Inc. – the only Mob leader to ever die in the electric chair – and Arthur Flegenheimer, later to achieve fame as Dutch Schultz.

Meyer soon realised that it would be better to have the Sicilian gangs on his side. So he and Charlie 'Lucky' Luciano, began forge an invaluable link.

It was for Luciano, in fact, that Bugs and Meyer carried out their first hit. Lucky was released from prison after serving six months of a one-year sentence for dealing narcotics, wanting revenge on the 19-year-old son of an Irish cop who had set him up. Lansky told him to relax; he and Benny would take care of it. They waited a year to let the dust settle and then instructed Luciano to get out of town, take a vacation. Not long after, the Irish cop's son disappeared and a massive manhunt was launched. Of course, Luciano was hauled in for questioning, but his alibi was watertight. The boy's body was never found.

When a woman told Luciano, Lansky and Bugsy that she knew about the boy's disappearance, trying to extort money from them to stop her going to the cops, the trio broke into her apartment and beat her savagely. Unfortunately, the police walked in on them and they were arrested. The woman was frightened enough not to show up in court, however, and the case was dropped.

When Siegel bumped into the same woman eight years later in a bar, she made the mistake of telling him that they had been wet behind the ears back then and wouldn't have known what to do with her, anyway. Bugsy decided to show her just how much he had grown up. He followed her home, dragged her into an alley and raped her. Again he was arrested and again the case never came to court.

By 1919, the Bugsy and Meyer Mob was making its money from floating crap games, trade unions and robbery. They were working in partnership with Luciano and his henchman Frank Costello, and showed no mercy towards anyone who stood in their way. Luciano and Lansky were inventing a new kind of racketeering. Never before had Sicilians and Jews worked together in this way.

But it was in the big time that their ambitions lay. They wisely put aside money from their robberies and their craps and protection rackets to be used at a later date to help them progress their ambitions. That money was invested in established bookmaking businesses and also found its way into the pockets of Lower East Side politicians and policemen who could provide them with protection to carry on their business.

Gradually they began to be an irritant to the real Mob bosses uptown who wanted to elbow in on the action. Mafia don Joe 'The Boss' Masseria demanded tribute payments from them. Joe was a gangster of the old school and wanted the Bugsy and Meyer Mob under his control. Anyway, the money would come in handy in his bid to become *capo di tutti capi* (boss of bosses) following the imprisonment of the incumbent, Lupo 'The Wolf' Saietta. But Bugsy and Meyer were not ready to hand over their hard-earned business to Masseria, letting him know by wiping out his soldiers in a huge fight, sending Masseria a clear message that the Lower East Side was not up for grabs.

When the Volstead Act became law in 1919 making the manufacture and sale of alcohol illegal in the United States, it was a red-letter day for racketeers everywhere, but especially for Luciano, Lansky and Siegel.

Arnold Rothstein, a major player in New York's organised crime world, was amongst the first to see the potential. He called in Luciano, Lansky and Bugsy and proposed that a bootlegging business be set up to provide good whisky for his high-class casinos. The operation involved Dutch Schultz, Longy Zwillman, Joe Adonis, Vito Genovese and Albert Anastasia, as well as the Bugsy and Meyer Mob.

Siegel and Lansky opened a car and truck rental business in a garage on Cannon Street, Brooklyn, as a cover and Bugsy became the mainstay of the bootlegging business, driving shipments of illegal hootch or, better still, hijacking it from another gang. Needless to say, Meyer, never one to miss out on an opportunity, also made the rental business work and that, too, brought in cash.

Their war with Joe Masseria continued and Bugsy and Lansky struck him a major blow when they ambushed a convoy of his trucks, carrying bootleg hootch, near Atlantic City. The booze was being transported from Masseria's boats to Irving Wexler, also known as Waxey Gordon, another partner of Rothstein. This venture was not without danger for Bugsy and Lansky. Waxey Gordon was an important and powerful player, the boss of Philadelphia, and he would be far from pleased to lose his whisky. Masseria, himself, had an army of 200 men. In addition, they were also two-timing Rothstein who had forbidden the people working for him from stealing from each other. The consequences could prove to be fatal.

The convoy stopped at a tree that Bugsy and his

men had felled across the road and as soon as Waxey's men climbed out of their cabs to move it, they came under fire. Three of them fell in the ensuing gun battle and when the survivors surrendered, they were beaten savagely. However, although Meyer Lansky was recognised by one of the beaten men, word never got back to Rothstein. Waxey did not want him to find out he was working with the Sicilians. Bugsy and Meyer lived to fight another day but Waxey, like Masseria, would not forget.

Business was booming by 1920 and Siegel, Lansky and Luciano moved into Chicago after sending Brooklyn mobster Frankie Yale to put a bullet in the head of the city's boss, 'Big Jim' Colosimo. Johnny Torrio and Al Capone, who took over there, were reluctant to get into the bootlegging business and invited Bugsy and Lansky and Luciano to do it. Profits were split and everyone was happy.

From about 1927 to 1931, the warring factions in New York went head to head and the Castellamarese War, as it came to be called, between Masseria and Sal Maranzano would define organised crime in America for decades to come. When Luciano changed his sympathies and went over to Maranzano's side, he did so on the understanding that he would deal with Joe Masseria once and for all.

On 15 April 1931, he invited Masseria to Scarpato's Restaurant in Coney Island. Towards the end of the meal, Luciano excused himself and went to the gents. As he closed the door, four gunmen burst into the room, guns blazing. They were Albert Anastasia, Vito Genovese, Joe Adonis and, leading the charge as ever, Bugsy Siegel. Masseria was hit six times and another 14 bullets lodged themselves in the restaurant walls.

Charlie Luciano completed his rise by rubbing out Sal Maranzano. After all, if he had not killed Maranzano, Maranzano would have killed him. That was the way it worked.

In 1934, when Dutch Schultz was being hotly pursued by New York City Prosecutor Tom Dewey, he lost the empire he had built since his days in the early Bugsy and Meyer Mob. The new man in charge was Bo Weinberg, another alumnus of the gang and the man Bugsy had recruited to kill Sal Maranzano on Luciano's behalf. Dutch was, understandably, furious. He explained his problem to Bugsy who offered to help his old friend.

Bugsy invited Weinberg to dinner but, on the way to the restaurant, stopped his car on a dark, empty street. He got out, went round to the passenger side, threw open the door and began beating Weinberg with his pistol. He then pulled a knife and stabbed the dazed

Weinberg, a schoolboy friend, in the throat. Bugsy was nothing if not meticulous in his killing and, having learned that intestinal gases often made a corpse float, he made sure he stabbed him in the abdomen to release those gasses. After that, it is likely that Bo ended up in the East River, but no one knows as his body was never found.

Not long after this, Waxey Gordon, by this time in prison, decided it was time to get even with Bugsy and Lansky. He hired the Fabrazzo brothers who planted a bomb in the fireplace of the Bugsy and Meyer Mob's Grand Street hideout. But Bugsy spotted the device and managed to throw it out of a window just before it exploded, escaping with only minor injuries. It did not take him long to catch up with the perpetrators. Andy Fabrazzo's body was later found in a sack in North Jersey and his brother Louis was gunned down in Manhattan.

The third brother, Tony, had not been involved in the hit, but just in case, he threatened to write his memoirs which would be delivered to the police in the event of anything happening to him. The Mob was concerned, but Bugsy decided to take matters into his own hands. First of all, he set about creating an alibi for himself.

In autumn 1932, he told his friends that he was ill and exhausted and in need of rest. He admitted himself to a local Catholic hospital and for the first few days lapped up the treatment. One night, however, he told a nurse he was going to bed early and did not want to be disturbed.

As soon as she left the room, so did Bugsy, by the fire escape, a couple of pillows stuffed under the covers to deceive anyone looking in into thinking he was still in bed. He met a couple of his guys and they drove to Tony Fabrazzo's house. When Fabrazzo came to the door he failed to recognise them, although he should have, given that he had acted as back-up when Bugsy had shot Vincent 'Mad Dog' Coll in a phone booth. Bugs wasted no time. He gunned down Fabrazzo in front of his mother and father.

The murder was a bad call, however. Fabrazzo's friends knew Bugsy had done it, even though he had his alibi. Added to this were the facts that Dewey was beginning to turn his beady eye on the Bugs and Meyer Mob and, in the years following the killing, cracks began to appear in Bugsy's friendship with Lansky. Bugsy was sick of playing second fiddle to the much smarter and more plausible Lansky. Four years after Fabrazzo's death, he was in trouble.

The Syndicate met to discuss him and could have been forgiven for deciding he was becoming too much of a liability. Instead, they decided to give him a break and send him out to the West Coast where the Mob's influence was nowhere near as great as in the east.

Bugsy arrived in California with his wife and kids and bought a $200,000 mansion in the upmarket area of Holmby Hills. He began moving in elite circles, hanging out with George Raft, an old friend from Williamsburg who had become a major movie star. Raft was a ticket for Bugsy into the high-octane world of Hollywood's movie stars and starlets. With his suave good looks, he began to occupy the gossip columns, being seen attending parties and premieres. He fell for a French actress, Ketti Gallian, and romanced a whole parade of starlets, including Jean Harlow.

But he was also busy during the day. He saw the unions as a big opportunity for the Mob, especially the extras union. Without extras the studio bosses had no movies and if they wanted extras, they had to pay Bugsy. He hit on actors too, sidling up to them at parties and telling them that if they wanted their next movie to happen, it would cost '$10,000 for the extras'.

In 1939, Harry 'Big Greenie' Greenberg had gone on the run when Tom Dewey had set his sights on him. The Syndicate wanted him killed because he knew too much and Lepke Buchalter, Bugsy's old boss in Murder Inc., asked Bugsy to help an associate, Allie Tannenbaum, to make the hit. But Bugsy, against the advice of all his friends, wanted to be directly involved in the contract.

Doc Stather writes: 'We all begged Bugsy to keep out of the shooting. He was too big a man by this time to become personally involved. But Bugsy wouldn't listen. He said Greenberg was a menace to all of us and if the cops grabbed him he could tell the whole story of our outfit back to the 1920s.' In truth, though, Bugsy wanted to be part of it just because he enjoyed killing.

The hit had problems from the start, but eventually 'Tick-Tock' Tannenbaum made Murder Inc.'s first hit on the West Coast. Later, Bugsy was arrested and acquitted for the murder of Greenberg, but in the course of the trial his reputation was torn to shreds, his sordid past exposed for the world to read about in the Californian papers.

His work on the West Coast also involved illegal wire services that gave the results of races before they were actually announced. He was making $25,000 a month from it but, inevitably, the Syndicate back in New York told him it would take the profits from now on. He told them to keep their hands off and, with that, probably began the process that would lead to his eventual elimination.

He had one last hurrah, though.

Las Vegas, back in the early 1940s when Bugsy first visited it, consisted of no more than a couple of dude ranches and resorts. It was searingly hot in summer and in the middle of nowhere. It did have one thing going for it, though. In 1931, the Nevada legislature had legalised gambling to raise revenue. In the 1940s, it also legalised off-track betting on horse races. That was what interested Bugsy. And opening a legitimate casino in Vegas had unheard of potential for making money for the Mob.

Siegel called his casino-hotel the Flamingo. It would be Las Vegas's most luxurious hotel by some way and it was hoped would bring customers down from the swanky watering holes in Reno. His dream was an oasis in the desert to which gamblers from both coasts would flock for fun and the finest entertainment.

But the Flamingo project had an inauspicious start. It was difficult and expensive to get building materials to and from Vegas and Bugsy, a gangster after all and not a construction expert, lost control of it. Materials would be brought in the front gate and driven straight out the back to be delivered again, and paid for again. The million dollars he had initially obtained from his Mob friends grew to six million. Lansky, Luciano and other investors became uneasy. Some had even used their own savings, persuaded by Bugsy's vision of quick profits and untold riches.

By 1946, the Flamingo had still not opened and Bugsy was asking for more and more money. Finally, at a Havana conference on 22 December that year, attended by the biggest names in the gangster pantheon – Meyer Lansky, Frank Costello, Lucky Luciano, Vito Genovese, Joe Bonnano, Albert Anastasia and Joey Adonis, amongst others – Lansky dispensed some bad news. Bugsy had been skimming from the cash provided by the Mob for the Flamingo. He was thought to be depositing it in Swiss bank accounts, ready to flee if all did not go according to plan. The Syndicate turned to Lansky for his opinion on what they should do. Lansky reluctantly told them that Bugsy had to be hit, a motion passed unanimously by the assembled mobsters. The contract was given to Charlie Fischetti but Lansky provided his old friend with a stay of execution, persuading the conference that the contract should be delayed until after the opening of the casino – Boxing Day – to see what happened. Who knows, he suggested, it might even be a huge success and they could get Siegel to pay back the money.

So, although he did not know it, Bugsy's fate would be decided by the success or failure of the Flamingo. Unfortunately, however, in spite of top-notch entertainment – George Raft, Jimmy Durante, Xavier Cugat's orchestra, all big names back then – and the presence at the opening of movie stars Clark Gable, Lana Turner, Joan Crawford and many more, the Flamingo was an unadulterated flop. After the second day, the one-arm bandits were more or less silent and the gaming tables were empty. 'We worked to 9 or 10 people a night for the rest of the two week engagement,' the actress Rose Marie said. 'The locals just didn't come out to the Flamingo. They were used to cowboy boots, not rhinestones.'

It was with a heavy heart that Lansky reported the troubling situation in Las Vegas and the Syndicate responded by demanding the fulfilment of the contract. Nonetheless, he gained another stay of execution and the Flamingo limped along until Bugsy closed it to enable the hotel part of his complex to be finished.

It reopened in March and by May it had started to work, returning a profit of $250,000. But it was all too late for the Syndicate

On 20 June 1947, Bugsy had just returned from having a manicure and a haircut. He felt good as he sank into the comfortable chintz sofa in his living room to read the papers. Things were getting better – his daughters were coming out to spend the summer with him and the Flamingo was finally proving him right. The money was pouring in.

Outside, in the garden, Charlie Fischetti squeezed the trigger of his .30-06 Springfield rifle and the sound of gunfire shattered the hot Las Vegas evening.

VITO GENOVESE

As his ship slid into New York Harbour from Naples in 1912, did Vito Genovese even then, at the age of 15, staring at the Statue of Liberty and the high-rise buildings of Manhattan, conceive the burning ambition to climb to the top of the heap, and to achieve it by whatever means necessary? From humble beginnings, he clambered up the greasy pole until he looked down on all of them, the ones who survived his fight for success.

When his family arrived in the New World in 1912, they quickly established themselves in the Queens area of New York, his father starting a small contracting business. For Vito it was not nearly enough, however. He was in a hurry to be someone and needed more excitement in his life. Soon, he moved out and went to live with relatives in the much more cosmopolitan and vibrant Little Italy in Lower Manhattan.

He started hanging around with a bad crowd as a youngster and, aged 20, had his first brush with authority when he was sent to jail for 60 days for carrying a gun. It was 1917. It was a slight hiccup, but his relentless climb up through New York's underworld had begun.

He launched his Mafia career serving New York boss Giuseppe 'Joe the Boss' Masseria during the early 1920s, working mainly in bootlegging and extortion. However, what Genovese really brought Masseria was a propensity for violence. Vito was afraid of nothing and no one. It was around this time that he met Charles 'Lucky' Luciano, the criminal visionary who would shortly become the lynchpin of the American Mafia, reshaping it at the end of the 1920s. While Luciano would become one of Genovese's closest allies, the two men had a complex relationship and would never be what could be called friends.

When Luciano organised the extermination of the old boss, Masseria, Genovese was one of the four gunmen who made the famous hit. Later that year, Luciano organised a hit on Salvatore Maranzano, the victor in the Castellamarese War that had split the Mafia for two years. With both Masseria and Maranzano dead, Luciano became boss of his very own crime family, appointing Genovese as underboss.

According to those who knew him, Vito Genovese was not a man to be trusted. 'Sly', 'devious' and 'cunning' are words often used in conjunction with his name. Joe Valachi, the first Mafia man to turn informant, famously said: 'If you went to him and told him about some guy doing wrong he would have the guy whacked. And then he would have you whacked for telling on the guy.'

And he had no compunction about using violence to deal with his problems. After the death of his first wife, he fell in love with another woman who, unfortunately, happened to be already married. No problem for Vito – he killed the husband.

In the 1930s, Genovese began to make serious money from the various rackets in which he was involved, but mainly from the Italian lottery which he had come to control. He invested this wealth in nightclubs in Greenwich Village.

Then, when Luciano was convicted and imprisoned on pimping charges in 1936, Genovese was made acting boss. He did not last long, however. In 1937, he was indicted for the murder of Ferdinand Boccia, a small-time gambling racketeer. Boccia and Genovese set up a rigged card game and, a few days later, Boccia demanded a third of the profits. He thought it was only fair as he had introduced them to the victim, a wealthy Italian businessman. Genovese refused to pay up, instead hiring Willie Gallo and Ernest 'the Hawk' Rupolo to murder Boccia. His body was pulled out of the Hudson River in May 1937, at which point Genovese offered Rupolo $175 to murder Gallo in case he talked. Rupolo made two bodged attempts before Gallo decided that this was getting ridiculous. He went to the police and implicated Genovese and Rupolo in the murder. Rupolo got 20 years, but Genovese took off before they could lock him up, too. He bought a house for his second wife in New Jersey, deposited money in various accounts for her and fled to Italy with a suitcase stuffed with $750,000. He settled in the town of Nola, not far from his home town Naples. Not a man to kick his heels when there was money to be made, he threw himself enthusiastically into the local narcotics trade.

So, when the Allies invaded Italy in 1944, starting their big push for Berlin and victory, who should they find waiting for them but Vito Genovese, an English-speaking American with lots of local knowledge and contacts. He got a job as an interpreter/liaison officer in the US Army headquarters, and turned himself into one of American Military Government of Occupied Territories' (AMGOT) most trusted employees. This was a bit of a turnaround as, just under a year previously, he had arranged the killing of Carlo Tresca, editor of an anti-Fascist Italian-language newspaper in New York, as a favour to his good friend, the Italian dictator Benito Mussolini. He was a friend of the family – he had also been supplying drugs to Il Duce's brother-in-law.

Ironically, Vito helped AMGOT to deal with crime in the Naples area, only, of course, so that he could clear out his rivals and take over their rackets. The opportunities were huge for a criminal mind such as Genovese's and he worked with the Italian Mafia, establishing a massive black market operation in southern Italy. However, the military police launched an investigation into his activities and he was arrested in August 1944 and held in a military prison in Naples. While he was detained they looked into his past, learning that he was on the run from murder charges back in the United States. Luckily, however, his friends in America had not forgotten him and they made sure that the key witness in the case was not around to testify against him when he was deported to the States. The witness died of 'an overdose of sedatives' while being held in protective custody. Therefore in June 1945 all charges against Vito were dropped, to the disgust of the judge who said: 'By devious means, among which were the terrorizing of witnesses, kidnapping them, yes, even murdering those who could give evidence against you, you have thwarted justice time and again.'

Genovese was free to return to business as usual, but things had changed. Luciano had by this time been deported back to Italy and, although he was still nominally in charge, the real boss was the man they called 'the Prime Minister of the Underworld', Frank Costello. This irritated Vito who, of course, thought he should be boss. After all, he had been acting boss before he had had to leave for Italy and he wanted all the wealth, power and prestige that the position brought. Even more irritating was the fact that he was not even given the position of underboss. That went to New Jersey racketeer Guarino 'Willie' Moretti, a cousin of Costello. Vito Genovese was now 52 years old and still only a capo.

As 1951 rolled around, Genovese made his mind up. He would take out Costello and his men and seize power.

Moretti was no problem. He had contracted syphilis from one of his many liaisons with prostitutes and was losing it. He talked too much, sometimes revealing Mob secrets to the press. When the US Senate Select Committee on Organized Crime started an investigation known as the Kefauver hearings, they called Moretti to testify. He hammed it up for the cameras and was too candid with the committee. Moretti had breached the Mafia code of silence, *omerta*. He was the first that Genovese dealt with. He spread word that Moretti was no good and had to be rubbed out. On 4 October 1951, three of Albert 'Mad Hatter' Anastasia's hitmen took him to lunch. Afterwards, they killed him with a number of shots to the chest. Interestingly, he had been due that day to have lunch with comedy duo Dean Martin and Jerry Lewis, but Lewis learned that morning that he had mumps and the pair cancelled. The first nail had been hammered into Frank's coffin.

Genovese now went after the Prime Minister. He sent out soldier Vincent 'Chin' Gigante to whack Costello. In spite of a shotgun blast fired at his head from close range, Costello survived. Genovese had to move fast. He said that it had been kill or be killed, that Costello had been coming after him. He began to cultivate a perception of Costello as an ineffectual boss and made it very clear that he was now top of the heap and if anyone was found trying to contact Costello he would be considered a traitor and dealt with accordingly. He made Jerry Catena underboss and Michael Miranda became his consigliere. Probably wisely, Costello decided to retire, but only after being demoted to the position of soldier in the Family.

Being head of the Luciano Family was still not enough for Genovese. He wanted the position of *capo di tutti capi*, boss of bosses. To do that he would have to whack the 'Mad Hatter', Albert Anastasia, a dangerous and violent individual who had been prominent in the legendary Murder Inc. in its heyday. Genovese persuaded Carlo Gambino that it would be beneficial to both of them if Anastasia was not around any more and the Mad Hatter was sensationally shot dead in a barber's chair in the Manhattan Park Sheraton Hotel on 25 October 1957.

Some three weeks later, Genovese organized the Apalachin Conference in the rural town of Apalachin, New York. It was at this meeting, attended by 58 top Mafiosi, that he hoped he would be enthroned as boss of bosses. But, it all went badly wrong. An eagle-eyed New York State Trooper, Edgar Croswell, had been observing the meeting house, which belonged to mobster Joseph 'Joe the Barber' Barbara, head of the Bufalino Crime Family. Croswell saw large numbers of mobsters arriving at the house, radioed in for reinforcements and they surrounded the farm. When the mobsters were alerted to the police presence, chaos erupted and they tried to flee. Some even ran off into the neighbouring woods. A number of men were arrested, amongst them Carlo Gambino and Vito Genovese. Aside from derailing Genovese's power plan, the most important consequence of the Apalachin Meeting was that J. Edgar Hoover, head of the FBI, had to admit to the power of organised crime in the States and declared war on it. Genovese had, unwittingly, brought Cosa Nostra out of the shadows and into the view of the public and law enforcement. More importantly for Don Vitole, he was not going to be boss of bosses.

In April 1959, it ceased to matter when he was convicted of selling a large quantity of heroin. He was fined $20,000 and sentenced to 15 years in the Atlanta Federal Penitentiary in Georgia. It was widely believed that he was set up by the authorities, especially as the Mafia had banned dealing in drugs as a part of its business. But another theory has it that Lucky Luciano, Meyer Lansky and Frank Costello were behind it, knowing that it would not be long before Genovese would come after them. They set up a drug deal that they knew Genovese could not resist and Puerto Rican drug dealer Nelson 'Melon' Cantellops, was paid $100,000 to stand up in court and testify against Genovese. When he told a Grand Jury that he had attended a meeting in which Genovese spoke of taking over the drugs trade in the Bronx, the game was up for Vito.

Prior to sentencing, he summoned his men and claimed that he would continue to run his empire from behind bars, as other bosses had done. His brother Mike would be the conduit for his orders and Tommy Eboli would be acting boss. He appointed a team of caretakers to oversee day-to-day matters.

He ruled the Genovese Family in this way until he finally succumbed to heart failure in the federal prison medical centre in Springfield, Missouri, on Valentine's Day 1969, aged 72.

JOE COLOMBO

Jo Colombo, boss of one of America's five crime families from 1964 to 1971, did not start out as a hood. Instead, he began his working life in the American Coast Guard, but was never really cut out for it and was soon getting into trouble. At one point he was diagnosed in a naval hospital as suffering from psychoneurosis, was given a medical discharge and started collecting disability allowance. By the end of the war, his real career path was becoming clear and he could be found flexing his muscles and organising rigged dice games on the piers of New York. Soon he was climbing the greasy pole within the Profaci Family, one of the five divisions of the Mafia created by Lucky Luciano in 1931.

Joseph Profaci headed the Profaci Family, a man loathed by his soldiers because of his legendary tight-fistedness and his heavy taxation of family members. He ran his branch of the Mob along the lines of the old Sicilian Mafia families, levying charges and tributes from family members. Nevertheless, under Profaci, the Brooklyn-based family business prospered through its labour rackets, extortion, gambling, hijacking and loan sharking. And Profaci, of course, prospered more than most. He was a flamboyant man, smoked big cigars, drove big, black cadillacs, and bought rows of tickets to Broadway shows. He owned homes in New York and Florida and a 328-acre estate in New Jersey.

Colombo was a well-spoken, articulate man with pots of charisma and flair, so it is no surprise that by the late 1950s he was a 'made' man – a full member of the Mafia family. His calm manner and gentlemanly behaviour belied his awful temper, however, and he could erupt into a terrible rage at any moment. But above all, Colombo was a survivor. After all he had survived the assassination of his father, Joe Sr.. He had been garrotted in his car, along with a lady friend, in 1928. Famously, when Joe Jr. was asked when he got to the top of the tree whether he was ever tempted to find the people responsible for his father's murder, he replied: 'Don't they pay policemen for that?'

Joe became a highly respected enforcer for Profaci, ensuring monies got paid and debts were settled. He was part of a five-man hit team, working alongside Larry and Crazy Joe Gallo, two of the Mafia's most efficient killers. It was a team credited with at least 15 kills. 'When you killed with the Gallo boys,' Carl Sifakis writes in *The Mafia Encyclopedia*, 'you killed with the best.' In addition to his hit-man duties, he worked as an enforcer on the docks, before moving on to running gambling dens, hijacking, and loan-sharking. He was seen as tough, smart and supremely capable. It did not take him long to achieve the senior Mafia position of capo.

In 1962, the unpopular Joe Profaci's 34-year reign finally ended when he succumbed to cancer. To the disappointment of many members of the Profaci Family, especially Joey Gallo and his family of violent street thugs and enforcers, Giuseppe Magliocco, a man very much in the Profaci mould, was given control. The war with the Gallos, which had gone on during Profaci's time, simmered on. Carmine 'Junior' Persico and Hugh McIntosh, two of Magliocco's chief enforcers, survived attacks by the Gallos. And they would, undoubtedly, have gone after many more of Magliocco's crew had 17 of them not been convicted on racketeering charges and two of them not been murdered by Magliocco's men. Meanwhile, leader Joey Gallo sat in prison, powerless to do anything.

So with the Gallos safely out of the way for a while at least, Magliocco could get on with running the business. Part of that business was doing a big favour for Joe Bonnano, known as 'Joe Bananas' and head of the Bonnano Family, another of the five divisions of the Mafia. Bonnano wanted to be *capo di tutti capi*, boss of bosses, and there was only one way he could achieve that; he needed to be rid of the bosses of the other three families – Carlo Gambino, Thomas Lucchese and Stefano Magadinno. There was really only one man for the job. The ever reliable and eminently capable Joe Colombo was to be entrusted with it.

But it did not work out quite the way Bonnano had planned. What he forgot was that Joe Colombo was very close to the Gambino Family. In fact, before joining the Profaci Family, he had been employed by the Pride Meat Company run by Paul Gambino, brother of Carlo. It was through Gambino, who had taken a shine to the bright young Colombo, that Joe had found a place in the Profaci Family. He had never had much to do with Magliocco or Bonnano. Consequently, he reckoned that his loyalties lay with the Gambinos and not with Bonnano. Joe went to Carlo Gambini and told him about Bonnano's plan. Gambino was, needless to say, furious and convened a meeting of the other families to which Bonnano and Magliocco were summoned to explain themselves. Bonnano failed to show but Magliocco attended, admitted the plan, was fined $50,000 and sent into retirement. He was already a sick man and he died a month later. Joe Bananas was removed from his position and his family broke into two groups. The press termed it 'The Banana Split'.

Gambino was now top dog and knew he owed it to Joe Colombo. He also thought that if Colombo became boss of the Profaci Family, he would be a mere puppet and Colombo would really be pulling the strings. So, he petitioned the Commission to put Colombo in charge of the Profaci Family. The decision was unanimous and Colombo, aged 40, became the youngest mob boss ever.

It was a decision not to everyone's liking. New Jersey Mafia boss Simone Rizz 'Sam the Plumber' DeCavalcante said at the time: 'What experience has he got? He was a bustout guy all his life . . . What does he know?' And within his own family, there were warring factions. However, the Gallos still did not have the strength to be in a position to challenge Colombo. But there was also the Persico crew who provided enforcement for the Profaci Family. None-theless, Joe's control was absolute and the press began to refer to the Profaci Family as the Colombo Family.

Joe Colombo's life was not just all about the Mob. He was a devout Catholic. One story alleges that when a valuable crown was stolen from a Brooklyn church, he was outraged. He put the word out that it should be returned immediately. The thief did so, but made the fatal mistake of keeping three of the diamonds from the crown. Not long afterwards his body was found with a rosary wrapped around his neck.

When Colombo's son was arrested in 1970 for melting down $500,000 of US coins for their silver content, Joe formed the Italian–American Civil Rights League, appointing himself leader. Its stated aim was to protest against the harassment of Italian Americans but his real objective, apart from skimming money from the organisation of course, was to portray anti-Mafia activities by the police and FBI as harassment of Italian Americans. Its benefit events – featuring stars such as Frank Sinatra – raised large sums of money which went straight into Mafia coffers, and by the end of the year the League had 150,000 members and 50 chapters across the country. But other Mafia bosses began to worry about what appeared to be Joe's obsession with the League. They also worried about the publicity he was attracting. He was giving interviews on television and making speeches. Throughout its history, the Mob has shunned publicity and has always dealt harshly with those of its members who courted it. Joe did not help by allegedly spitting in Carlo Gambino's face when Gambino complained about the publicity surrounding Joe.

The situation was complicated by the release from prison of Joey Gallo. Gallo had already gone to war once, with Joe Profaci, over the leadership of the family, and he hated Colombo for his activities during that war. He had made good use of his prison time, building alliances with other ethnic criminals. He courted, in particular, the Afro-American criminal elements in Harlem and the Bedford-Stuyvesant area of Brooklyn. He was using these contacts to disrupt Colombo's activities in Brooklyn.

Joe had organised the League's second big rally for 28 June 1971. The day dawned bright and sunny and when he was picked up by his driver that morning, he felt good. The League was the perfect scam – it had the air of a legitimate organisation, it made him look good and, above all, it made him lots of money, more than $1 million in its first year. He would make still more today.

He arrived at the venue at Columbus Circle and made for the platform where his sons, Anthony and Joe Jr., were working, along with around 50 of his men. There were police, TV reporters, photographers and around 4,000 people in the audience. As Joe approached the stage, a young black man filmed him up close and as he reached it, the black man, only a few feet away, suddenly dropped his camera, whipped out a pistol and fired three shots into Colombo's head and neck. Mayhem broke out as Joe stumbled onto the steps. Joe Jr., another Colombo Family soldier and a couple of cops roughly wrestled the black man, Jerome Johnson, to the ground but as the cops pulled out their handcuffs and struggled to cuff Johnson, a short, stocky man with a pistol in his hand, pushed through the baying crowd now surrounding the assassin and leaned forward, shooting him dead. Then he was gone in the crowd.

Colombo was rushed to Roosevelt Hospital where surgeons fought to save his life. He survived, but remained in a coma for the seven remaining years of his life.

As Joe Gallo said: 'He was vegetabled.'

CARMINE 'THE SNAKE' PERSICO

Carmine Persico is not the best-looking guy in the world. But, small and scrawny though he is, with one hand mangled from a bullet wound, he is not a man to tangle with and he has been known to carry an ice-pick around with him just in case someone annoyed him. His hand-wound is not the only injury, for Carmine has been shot some 20 times in his long and illustrious Mafia career. He is sometimes known as 'Immortal' on account of his ability to survive the countless attacks on him, one of which was a bomb in 1963 from which he escaped with minor injuries. However, the most popular nickname for this Mob veteran is pretty unappetising – 'The Snake'. He was given this as a youngster because of the slyness of his crimes.

Persico is as tough as they come. Once, during the first Gallo Wars, when the brothers Joey and Larry Gallo were trying to take over the Colombo Family, of which Persico is a made member and currently head, he and an associate, Alphonse D'Ambrosio, were sitting in a car, minding their own business. Suddenly, a carful of Gallo loyalists drove by and opened fire on the car with a semi-automatic M-1 carbine. D'Ambrosio was hit in the chest and Persico took bullets in hand, shoulder and face. However, tough as old boots, Persico calmly spat the bullet out that had hit his face, started the engine and drove the car to the nearest hospital.

But you messed with The Snake at your peril. 'Crazy' Joe Gallo was gunned down in a clam restaurant in April 1972 as he celebrated his 43rd birthday. Persico is a suspect in that death as well as the death of 'Crazy' Joe's brother Larry.

Born in 1937 in the Mafia's top breeding ground of Brooklyn, Carmine Persico's father was a soldier in the Genovese Family. Carmine was a chip off the old block and was known at first as 'Junior' in the streets of Brooklyn. As a teenager, he joined a gang known as The Garfield Boys, roaming the streets of the Red Hook district with a bunch of like-minded young thugs and hooligans. The Garfield Boys had terrorised Brooklyn since the early 20th century, only disappearing from the streets in 1971, and Persico soon became its leader.

He killed his first man at the age of 17 and with a witness known only as the Blue Angel identifying him as the shooter, it looked as if he would go to prison.

However, before the Blue Angel's testimony could be used to convict him, his older brother confessed to the murder. Taking the rap for his younger brother cost Alphonse dearly – 18 years in prison.

Persico became a made member of the Profaci Crime Family under Joe Profaci who reigned from 1928 to 1962. When Joe Colombo took over at the top, re-titling the Family in his name, Persico was promoted to capo. Meanwhile, his reputation as an enforcer and loan shark became fearsome on the streets of New York.

His team consisted of some of the most ruthless killers of the time – his brother, Alphonse, now out of jail, Gennaro 'Jerry Lang' Langella, Anthony Abbattermarco, Joey Brancatto and Hugh 'Apples' Mackintosh who, although not a made man due to his father not being Italian, was a hugely effective enforcer. A giant of a man who wore a size 52 suit, he was so valued that he became Carmine Persico's bodyguard.

When Thomas 'Old Man' DiBella stepped down in 1977 as boss of the Colombo Family after five years at the helm, the Family descended into anarchy. The obvious choice as replacement was The Snake. He was the Family's most powerful capo, but he had been pursued relentlessly by the authorities and served time in prison between 1973 and 1979 and then 1981 and

1984. Nevertheless, he held on to power, even behind bars, controlling Family affairs through his brother Alphonse and Langella. Those affairs consisted of narcotics-trafficking and labour racketeering.

When he was not in prison, Persico ran things from the Diplomat Social Club on the corner of 3rd Avenue and Carroll Street in the Van Brunt district of Brooklyn. This was where the top echelons of the Colombo Family could be found – his son, Ally, Langella, 'Apples' Mackintosh, Greg Scarpa, Carmine Franzese and Joe Colombo's sons, Anthony, Vincent and Joe Jr. If you had business with the Colombo Family, that was where you went.

For years the US government had been wielding the Rico (Racketeering Influenced and Corrupt Organization) statutes against organised crime figures and in 1985 it was using them to remove leading New York Mafiosi from the scene. Persico had been out of jail for less than a year when, faced with racketeering charges, he went on the run. He was arrested in February 1985 in Wantagh, New York, but not before his name had been added to the FBI's Ten Most Wanted List, the 390th fugitive to be listed.

A total of nine gangsters were being tried on racketeering charges in what became known as 'The Commission Trial'. Persico, stupidly some thought, had studied law while in prison and decided to represent himself in the trial. His defence was that he should not be prosecuted just for being a member of Cosa Nostra. 'Without the Mafia, there wouldn't be no case here!' he stormed at one point. But there was a case and a successful one at that. He was sentenced to 100 years in prison and would never be released.

However, he wanted to remain in control of the organisation, especially as he wanted his son, Alphonse, aka 'Ally', to take over from him when he was ready. Anyway, he had run things from prison before and did not see why he could not do so again. Victor 'Little Vic' Orena was chosen by Persico to deputise for him on the outside.

The trouble was that Orena enjoyed being top dog too much and wanted to do it full time. He lobbied Crime Commission members to remove Persico and make him head of the Family in his place and was supported in his efforts by the Dapper Don, John Gotti, head of the Gambino Family.

The Colombo Family inevitably split into warring factions, those who wanted Orena at the top and those who supported the status quo.

But, living up to his nickname, Persico struck quickly before the other side were ready.

In June 1991 Persico's Consigliere, Carmine Sessa, led a five-man crew in an attack on Vic Orena's home on Long Island. Sessa was a formidable hitman, with some 13 murders to his credit during his mobster career. This time it wasn't to be, however. One of the team got nervous and let off a round before the other members of the team had taken up their positions. Orena was alerted to the danger and succeeded in making his escape.

Orena now sought help from the other Families and made fresh overtures to the Commission to have Persico removed as head of the Colombo Family. Sessa, on the other hand, petitioned on behalf of Persico, calling Orena a traitor and a usurper.

On 18 November 1991, Persico capo Greg Scarpo Sr. was driving his daughter and granddaughter home. Cars pulled up around his vehicle and gunmen jumped out, guns drawn and ran towards him. Scarpo was fearless and hit the accelerator, driving off at speed and hitting anything that got in his way. As the bullets flew, some passers-by were injured, but Scarpa, one of the toughest men in the history of the Mafia, got away.

Five days later, Orena's men were out in force again, led by William 'Wild Bill' Cutolo. They gunned down Persico man Henry 'Hank the Bank' Smurra outside a Brooklyn doughnut shop.

War broke out and 12 men lost their lives in it, Cutolo and Scarpo killing three men each. Two of the other victims were innocent bystanders, caught in the crossfire. Fifteen people were seriously wounded.

The last man to die was an Orena capo by the name of John Scopo. His killer was one of Greg Scarpa's men – 18-year-old John Pappa. Pappa is a piece of work. He has the words 'Morte prima di dishonore' (Death before dishonour) tattooed across his back. He showed his belief in this motto when he shot dead his two accomplices in the Scopo hit because they took all the credit for it when he had been the actual hitman.

At the end of the two-year war, Persico claimed victory but it was a hollow one. The police had arrested Orena, who went to prison for life, effectively removing the threat to Persico, but numerous loyalists from both sides also went to jail. The Family emerged from the war, battered, bruised and weakened.

Persico has been incarcerated for the bulk of his time as leader of the Colombo Family and has become well used to using deputies to manage the day-to-day business while in prison. Recently, Persico's cousin Andrew Russo and his son Allie have been running the Family. There is, currently, one slight problem though. Like Carmine Persico, both are behind bars, Allie in serious trouble and possibly facing the death penalty for his part in the murder of 'Wild Bill' Cutolo, a staunch Orena loyalist during the war. Cutolo had been made underboss by Allie as a peace gesture in 1999, but then suddenly disappeared on his way to a meeting with the boss.

The 'street boss' is now Thomas 'Tommy Shots' Gioeli, a loyal Persico ally during the war. Gioeli has suffered from chronic back problems for decades, but that did not stop him in his efforts to deal with Orena's troops, even when, in March 1992, he was wounded in a car chase and shootout in Brooklyn. The last time he saw the inside of prison was in 1980, for robbery, and his strength lies, according to one source, 'in his ability to bridge the gap between mobsters who were shooting at each other a decade ago'.

Meanwhile, Carmine 'The Snake' Persico, in the 22nd year of his incarceration, nods to a guard and sniffs the fresh air at Lompoc Federal Prison in California where he spends his time playing drums, riding the mechanical bull in the prison yard and tending his rose garden.

ANTHONY 'THE ANT' SPILOTRO

It wasn't much of a crime. A T-shirt worth a couple of dollars from a low-rent shop in the neighbourhood. It was 1955 and the law was making acquaintance with Anthony 'the Ant' Spilotro, by slapping a $10 dollar fine on him and sticking him on probation. It would be a long and varied relationship, though. He and the law would be rubbing up against each other for years to come.

Spilotro was born and raised in Chicago, the fourth of the six sons of Pasquale and Antoinette Spilotro who ran Patsy's Restaurant, an establishment renowned for its meatballs, which were a magnet for business from all over town. Patsy's was also a haunt of big-time gangsters such as Sam Giancana, Jackie Cerone, Gussie Alex and Frank Nitti. It is reported that the Mob would convene meetings in the restaurant's car park.

Five of the Spilotro brothers – John, Vincent, Victor, Michael and Tony liked what they saw when the hoods swaggered into Patsy's in their expensive suits, smoking fat cigars, and became involved in petty crime at an early age. The sixth brother, Pasquale, chose a different path, becoming one of Chicago's most highly respected oral surgeons. At school, Anthony was a bully and he dropped out of High School at the age of 15, turning his attention to petty theft and mugging. He was arrested no fewer than 12 times in the next five years. In the ensuing years he would be given the nickname, 'Tony the Ant' by the press, after FBI agent William Roemer referred to him as 'that little pissant'.

In the course of his activities, the young Spilotro befriended Vincent 'the Saint' Inserro, a crook with Mob connections, and soon he was mixing with the cream of the Chicago underworld, hanging out with figures like Joseph Aiuppa, Jimmy 'the Turk' Torrello, Joey 'the Clown' Lombardo and William Daddano Sr., most of whom would climb through the Mafia ranks in the coming years.

His mentor in the Mob was a bit special, however. 'Mad' Sam DeStefano was one of the Chicago outfit's most notorious hitmen, considered by some in the CIA to be the worst torture-murderer in the history of the United States. It was a lethal pairing, a mentally unstable sadistic killer and a ruthless young criminal on the make.

Spilotro did well in his first few years, moving

quickly through the ranks, and in 1962 was entrusted with his first hit. He was contracted along with 'Mad' Sam and a couple of others to take care of those responsible for robbing and killing Ron and Phil Scalvo, Mob associates, after a bar-room fight. To make matters worse, the murder was carried out in Elmwood Park, a neighbourhood on the outskirts of Chicago where a number of the members of the Chicago operation had their homes. This made Elmwood strictly off-limits for Chicago's criminals as the last thing the mobsters wanted was to draw police attention to the area in which they lived. Bill McCarthy and Jimmy Miraglia, a couple of small-time crooks, were known to have been responsible and they had the added misfortune to be in debt to DeStefano. Miraglia immediately went into hiding, but McCarthy was captured and taken to the basement of 'Mad' Sam's house where he was tortured in an effort to get him to spill the beans on his accomplice. At one point, to hurry matters along a little, Spilotro put McCarthy's head in a vice and began to tighten it. He tightened it so much that McCarthy's eye popped out of its socket. Needless to say, McCarthy began to talk.

A few days later, the bodies of the two men were found in the boot of a car, badly beaten, with their throats slit ear to ear. Spilotro's stock rose in the circles in which he moved and in 1963 he became a made member of the Mafia, working for Felix 'Milwaukee Phil' Alderiso, an underboss for Mafia Godfather Sam Giancana.

When a former associate of 'Mad' Sam DeStafano, Charles 'Chuckie' Crimaldi, became an informer for the FBI, he gave evidence against Spilotro and DeStefano at their trial for the murder of an estate agent, Leo Foreman, who had made the mistake of throwing Sam DeStefano out of his office in May 1963. Foreman had been lured to the home of Sam's brother, Mario, to play cards and, before being shot, was tortured, stabbed countless times with an ice-pick, and had pieces of his flesh cut out while he was still alive.

Nonetheless, they were both acquitted.

Spilotro was given responsibility for a large bookmaking territory and did so well in his first year that he was sent to Miami to provide protection for sports handicapper Frank Rosenthal, the man on whose career Martin Scorsese's film Casino was based. (Joe Pesci played Nicky Santoro, the Spilotro character.)

The year 1967 saw Spilotro back in Chicago, but in 1971 he landed a big job when he was sent to Las Vegas to replace Marshall Caifano as overseer of the Mob-controlled casinos there, setting up his office in the gift shop of the Circus Circus casino. It was handy having a desert nearby as that is where several of the people he tortured and murdered during this period ended up. In fact, immediately following his arrival in Vegas, the murder rate increased by 70 per cent.

Spilotro's job here was to manage the 'skim' operation that brought millions of dollars to the Mob every year. He oversaw the employees of the casinos who were embezzling money and ensured that it made its way back to the Mob in the mid-west.

In 1972, 'Mad' Sam was living up to his reputation, behaving bizarrely and drawing attention to himself and his associates in his various trials. It was decided to eliminate him and Spilotro was selected to make the hit. He shot Sam twice with a shotgun in the garage of his Northwest Side home, fatally wounding him. 'Mad' Sam's brother, Mario, was convicted of complicity in the murder and was a sentence of 20 to 40 years in prison. Amazingly, Spilotro walked again.

In late 1974, the manager of the International Fiber Glass Company Danny Siefert, was to be a principal witness in a fraud case involving Joey 'the Clown' Lombardo, later to become head of the Chicago Mafia, and insurance agent Allen Dorfman. These two men were accused of syphoning off $1.4 million from the Teamsters Union pension fund. But Siefert never had his day in court; he was shot in front of his wife and four-year-old son in September 1974 by Anthony Spilotro and, needless to say, he got away with this one, too.

In 1975, Allen Glick, front man for the Mafia-controlled Stardust and Fremont Hotel and Casinos in Vegas, was having problems with wealthy real estate owner and investor Tamara Rand, over a $2 million loan she had made to him. Rand claimed to have been threatened in May of that year after filing suit against him, although she never made clear by whom. To make matters worse, a couple of months previously she had also filed criminal fraud charges against Glick. Glick complained to Mafia boss Joe Aiuppa about Rand and in November of that year she was shot dead in the kitchen of her home in Mission Hill, San Diego by Tony Spilotro with the help of Frank 'Bomp' Bompensiero, another well-known Mafia hitman.

Shortly afterwards, it was Bompensiero's turn. Consigliere of the Californian Cosa Nostra – known as the 'Mickey Mouse Mafia' – 'Bomp' was believed to be an FBI informant and was becoming something of an embarrassment. He was shot to death at close range with a silenced .22 calibre handgun while standing in a phone booth in San Diego. The killer? Anthony Spilotro, of course.

The biggest hit of Spilotro's illustrious career, if indeed he did it, involved the Godfather himself. Sam Giancana had been head of the Chicago Mafia for ten years, from 1956 to 1966. But he had become unpopular due to his lavish lifestyle and his refusal to cut underlings into the profits of his highly lucrative gambling operations in Iran and South America. 'Momo', as he was known, was eventually deposed and went into exile in Mexico. A few years later, however, he was arrested by the Mexican authorities and deported back to the United States.

Not long after his return, in June 1975, Momo was frying Italian sausages and peppers in the basement of his home in Oak Park, Illinois, when he was shot in the back of the head. When he fell to the floor, the body was turned over and shot a further six times in the face, just to be sure. The assassin had to be someone that Giancana knew well for him to be in such close proximity to his victim. It is believed to have been Anthony Spilotro working under the orders of the new boss of the Chicago Mafia, Joey Aiuppa.

In 1976, Spilotro opened The Gold Rush Ltd with his brother Michael and Chicago bookmaker Herbert 'Fat Herbie' Blitzstein. The Gold Rush, located one block from The Strip, purported to be a combination jewellery store and 'electronics factory', but was mainly a place for the trio to fence stolen goods. It became the HQ of a gang Spilotro put together with his boyhood friend Frank Culotta, which became known as the Hole in the Wall Gang, due to their habit of stealing jewellery from stores by drilling a hole in the wall. The gang consisted of Spilotro, his brother Michael, Samuel and Joseph Cusumano, Ernesto 'Ernie' Davino, Lawrence 'Crazy Larry' Neumann, Wayne Matecki, Salvatore 'Sonny' Romano, Leonardo 'Leo' Guardino, Frank Culotta, Herbert 'Fat Herbie' Blitzstein and former Las Vegas detective Joseph Blasko. Culotta, Blasko, Guardino, Neumann and Matecki were all arrested while carrying out a robbery on Bertha's Household Products in July 1982.

Another of Spilotro's hits was brutal in the extreme. William 'Action' Jackson worked as a loan-shark enforcer for Sam DeStefano. Following his indictment on a hijacking charge, he was seen with FBI agents in a Milwaukee restaurant and DeStefano surmised that he had cut a deal with the FBI in return for a lighter sentence. Spilotro was enlisted to deal with Jackson and he abducted him, driving him to a meat-packing plant in Chicago. There, he hung him by a meat-hook which had been inserted in his rectum. Spilotro tortured him further by smashing both his knees with a hammer and prodding his genitals with an electric cattle prod. Jackson was left to die and it took him three days.

By the early 1980s, however, drugs were beginning to play an increasing role in Spilotro's life. He had also been having an affair with Frank Rosenthal's wife,

Geri. In addition to the troubles piling up around him, testimony by Aladena 'Jimmy The Weasel' Fratianno, following his arrest in 1977, ensured that the name of Anthony Spilotro was registered in the Black Book. This was the list of people who were legally banned from casinos, either because they were known to be associated with organised crime or because they were known gambling cheats. When Spilotro's name was put in the book and he was no longer able to set foot in any of Vegas's casinos, he was furious. Not as furious, however, as the new boss of the Chicago crime family, Joe Ferriola. The blacklisting from the casinos he was supposed to be supervising, the high profile jewel robberies, the drugs, sleeping with an associate's wife – these were not the type of activities the Mob condoned.

Ferriola decided that it was time that Tony 'the Ant' was taken care of.

Sam 'Wings' Carlisito called Spilotro and his brother Michael to a meeting at a hunting lodge in Indiana, owned by Joey Aiuppa. There, the Spilotros were savagely beaten and buried in a cornfield.

In September 2007, after a trial lasting three months, Joey 'the Clown' Lombardo, 78, James 'Little Jimmy' Marcello, 65, Frank Calabrese Sr, 70, and Paul 'The Indian' Schiro, 70, were found guilty of the murder of Anthony Spilotro. The convictions, which also included racketeering, loan sharking, extortion and 17 other murders, followed the admission of Nicholas Calabrese that he had helped to kill Spilotro 30 years previously.

In the film *Casino*, the Spilotro brothers are buried alive after being severely beaten. In reality, said Calabrese, the brothers were killed before being buried. He told the trial about Spilotro's demise: 'He came into the basement and there were a whole bunch of guys who grabbed him and strangled him and beat him to death ... Tony put up a fight. He kept saying, "You guys are going to get in trouble, you guys are going to get in trouble".

ROY DEMEO AND THE GEMINI CREW

A recipe for murder:

First take your victim. Make him feel relaxed by plying him with booze in the Gemini Lounge. Then lure him through the side door – game of poker, bit of food, women; anything will do, most people are weak for something – and into the apartment that joins on to the building out back. Approach victim from behind with a gun fitted with a silencer in one hand and a towel in the other. Add one bullet to victim's head, quickly wrapping your towel round the head like a turban to staunch the flow of blood. As you hold the towel around the head, another person stabs the victim through the heart, severing arteries and stopping blood from pumping around the body and out of the head-wound. Make sure your victim is dead and then remove all his clothing and leave him hanging like a game bird over the bath to drain all remaining blood out of the body. Return the body to the living room and place on large swimming pool liner. Remove arms, legs and head and then seal all parts in separate bags that are then placed in boxes and sent to the Fountain Avenue Dump in Brooklyn.

That was the preferred method – the Gemini Method as it was known – of Roy DeMeo and his crew, although they did use other methods as the situation demanded. Want to send a message out to everyone to say 'don't mess with us'? Leave the body on a street. Victim could not be lured to the Gemini Lounge? There were lots of other places the dismemberment could be carried out – on a yacht, in a hideout, in the meat department of a supermarket, anywhere.

The head killer of this murderous crew, Roy DeMeo, was born in Brooklyn, New York, in 1940 to working-class Italian immigrants. He learned about loan-sharking as a teenager from the sons of his neighbour, Mafia boss Joe Profaci. By the age of 17 it had become almost a full-time occupation for him. He was good at it too, mainly because he had no qualms about using violence to 'persuade' his debtors to pay up in time. He graduated High School in 1959, marrying not long after, and carried on with his criminal activities. He prospered so well through them, in fact, especially through loan sharking, that he gave up his day job at the Banner Dairy Supermarket in the early 1960s, focusing instead on making money in any way he could.

DeMeo's place of business was Phil's Bar, later to become the Gemini Lounge, which occupied the front half of a two-storey building located on a street corner in Flatlands, Brooklyn. Here he would pursue his loan-sharking activities and fence stolen goods and, in 1965, he bought a chunk of the bar.

He had hovered around the edges of the Lucchese Crime Family for a number of years, but in 1966 he befriended Anthony 'Nino' Gaggi, a high-ranking member of the Gambinos who had been inducted into the Family after taking part in the 1960 hit on Vincent Squillante, the killer of Frank and Joseph Scalise. Much of Gaggi's money also came from loan sharking, but he also dipped his toes in a number of legitimate businesses in which he had become a silent partner. DeMeo saw a better future for himself with the Gambinos than the Luccheses and cultivated his friendship and business relationship with Gaggi.

He diversified his interests throughout the sixties, assembling a crew of young crooks and moving into car theft and drug trafficking. Among his gang were Harvey 'Chris' Rosenberg, a friend whom DeMeo had met when they were both teenagers. Rosenberg had been dealing drugs and the young DeMeo had provided funds for him so that he could deal in larger quantities. Joey 'Dracula' Gugliemo, DeMeo's cousin, was a pornographer and killer whose strange rituals with the blood of victims in the rooms behind the Gemini Lounge earned him his nickname. Other members included Joseph Testa and Anthony Senter who were known as the Gemini Twins because they were inseparable and could always be found in the Gemini Lounge, and Joey's younger brother, Patrick Testa.

The Brooklyn Credit Union, of which DeMeo became a director, offered ample opportunity for laundering the proceeds of his loan-sharking activities and he stole funds from the Credit Union reserves which he used in his business.

It was not until 1972 when he was aged 32, that DeMeo carried out his first murder. Like Gaggi, he had become a silent partner in a number of businesses, one of which was a pornography film lab owned by a man called Paul Rothenberg. The lab had been raided by the police and Gaggi was concerned that Rothenberg was about to cooperate with the cops, a fear that was confirmed when Rothenberg informed the authorities that he was being extorted by two men called DeMeo and 'Nino'. DeMeo arranged a meeting with Rothenberg for Sunday, 29 July, at a local diner. As soon as he arrived outside the diner, DeMeo approached him, ordering him out of the car and into a nearby alleyway at gunpoint. He shot him twice in the head.

Rothenberg's murder paid off for DeMeo in several ways. Firstly, of course, he had divested himself of the problem that was Rothenberg. Secondly, and much more importantly, Gaggi and the Gambino Family were impressed.

A couple of years later, in 1972, Andrei Katz, a young Jewish Rumanian immigrant who ran a bodyshop known as Veribest Foreign Car Services in Flatlands, Brooklyn, became DeMeo's next victim. Katz had become involved with the DeMeo crew in some drug business as well as in a deal involving a number of stolen vans. He rented one of these vans out, but the customer to whom it was rented was stopped by police who discovered the van was stolen. Katz was arrested and offered a deal to cooperate by telling them where he had got the van. He refused, but when he was out on bail, he was threatened by members of the DeMeo crew and was then beaten up by two masked men whom he recognised as Joey Testa and Tony Senter. Foolishly, Katz tried to take revenge on Rosenberg, taking a shot at him with an automatic rifle. Rosenberg was wounded, but survived.

By this time, Henry Borelli, a Gambino man who was an expert marksman, had joined the crew. They wanted to take care of Katz once and for all, but he was careful, never going anywhere alone. Borelli dreamed up a plan whereby a female acquaintance of his would lure Katz to a place where he could be dealt with by the crew.

In June Katz met the woman at her apartment, but the Gemini Crew was waiting for him. He was abducted and driven to the meat department of a supermarket where he was stabbed in the heart and back with a butcher's knife. DeMeo and Joey Testa, who had both in their youth worked as butcher's apprentices, dismembered the body. He was decapitated and his head was crushed in a machine used for compacting cardboard. The remainder of the body was then put in bags and thrown into a skip behind the store. A few days later, a woman walking her dog was horrified to find one of Katz's legs lying on the pavement close to the supermarket. The body was identified through his dental records.

They had carried out their first murder as a team, but it may not have been their first dismemberment. In 2003, Salvatore Vitale, a former Bonanno underboss, claimed that in 1974 he had had to drive a body to a garage in Queens where Roy DeMeo and a few others waited. Vitale claimed he saw DeMeo with a large knife, presumably to be used in the dismemberment and disposal.

In 1975, DeMeo began to transgress against customary Mafia rules, involving himself in a peep show and prostitution establishment in New Jersey.

He was also dealing in pornography of the most graphic kind, including bestiality. Nino Gaggi warned him about this and even threatened him if he persisted with it. But DeMeo carried on and, luckily, Gaggi ignored it, presumably happy to continue receiving his increased weekly payment.

DeMeo was also heavily involved in drug trafficking, another area that was taboo for the Mafia, but only if you were caught. The profits were huge and DeMeo was dealing cocaine out of the Gemini Lounge and importing marijuana from Colombia in 25-pound bails. The money rolled in and as long as Nino got his share, he was prepared to turn a blind eye to its source.

In May 1976, Joseph Brocchini, a made man in the Mafia, made the mistake of punching DeMeo in the face when an argument they were having about a pornography business in which they were both involved got out of hand. DeMeo was prevented from killing Brocchini by Mob protocol, but swore revenge anyway at a meeting about it with Gaggi. On 26 May, he and Borelli cold-bloodedly shot Brocchini five times in the back of the head in the office of his used car dealership, making it look like an armed robbery gone wrong, blindfolding the employees and ransacking the office. DeMeo was on a roll. Next month, a young man, Vincent Governara, with whom Gaggi was in dispute, was shot several times by DeMeo and

Gaggi and died in hospital a week later.

In July, DeMeo and Gaggi flew to Florida to kill another enemy, George Byrum, who had stupidly given burglars information to help them rob Gaggi's house. He was lured to DeMeo's hotel room and shot as soon as he walked in. The plan had been to dismember him in the hotel room with the help of a local Gambino man, but there was construction work going on and they fled the scene leaving the body in the bath, its head half-sawn off.

The body count rose. An informer who had described DeMeo to the FBI as a 'ruthless killer' who had killed at least a dozen people and dismembered their bodies, had this fact confirmed for himself not long after when he was murdered. Nino's nephew, who was acting as DeMeo's driver, said that DeMeo had pointed out a newly built gas station and told him that he and the boys had buried two people under its foundations.

In 1976, when Carlo Gambino, head of the Family, died, Paul Castellano took over and Nino was promoted to capo. But Castellano was a different kind of boss. He behaved more like a businessman than a gangster and was contemptuous of the type of street crime that DeMeo specialised in – car theft and hijacking. Besides, DeMeo was a violent and un-predictable individual. For these reasons he opposed

DeMeo ever becoming a made member of the Family. DeMeo was devastated, but continued to try to impress by finding more ways to bring cash into the Family.

He finally managed it with a bold plan to broker a partnership between the Westies, an alliance of Irish-American gangs, and the Gambinos. This alliance brought in a lot of money, and he was finally inducted in 1977 and made responsible for all the business the Family did with the Westies. But he still ignored the customary Family rules regarding drug trafficking and persisted in selling large quantities of coke and marijuana, as well as pills. However, he was not the only one who flaunted this rule.

Neither did he bother too much about the rule that said members should seek permission before killing anyone. In June 1977, the crew took care of Johnathan Quinn, a car thief suspected of informing, and Cherie Golden, his 19-year-old girlfriend who just happened to be there at the wrong time.

By 1978, DeMeo was claiming to have committed 100 murders and he let it be known that he and his crew were open to contracts. They carried some out for as little as $5,000. Some were even done for free – 'personal favour', he would say.

They also killed their own. Edward 'Danny' Grillo had joined the team, but was heavily in debt to DeMeo. DeMeo and Gaggi suspected he would cooperate with police and so he was disposed of. Chris Rosenberg, original Gemini Crew member, was next. He had done a drug deal down in Florida, but had murdered the people he was buying from, a Cuban and his associates, and walked off with the money as well as the drugs. The Cuban had connections with a Colombian drug cartel and they insisted that Rosenberg be killed. DeMeo was given the contract, but weeks passed and he failed to carry it out.

In the meantime, he made a tragic mistake when he killed Dominick Ragucci, a college student who was working part time as a door-to-door vacuum cleaner salesman. When DeMeo saw Ragucci's car outside his house one night, he thought he was an assassin from the Colombian cartel and shot him to death after a car chase. This killing irritated Gaggi and he ordered DeMeo to get on with killing Rosenberg. He finally summoned him to a meeting and after Rosenberg had kissed him on the cheek, he shot him in the head. It was a killing that affected DeMeo deeply, probably the only one that ever did.

The money continued to pour in through his numerous enterprises. He now controlled the biggest car theft operation in New York's history. Hundreds of cars stolen on the streets of New York were being shipped from ports in New Jersey to Kuwait and

Puerto Rico. The profits were huge and the Family benefited as much as he did.

He was still not liked, however, even within his own organisation. Gambino man James Eppolito went to Paul Castellano in 1980, claiming that DeMeo and Gaggi were involved with drugs. But Castellano liked Gaggi and chose not to believe Eppolito. He gave Gaggi permission to kill him which he and DeMeo duly did, shooting him and his son to death in their car. A witness was able to alert a nearby policeman and Gaggi was shot and arrested after a shoot-out. Meanwhile, DeMeo got away without being seen. Nino was charged with murder, but only sentenced to 5–15 years for assault after the jury was got at. Needless to say, shortly after the trial, DeMeo murdered the witness.

In 1981, the car operation began to fall apart when Henry Borelli and another crew member, Frederick DiNome, were arrested. But luckily for the rest of them, there was not enough evidence to make further arrests. DeMeo ordered the two men to plead guilty and he hoped that their convictions might bring an end to the FBI's investigations into his affairs.

It did not, however. The FBI became curious about the number of people who had disappeared after last being seen entering the Gemini Lounge. To make matters worse for DeMeo, Paul Castellano, fed up with DeMeo's activities, put out a contract on him.

However, he could not find anyone willing to carry it out. Eventually, it was handed to Frank DeCicco but he passed it on to DeMeo's own crew.

DeMeo, aware of what was going on, began wearing a leather jacket with a shotgun hidden under it. It wasn't enough, however, and on 10 January 1983, he went to a meeting at Patrick Testa's bodyshop and disappeared. Eight days later, police responded to a call saying that a car appeared to have been abandoned in the car park of the Varnas Boat Club in Sheepshead Bay, Brooklyn. When they opened the boot, they were surprised to find a large chandelier and underneath it Roy DeMeo, his hand frozen in rigor mortis with a bullet hole right through it, as if he had raised it to protect himself. His leather jacket was wrapped around his head and he had been shot a number of times in the head and in the hand. At least they did not dismember him.

Although the government had lost Roy DeMeo, they were not to be defeated and continued to look for evidence against the remainder of the Gemini Crew. Anthony Gaggi was suspected of having personally carried out DeMeo's murder, but although he was charged with a number of other murders, that was not one of them. He died of a heart attack during his trial in 1988.

Henry Borelli, Joseph Testa and Anthony Senter (the Gemini twins) were sentenced to life for a collective total of 25 murders. Paul Castellano was indicted for ordering the killing of DeMeo, but was gunned down before the case came to trial.

The FBI and New York Police Department estimate that DeMeo and his crew were responsible for at least 70 murders, although the true total could be closer to 200. Most were never found.

NICODEMO DOMENICO SCARFO

Nicodemo Domenico Scarfo's family had Mafia blood running through their veins and within a couple of decades of his birth, 'Little Nicky' had it running in the streets of Philadelphia.

His father was a made member of the New York-based Genovese Crime Family and his son, Nicky Jr. became a made member of the Lucchese family, while Nicky himself was boss of the Bruno or Scarfo Crime Family which ruled the roost, in organised crime terms, in Philadelphia and parts of southern New Jersey, including Newark. This makes them probably the only men to have the distinction of being made members of three entirely different families.

Nicky was born into this Mafia dynasty in 1929 in Brooklyn and before long had attracted the sobriquet 'Little Nicky' on account of his diminutive stature; fully grown, he stood a mere five feet six inches tall.

While a young man, he made a living as a car valet, parking cars at clubs, but was introduced into the Bruno Family by his uncle, 'Nicky Buck' Piccolo, known as one of the last of the 'gentlemen gangsters'. This contrasted with his nephew Nicky, who was anything but a gentleman and was, instead, renowned for his volatile temper and violent ways.

'Little Nicky' was also known to be a narcissistic individual. There are countless reports of him gleefully scanning the crime reports in the newspapers to see if he had rated a mention. This was, of course, contrary to the customary Mafia way. Mobsters tended to be media-shy. It was good for business if nobody knew who you were.

In the 1970s Scarfo was working in Atlantic City. He had been sent there long before casinos had been legalised but had established a network of contacts so that by the time the New Jersey legislature decided in 1976 that gambling could provide the state with some easy income, Scarfo was in a good position to create the steel and concrete companies that would be contracted to lay the foundations for the 35 casinos that would be built in the last few years of the seventies. The Scarfo and Bruno families controlled the unions and if casino developers caused them any trouble, all it took was the threat of a strike which would delay their projects and, ultimately, lose money for everyone; a 30-day delay, for instance, could cost a casino owner $15–20 million.

Scarfo and Bruno also ensured that a man called Mike Matthews was elected as mayor of Atlantic City. Matthews would present them with no problems as they went about their business and he understood very well that if he did, he would be trying a concrete overcoat on for size. Eventually, Matthews was found guilty of accepting a $10,000 bribe and went to prison for 15 years.

When Bruno Family boss Angelo Bruno was murdered in the summer of 1980, his underboss Philip Testa and his *consigliere* Anthony Campanegra were left in charge, but when Campanegra was himself murdered a month later, Testa named Scarfo as the new *consigliere*.

Testa himself did not last long. He believed that a captain in the Bruno Family, Chickee Narducci, was robbing the Mob through his numbers business and, in addition, the two men were having disagreements about loans. Narducci had a bomb packed with roofing nails and explosives placed under the porch of Testa's home, because he thought, probably correctly, that if he did not murder Testa, Testa would murder him.

The Crime Commission realised that Narducci must have called the hit on Testa and what's more, he had done it without their authority, a serious breach of the rules. They contracted Scarfo to take care of Narducci and before too long he was found in a pool of blood in the back of his Cadillac. Scarfo also took care of one of Narducci's men who had been involved in the Testa murder. He placed a home-made bomb in the man's mouth and set it off.

Peter Cassella, Testa's underboss, called a meeting of the Family and said that he had been cleared by New York to be the next boss of the Family. Scarfo did not believe him and, on the day of Testa's funeral, travelled to New York to meet the heads of the Genovese and Gambino Families. He was told that Cassella was lying and no approval had been given for his assumption of leadership of the Family. Scarfo persuaded them to make him the next boss of the Family. He was invited onto the Crime Commission in 1981, becoming an ally of the powerful Genovese Family.

As a soldier, Scarfo was ruthless. In 1962, a man called Dominick 'Reds' Caruso had shown fatal disrespect to Bruno Family *consigliere* Joe Rugnetta by slapping him on the face. Scarfo, along with Sal Merlino, Santo Idone, Anthony Cassella and Santo Romero, was ordered by the then boss, Angelo Bruno, to strangle him. One of the secrets of a successful hit is to get close to your target and Scarfo was already friendly with Caruso. For a few weeks he kept his company, eating and drinking with him. Consequently, it did not seem at all out of the ordinary to Caruso when Scarfo invited him to Anthony 'King Kong' Perella's Bar in Vineland, New Jersey. Idone was going to carry out the hit according to the orders of their boss, by strangling Caruso. But he was late and Scarfo reached for his gun and shot Caruso five times, but without killing him. Scarfo reached for what was to hand which happened to be an icepick. He buried it so deeply in Caruso's back that it would not come out and had to be broken off. Idone eventually appeared with a rope that they wrapped around Caruso's neck. They then took the body for perusal by Bruno. He ordered it to be buried in rural Vineland and then removed and reinterred, just in case one of the original gravediggers decided to inform on them. You could never be too careful.

As boss, Scarfo was even more ruthless. He broke all the records for mob violence, having at least 30 members of his own crime family rubbed out in the four years following Testa's murder. They were killed for failing to obey orders or simply because he suspected them of being disloyal to him. He also homed in on the Riccobene faction of the former Bruno Family that was vying for control of Atlantic City. More than 24 Riccobenes were targeted in a war that went on for months.

He drove a white Rolls-Royce and took the entire

Bruno Family on holiday to Florida where he had a yacht, *The Casablanca*, much photographed by the FBI as hoods came and went. They were able to make connections from these images which could be used as evidence that individual crooks were, in fact, working for one organisation.

Scarfo learned from the methods of the Families in New York and Chicago, running loan-shark operations and providing protection. On pain of death, they demanded a piece of the action from every independent business in their area. He moved his Family's business affairs into narcotics – once taboo for the Mafia – and, by 1984, Philadelphia was the United States' amphetamine capital.

There are stories of Scarfo's out-and-out love for killing. It is said he loved it so much that, even when he was boss, he would accompany his soldiers on hits. Bosses of Families never did this and it is testament to his bloodlust. At the trial of Scarfo, his underboss Philip Leonetti and capo Lawrence Merlino for the murder of Vincent Falcone, Joseph Salerno, a former associate of the Mafia boss, testified for the prosecution. Falcone was Scarfo's partner in his construction company but, unfortunately for Falcone, Scarfo believed he was ripping him off. In reality, Falcone's biggest mistake was to be critical of the workmanship of Scarfo's men.

Scarfo and Leonetti invited him to a hideaway where they all had dinner. After the meal, Leonetti stood behind Falcone and shot him in the back of the head. Scarfo celebrated the hit with more alcohol, but putting his hand on Falcone's body he felt a heartbeat and ordered Leonetti to finish him off with a bullet in the heart. Scarfo then mocked the dead man, calling him a 'no-good motherfucker'. Chillingly, Salerno related that Scarfo exclaimed: 'I love this!' during the killing, as if he were playing a game of pool.

Scarfo and Leonetti were arrested and charged with Falcone's murder in 1983 and Salerno became a star witness for the FBI under the witness protection programme. However, a local cop who was on the Bruno Family payroll testified that Scarfo's car was not at the property where the murder was committed, contradicting Salerno, who testified that Scarfo had parked his black Cadillac in front of the building. As a result of his testimony, the cop was thrown off the police force but it sowed enough seeds of doubt to mean that the two men were found not guilty. With a grin on his face, Scarfo declared after the trial, 'Thank God for the American jury system. And an honest jury.'

Scarfo could be dangerously unreliable. Even his closest friends were reluctant to trust him. Salvatore Testa, son of Phil Testa, was a good example. In the months following his father's murder, Salvie was promoted through the ranks to the position of capo. He was an extremely violent man, a violence exploited by Scarfo who used him in 15 different hits. But this was Scarfo and with him there was always danger. Salvie was a childhood friend of Leonetti, now underboss to Scarfo, and he relied on his friend to give him a warning if anything bad was going down. Leonetti failed to do so, however, when Salvie made the mistake of falling for the wrong girl. He had been engaged to Leonetti's daughter, but when he broke it off in favour of another girl, his reliability and unflinching obedience counted for nothing. Scarfo ordered his death and Salvie was eliminated by Nicky 'The Crow' Caramandi in September 1984.

Caramandi was worried, however, that Scarfo had, in turn, ordered that he be hit and went to the FBI who put him into the Witness Protection Programme.

Scarfo relied on fear but it eventually backfired on him when, between 1987 and 1989, no fewer than five of his trusted lieutenants, who could not stand working in such an atmosphere, turned against him and became government informers.

The FBI played on the insecurity felt by members of the Family as their colleagues were rubbed out by Scarfo. In the summer of 1989, they arrested Leonetti for the murder of Salvatore Testa. He contacted the FBI before his trial, but they told him to wait until he had been sentenced. He was given 45 years' imprisonment, but as soon as the trial was over he began talking. He went into protective custody with his wife and children and served only five years of his sentence.

Capos, Tommy DelGiorno and Lawrence Merlino, plus soldier Gino Milano, joined Leonetti and Caramandi on the programme. By the end of 1989, no fewer than 20 members of Scarfo's Family were incarcerated and an additional ten were under indictment or awaiting Grand Juries.

As for Scarfo, already serving 14 years for extortion, he was convicted in 1989 of the murder of Frank 'Frankie Flowers' D'Alfonso.

D'Alfonso had refused to pay tribute to Scarfo and Scarfo had ordered Salvie Testa and another soldier, Gino Milano, to persuade him to come into line. D'Alfonso was beaten with a steel rod and a baseball bat and received a fractured skull, broken jaw and a broken kneecap. The bones under both eye-sockets were shattered and two bones in his left leg were broken. He needed 64 stitches in a head wound. When asked by police officers what had happened, he merely replied that he had been hit by a truck.

The beating did not yield the correct response, however, and several years passed during which D'Alfonso continued to refuse to pay tribute. One day in July 1985, when he went out to buy cigarettes, two men walked up to him and fired five bullets into his back and head.

Scarfo was sent to prison for life and is scheduled for release in 2033 when he will be 104 years old.

JOHN GOTTI, 'THE DAPPER DON'

It was Monday, 16 December 1985. The black Lincoln negotiated the driveway of the mansion, known as the White House, in Staten Island and pointed its nose towards Manhatten. Paul Castellano, owner of the mansion and head of the Gambino Crime Family, was relaxed. Christmas was only nine days away and, on his way to dinner, he was going to stop off at his lawyer's office to distribute a few presents to the staff. Then he would do a little Christmas shopping before heading for the restaurant. He sat back in the front seat of the Lincoln as his driver and bodyguard, Thomas Bilotti, guided it sedately through the late afternoon traffic. Neither man was carrying a gun.

Dinner was at 5 p.m. at Sparks Steak House restaurant on 46th Street, between Second and Third Avenue, and his guests would be three of the capos of the Gambino Family of which he was head – Thomas Gambino, son of Carlo and head of a successful trucking company, James Failla whose interests lay in rubbish disposal and Gambino soldier Frank DeCicco.

As they drove into town, they hit heavy midtown traffic as the evening rush hour began to build. Christmas shoppers, out in force, did not help. Eventually, however, having done their other chores, they arrived at the restaurant and Bilotti nosed the Lincoln into a space which said 'No Parking'. It's amazing the effect a Police Benevolent Fund sticker on the windscreen could have on parking wardens. It was 5.45 p.m.

As the two men climbed out of the car, three other men who had been hanging about outside the restaurant straightened up and approached them. The men were dressed oddly, in Russian-style fur hats and white raincoats. Castellano and Bilotti, straightening their suits on the sidewalk, looked up and were horrified to see pistols, .32s and .38s, in the hands of the three men who stopped not too far distant and, raising the guns, opened fire. Numerous bullets thudded into the bodies of Castellano and Bilotti before they could react. Castellano was hit six times in the head and chest and Bilotti took four bullets. They fell to the ground and one of the fur-hatted men stood over Castellano and delivered the *coup de grâce*, a final bullet in the head. The three then ran off in the direction of Second Avenue.

It was the first assassination of a Commission member since Alberto Anastasia had been rubbed out in the barbershop of the Park Sheraton Hotel in 1957. And with Big Paul out of the way, John Joseph Gotti was now top of the heap in the Gambino Family, one of the Mafia's five Families.

He had been born 45 years previously in the Bronx to Naples-born John Gotti Sr. and Philomena 'Fannie' Gotti, the fifth of their 13 children, and when he was 12 the family moved to the rough Italian neighbourhood of Sheepshead Bay in Brooklyn. They were poor which gave Gotti something of an inferiority complex, especially around anyone more fortunate than himself. He had a quick temper and envied the gangsters he saw strutting around the neighbourhood in their $100 suits and fancy cars. He wanted nothing more than to be one of them when he grew up.

School was only a minor irritant to Gotti and, generally speaking, he ignored it and it ignored him. On the rare occasion he did attend, he distinguished himself by being the class bully and by being disruptive. So he got his education on the street where he ran messages for the local hoods and hung out with a gang.

His first real criminal act took place when he was 14 – a robbery at a construction site. It ended in farce, however, when a cement mixer he and some acquaintances were trying to steal tipped over and crushed his toes. The remainder of his summer was spent in hospital.

At the age of 16 he became a fully-fledged member of the Fulton-Rockaway Boys, a local teenage gang that stole cars, fenced stolen goods and mugged drunks. It was around this time that he first met two men who would become long-term associates – Angelo 'Quack Quack' Ruggiero and Wilfred 'Willy Boy' Johnson. Gotti was arrested five times while he ran with this gang, but true to one of the nicknames given to him later in his career, 'the Teflon Don', he got no more than probation.

He married in 1962 and had five children – Angela 'Angel', Victoria, John A., Frank and Peter, named after Gotti's brother Peter, a minor gangster who hung around with the Gambino Family. He also had three illegitimate children with a Staten Island woman, Shannon 'Shady' Connelly, wife of a Gambino soldier, Ed Grillo.

Marriage straightened out the 22-year-old Gotti . . . for a short while. He got work as a presser in a coat factory and was also a truck driver's assistant for a while. But it did not last and after a year or so he was arrested for being in a stolen hire car. This resulted in his first jail term, but he was only inside for 20 days. His arrest record quickly began to grow, however, and he was picked up often, for crimes such as burglary, larceny and bookmaking. He did some more time in jail in 1966 – a couple of months for attempted theft. In that same year, however, he became involved with the Mob, working for Carmine Fatico, a Gambino capo who reported to underboss Aniello Dellacroce.

Gotti started out pretty low in the pecking order, fencing goods stolen from Idlewild Airport, later to be known as Kennedy Airport, but was soon doing well enough to move his family to a better apartment in Brooklyn. In 1967, however, he was arrested by the FBI while hiding in the back of a truckload of stolen merchandise. They charged him with three hijackings and he was sentenced to four years at Lewisburg Federal Penitentiary. He was inside for less than three.

Released from prison, he was put on probation and ordered to get a job. His wife's stepfather's construction company provided the job, but Gotti, of course, never did a single day's work there. He returned to his old ways, hanging out with the Gambinos at their headquarters, the Bergin Hunt and Fish Club in Queens. He got lucky when his boss, Fatico, was indicted for loan sharking and, although he was not a 'made' man – a full member of the Mafia – neither were any of the other guys on the crew. So Gotti was asked to mind the shop which brought him to the attention of the Gambinos and Aniello Dellacrace, a man just as foul-mouthed and vicious as Gotti. Dellacroce made him acting capo, at the age of 31. He began to cultivate friendships in high places. He became a good friend of the powerful Dellacroce and was close to the head of the Family, Carlo Gambino, until his death in 1976.

Gotti was now involved in much more serious matters than just hijacking trucks or fencing stolen goods. In 1973, when a nephew of Gambino's was kidnapped and found dead, even after a ransom of $10,000 was paid, the boss called on Gotti to wreak revenge. A couple of men, Edward Maloney and James McBratney, were linked to another kidnapping, but were almost certainly not the abductors of the boy in question. That was a mere detail to Gambino. He ordered Gotti to go after them.

On 22 May 1973 McBratney was sipping a crème de menthe at Snoop's Bar and Grill on Staten Island when three men entered the bar and surrounded him. They told him they were detectives and that he was under arrest. When they tried to put handcuffs on him there was a vilolent struggle. When a bystander shouted out to them to show some ID, one of the men did indeed show his credentials. He pulled out a gun and fired a slug into the ceiling. Then the two others held McBratney and he fired three shots into his body. McBratney's crème de menthe was left unfinished.

Witnesses to the murder picked two men out of the police mugshot book immediately – Angelo Ruggiero and Ralph Galione – and the third man was identified as John Gotti. The three were arrested and pleaded guilty to manslaughter – it had just been a bar-room brawl after all, they claimed. Gotti was sentenced to two years, but when he was released he achieved his life's ambition – he became a 'made' member of the Mafia.

But, suddenly it all started to go wrong.

Paul Castellano was now in charge and when Gotti's crew were caught selling heroin he disbanded them. It had been decreed at the infamous Apalachian summit of Mafia heads that drugs were off-limits – 'if you deal, you die'. So, in reality, Gotti was lucky to get away with his life.

But then Castellano decided to have dinner at Sparks Steak House.

As head of the Gambino Family, Gotti began to walk the talk. He took to wearing $10,000 suits tailored by Brioni in Rome, tailor to kings, earls and the super-rich. So why not a Don, a Dapper Don as they started to call him in the press? His picture appeared in magazines and on television and he loved it. He would pose outside his hang-out, the Ravinelli Club in Manhatten, shaking hands and posing for photographs with tourists. In Queens he threw lavish street parties and made sure that his was the only crime taking place on its streets. He was adored for it.

In the 1980s, he escaped conviction on racketeering and assault charges several times by bribing and threatening jurors. He became 'the Teflon Don' – nothing would stick and he used police informants to make sure it stayed that way.

He remained a vicious, cold-blooded killer though. In 1980, his 12-year-old son Frank was run over and killed when he ran out from behind a parked car. The man driving the car that hit him, a salesman named John Favara, was warned that he should move out of the area. He did not, and a few months later disappeared, never to be seen again.

As the 1990s arrived, Gotti had to be increasingly on his guard. The FBI were on his case, following him wherever he went and listening to him non-stop. Everywhere was bugged. He was forced to hold meetings walking in the street or to play loud tapes of white noise when he was having a conversation. Eventually, of course, he made a mistake. He was heard in an apartment above his club discussing a number of murders as well as other criminal dealings. They arrested him on 11 December 1990 and threw the book at him; several books in fact. He was charged with 13 counts of murder, conspiracy to commit murder, racketeering, loan sharking, obstruction of justice, illegal gambling and tax evasion. Amongst the murders were those of Paul Castellano and Thomas Bilotti. A witness placed Gotti outside the steakhouse immediately before Castellano and Bilotti were shot.

He was hung out to dry. Former Philadelphia underboss Philip Leonetti testified that Gotti had boasted about ordering Castellano's murder. Sammy 'the Bull' Gravano testified against his boss and went into witness protection. He detailed 19 murders for 'crimes' such as cheating, failing to show respect, lying, giving false evidence to a grand jury and so on. The jury found him guilty on all 13 charges and he was sentenced to life without possibility of parole.

He went to the penitentiary at Marion, Illinois, where he was kept in strict conditions of maximum security. His cell, measuring just eight feet by seven, was underground and he was locked in it for 23 hours a day, being allowed out to exercise for just one hour a day in a concrete-walled enclosure. He was permitted to shower twice a week and could have a radio and a black and white television. Meals arrived through a slot in the door. However, illness struck and in September 1998, The Dapper Don had to undergo an operation to remove a cancerous tumour.

The Dapper Don never did complete his time. He died of throat cancer on 10 June 2002 at the United States Medical Center for Federal Prisoners at Springfield, Missouri and was buried in Queens, next to his son, Frank.

JOEY 'BIG JOEY' MASSINO, THE LAST DON

When Joey Massino was convicted in New York, in 2004, his charge sheet was a roll-call of Mafia crimes of the past 100 years – murder, racketeering, arson, extortion, loan-sharking, illegal gambling, conspiracy and money laundering. This head of the Bonanno Crime Family had certainly come a long way.

Although Joey later became a restaurateur, his catering career had humble beginnings – a mobile food-wagon in the Queens area of New York, selling coffee and pastries to workers in the docks. He began his Mafia career in the 1960s as a protégé of Philip 'Rusty' Rastelli and his brothers. Rastelli was a nasty, violent individual who, a few years later, would rise to the top of the heap in the Bonanno Family. With the Rastellis, he got into running numbers, hijacking trucks and fencing stolen goods.

In 1975, Paul Castellano, who would in the future become head of the Family, ordered Massino to carry out a hit on Vito Borelli. Borelli was dating Castellano's daughter and had made the fatal mistake of insulting Castellano in front of her by comparing him to a man called Frank Perdue, a businessman with a cooked chicken brand who used to advertise it personally on television. The fact that Perdue himself resembled a plucked chicken, did not endear Borelli to Big Paul. So Massino, accompanied by John Gotti, another future Family head – the Gambinos in his case – killed the unfortunate Borelli at a Manhattan cookie business owned by Bonanno soldier Anthony Rabito. Other men involved were Dominick 'Sonny Black' Napolitano, Rabito and Angelo Ruggiero, Roy DeMeo and Frank DeCicco. Massino's brother-in-law, Salvatore Vitale, was asked to drive the body to a garage where they were waiting. Borelli had been shot in the face and body and he was wearing only his underpants. Vitale noticed that one of the men was holding a knife and speculated that the man with the knife was Roy DeMeo whose speciality was cutting up bodies like a Perdue chicken.

Borelli's murder provided a boost to Massino's career and in 1976 he became a made man of the Bonanno Family, reporting to Philip 'Lucky Phil' Giaccone. Best of all, he was still a complete unknown to the Federal authorities. In June of that year, the body of Joseph 'Doo Doo' Pastore was discovered in a dumpster, round the corner from Massino's restaurant in Maspeth. He had been killed with two shots to the head. There was a connection to Massino because Pastore was a truck hijacker who supplied Joey with stolen goods that Massino fenced for him. It did not take police long to make the connection and he and Richard Dormer, Pastore's half-brother, were taken to the morgue to make an identification of the body. It was no coincidence that, just before the murder, Massino had asked his brother-in-law, Salvatore Vitale, to borrow $9,000 from Pastore for him. It looked like he would never have to repay that particular debt.

Massino was in court in 1977 on a charge of hijacking a truck but was acquitted while his co-defendant Raymond Wean went to jail for three years.

In 1979, Rusty Rastelli took over at the top of the Family following the killing of Carmine Galante in his favourite restaurant, Joe and Mary's Italian-American Restaurant at 205 Knickerbocker Avenue in Bushwick, Brooklyn. The 69-year-old Galante died with his trademark cigar in his mouth, blasted in the face and chest at point-blank range with a shotgun. Although Massino was not one of the shooters, he is reported to have been seen outside the restaurant on the day of the shooting. Whatever his involvement, Rastelli's promotion was good for Massino – he was advanced to the rank of *caporegime*, just three years after becoming a made man.

In 1989, when Massino heard that Alphonse Indelicato, Dominick Trinchera and Philip Giaconne were plotting to take over the Bonanno Family by purging Rastelli's men, he went to Family bosses Carmine Persico and Paul Castellano for advice. They told him that he had only one option; kill them or be killed himself.

Sonny Red Indelicato, Giaccone and Trinchera were lured to a meeting with their rival factions, accompanied by capo Frank Lino. Gerlando 'George from Canada' Sciascia, Vito Rizzuto and Sonny Black Napolitano burst out of a closet in the room where the meeting was taking place and gunned down Trinchera, Indelicato and Giaccone. Lino escaped.

Napolitano would, himself, suffer at Joey Massino's hands in 1981 when he made the mistake of proposing a man called Donnie Brasco to become a made man in the Family ahead of Salvatore Vitale, Joey's brother-in-law. Vitale, Joey said, had been involved in killings for years, whereas Brasco had not been around for more than a few years and had not been part of any hits for the Family. Unfortunately for Napolitano, Brasco

121

turned out to be Joe Pistone, an undercover FBI agent, a fact confirmed when he disappeared from view. Sonny Black Napolitano also disappeared from view in August of that year. He was taken to a meeting at the house of a Family associate. Frank Coppa, a Bonanno capo, greeted him and threw him down a flight of stairs into the basement of the house. He was shot dead and when Frank Lino handed Sonny's car keys over to a group of men in a waiting car, he noted that one of them was Joey Massino.

Another victim of the Donnie Brasco embarrassment in February of the following year was the widely feared street soldier Tony Mirra. Mirra had been the one who had introduced Brasco to the Family. Massino handed the contract for the killing to Mirra's cousin, Richard Cantarello. Mirra was lured to a parking garage in Lower Manhattan where another cousin, Joseph D'Amico, climbed into his burgundy Mercedes beside him and shot him in the temple. When the police found Mirra hours later, he had been shot twice behind his ear and once in the face.

When a number of the Bonanno hierarchy were arrested, Massino became a fugitive, indicted by a Federal Grand Jury in Manhattan along with five other men on a charge of conspiracy to murder Indelicato, Giaccone and Trinchera. On the run, his associates kept him in funds and many of his colleagues, including John Gotti, made the trip to visit him.

Massino was now running the Family and, even though Rusty Rastelli had been released from a spell in prison, it was Joe calling the shots.

His next hit was Cesare Bonventre who had been Carmine Galante's – unsuccessful – bodyguard on the day he had been killed. Bonventre was invited to a meeting with Rastelli in Queens, but was picked up by Salvatore Vitale and Louie Attanasio and never made it to the meeting. They drove into a garage where Attanasio shot him twice in the head. Bonventre was a strong guy and he struggled, despite his wounds. They had to pull into a car park where Bonventre crawled out of the car. Attanasio jumped out and pumped another two bullets into him. Gabriel Infante was given the job of getting rid of the body, but it was found shortly after, in April 1984, cut in two and stuffed into 55 gallon oil drums in a warehouse. It was the last mistake Infante made.

Things were becoming a little hot and Massino decided that the best thing would be to turn himself over to the police. He was given bail and released. In 1985, he was indicted for labour racketeering along with Rastelli, Carmine Rastelli, Nicky Marnagello and 13 others. Then in October of the next year he was found guilty of violations of RICO Law, the Hobbs Act (robbery or extortion) and the Taft-Hartley Act (labour racketeering). In January 1987, he was sentenced to ten years.

As if that were not enough, April 1987 saw him in court again, on hijacking and murder charges. Joe Pistone/Donnie Brasco testified against him, tried to implicate him in a triple murder as well as the conspiracies to kill Pastore and Indelicato. He was acquitted of the hijacking charges due to a legal problem, but went to prison until 1993.

Rastelli had died in 1991, and when Massino came out of prison, he seemed to be the only man who could fill his shoes. He made Salvatore Vitale his underboss and Anthony Spero *consigliere*. He gained a reputation for living according to the old rules, keeping Cosa Nostra and membership of it secret. He accused the government of being biased towards Italian-Americans. He was doing a good job. The Bonanno Family regained its seat on the Crime Commission and business was looking up. It did not last long, however. Spero was given life for racket-eering and murder and his replacement, Anthony 'TG' Graziano, was indicted for murder, drug trafficking, extortion and illegal gambling.

Joey was, himself, indicted again in January 2003 and amongst the charges lurked seven murders: Alphonse 'Sonny Red' Indelicato, Philip 'Lucky Phil' Giaconne, Dominick 'Big Trin' Trinchera, Dominick

'Sonny Black' Napolitano, Tony Mirra, Cesar Bonventre and Gabriel Infanti. Things began to go very wrong when eight Bonanno men decided to give evidence for the prosecution, including Salvatore Vitale, his loyal associate of so many years. Massino had been best man at his wedding and was godfather to one of Vitale's sons.

In July 2004, he was found guilty on all counts and faced at least life or possibly execution. To the Mob world's horror, it was announced in February 2005 that Joey Massino had turned and was cooperating with the authorities, the first Mafia boss to do so.

As a result of his cooperation he succeeded in escaping the death penalty, instead being sentenced to life. He also admitted ordering the killing of Bonanno capo Gerlando Sciascia, waiving his right to appeal his conviction for the seven other murders.

Meanwhile the Mafia reeled.

PART TWO

OTHER AMERICAN KILLERS

FUNG JING TOY, 'LITTLE PETE'

It must have been quite a sight back in the late 1800s – Fung Jing Toy, better known as Little Pete, processing through San Francisco's Chinatown, one minder walking in front of him, one at his side and one behind him. Accompanying them was a trusted servant carrying a jewel case and Pete's toilet articles so that he could maintain his appearance. Alongside Little Pete was his interpreter, for, bizarrely, this Chinaman spoke no Chinese and could only bark his orders to his henchmen by way of a third party. Hovering in the shadows were half a dozen *boo how doy*, 'hatchet men', who would bury a hatchet in the head of anyone who so much as approached the little man. He took no chances, Little Pete. At night, he and his family slept in a windowless room behind a heavily built door that was both barred and bolted. As an added security measure, a vicious dog was chained on either side of the door to deter break-ins.

Little Pete himself was quite a sight. On his fingers he wore several of the numerous, expensive diamond rings he possessed and which he would change several times a day. As a protection against assassins, he wore a coat of chain mail over one of the 40 suits he owned, none of which he wore two days in succession. If his hat looked a little strange and uncomfortable, it was because inside it lay a protective thin sheet of metal, curved to the shape of his head. From under his hat grew a glossy queue – a pigtail – of which he was extremely proud. In fact he was so proud of it that every morning he would spend at least two hours brushing, combing and oiling it.

Although responsible for the deaths of at least 50 men, Little Pete was a cultured man. He played the zither and wrote comedies in his spare time which he had translated into Chinese and staged at the Jackson Street Theatre. It was never a problem getting them put on – he owned the theatre after all. Little Pete had reason to be cautious as he went about his business in Chinatown for he was, at the time, the most powerful Chinaman on the entire Pacific Coast. He ruled his own gang or Tong, the SumYops, with a rod of steel and exercised control over a number of other Tongs that were allied with his. The world of the Tongs was a violent one and careers were often short-lived, especially careers such as Little Pete's.

The first Chinese immigrants arrived in America in 1820, but until the California Gold Rush in 1848, fewer than 1,000 had settled in the United States. The Goldrush, however, provided plenty of work for them as labourers for the gold prospectors who had flooded into California. By 1852, 25,000 Chinese had arrived and by 1880 more than 100,000 Chinese immigrants had decided to make their future in America. They settled mostly on the Pacific Coast, and consisted mainly of poorly educated young men from the province of Guangdong on China's south coast.

Chinese immigrants often suffered at the hands of other ethnic groups and Tongs, and benevolent organisations were created for the support and protection of Chinese–American communities. Originally, the Tongs emerged in 17th-century China as political–religious bodies, but the 19th-century American versions were often special fraternal groupings of merchants, craftsmen and tradesmen. However, along the Pacific coast of America, criminal Tongs also sprang up, dealing in opium and gambling, activities accepted in China but illegal in the United States. Further revenue was derived from prostitution and protection.

As the number of criminal Tongs grew, so, too, did quarrels and territorial disputes, resulting in bloody feuds and violent clashes between rival gangs. These gang wars spanned a period of some 70 years, starting in the 1850s and not fading out until the 1920s by which time the Chinese–American community had grown wealthier and had begun to feel more secure in its adopted country.

Fung Jin Toy arrived in America with his merchant father when he was five years old, in 1869. That year, as Ulysses S. Grant succeeded Andrew Johnson as President of the United States, Little Pete began work as an errand boy, working for a Chinese shoe-manufacturer. By the age of 21, he owned his own shoe company, J.C. Peters & Co, the only legitimate business with which he was ever involved. He had become attracted to the profits to be made from gambling establishments and opium dens and had also begun to dabble in the slave trade. By 25 he was head of the Sum Yop Tong and intent on expanding his business interests.

The Su Yop Tong were one of Chinatown's most powerful criminal organisations and when Little Pete began stealing girls from Sue Yop members, animosity broke out between the two Tongs. Soon, they were at each other's throats, engaged in a bitter and bloody war, a war in which, it is reported, Little Pete hacked to death 50 members of the rival Tong. In the midst of all this, however, he made a grave error, foolishly trying to bribe the jury and the entire prosecution team, including the District Attorney, when one of his killers was put on trial for the murder of a Sue Yop man. His mistake cost him the next five years which he spent in San Quentin State Prison.

On his release, Little Pete picked up where he left off, escalating once more the war with the Sue Yop whhich had died down considerably during his incarceration. Having been to prison once, he sought legal protection, retaining the noted criminal lawyer Thomas D. Riordan. Critically, however, he forged an alliance with the blind saloonkeeper and Democratic Party political boss of San Francisco, Christopher A. Buckley, nicknaming him the Blind White Devil. Buckley ruled the city for some 20 years, the most corrupt years in San Francisco's history. Soon, with friends in such high places, Little Pete was riding high as the undisputed boss of Chinatown, with tribute being paid to him by every business, legal or illegal. If payments were not paid, establishments would receive a visit from the San Francisco police and would be closed down, to be reopened a few days later with Pete and his gang in charge.

By now, Little Pete was an enormously wealthy man. Revenues from his business interests flooded in, but he always wanted more. Horse racing was the next thing to take his fancy and in 1896 he could be found in the betting rings of the Bay District and Ingleside tracks placing very large bets, sometimes amounting to as much as $8,000 a day. He never lost and within two months had won over $100,000. Naturally, it was not long before stewards became suspicious of the epidemic of sick horses and inept rides by previously talented jockeys and wondered if perhaps it might have something to do with Little Pete's success. When private detectives followed jockeys to the offices of his shoe company, J.C. Peters, it became evident that he was bribing them to throw races and paying trainers and stable boys to poison their horses. But although the racing establishment was outraged and jockeys were banned, they were unable to pin anything on Little Pete and he pocketed his winnings and carried on as before.

The Sue Yops were still smarting over his success and decided to finally bring an end to his reign in Chinatown, joining forces with 12 other Tongs to engage the Sum Yop in a war of extermination. Little Pete was, naturally, the principal trophy in this war and a record-breaking price of $3,000 was placed on his metal-covered head.

Three thousand dollars was a significant amount of money and would guarantee a comfortable old age back in China. Consequently, the race was on to win the money and Little Pete was pursued everywhere by assassins – the *boo how doy* of the enemy Tongs were out in force as were numerous freelance professional killers. Little Pete's iron curtain of bodyguards and hatchet men could not be penetrated, however.

Lem Jung and Chew Tin Gop were two young Chinese men who had arrived from China to find their fortune prospecting for gold in Oregon. Having made a considerable sum of money, they headed for Chinatown in January 1897, to see the sights before returning home to China. Both men were members of the Suey Sing Tong that was opposed to Little Pete's Sum Yops. But they were peaceful men and neither had ever fired a pistol or swung a hatchet in anger. Neither had they heard of Little Pete before their arrival in San Francisco.

It was their cousin, Lem Jok Lep who first told them of the head of the Sum Yop Tong, his criminal activities and the high price that had been put on his head. Lem Jok was an important man, occupying, on behalf of the Suey Sings, a seat on the strategy committee that had been set up by all the Tongs opposed to Little Pete and his men. As he explained the way Little Pete operated to his two cousins, they became angry and decided that there was no reason why they should not kill him and claim the substantial reward.

You would be excused for believing their decision to be a little foolhardy, given the number of people protecting Little Pete and the fact that many of the most efficient hatchet men and assassins had failed so far in the task. Nonetheless, on 23 January 1897, Chinese New Year's Eve, Lem Jung and Chew Tin Gop strolled into the barbershop which occupied the ground floor of Little Pete's building at the corner of Waverley Street and Washington Street in San Francisco. Little Pete, ever careful about his appearance, was, at that moment, bent over a sink, the barber wetting his hair under a tap before plaiting it into the queue of which the little man was so proud.

For once, however, his cautious nature had failed him. He had been running late that morning and had hurried out of his apartment accompanied by only one of his bodyguards. He had then sent this man out to buy a newspaper for him to read while the barber worked on his queue. So, when the two young men entered the barbershop, Little Pete was utterly defenceless. Chew Tin Gop stayed at the door watching out for the returning bodyguard, while Lem Jung walked up to the Sum Yop leader and grabbed a handful of his hair, at the same time pushing the barber to one side. He pushed the barrel of the revolver he was carrying down the back of Little Pete's neck, inside the coat of chain mail and pulled the trigger again and again. Little Pete fell to the floor with five bullets lodged in his back.

The two men fled the barbershop to be hailed as

heroes. They received their money before escaping to Portland where they boarded a ship for China. Meanwhile, other assassins who had been loitering in the vicinity of the barbershop, armed to the teeth with knives, guns and hatchets, were arrested and charged with the murder, only to be acquitted later.

Little Pete's death marked the end of the Sum Yops and the other Tongs took savage revenge, slaughtering their enemies. It was a slaughter that was ended only by the intervention of the Emperor of China himself. Thomas Riordan, Little Pete's attorney, sent a cable to Emperor Kwang Su pleading for help, and the Emperor consulted with the great Chinese statesman, Li Hung Chang. Li Hung Chang ordered the arrest of all relatives of the Sue Yops living in China and threw them into prison, threatening to behead them if one more Sum Yop was murdered in San Francisco. The war ended abruptly and a peace agreement was signed by the Sum Yops and the Sue Yops. It is a peace that has never been violated.

The funeral of Little Pete was one of the most lavish ever seen on the Pacific Coast. The funeral cortège was more than a mile long and firecrackers exploded the length of the procession. There were three Chinese bands, and numerous black-gowned priests swung noisy rattles. A huge quantity of baked meats, rice, gin and tea was hauled by a dozen express wagons. At the cemetery, however, there was a riot when a party of thugs threw themselves on the cortège and gorged themselves on the food.

GEORGE 'BUGS' MORAN

George Clarence Moran was born Adelard Cunin on 21 August 1891 on a farm near Minneapolis, Minnesota, to Jules Adelard Cunin and Diana Gobbeil, giving him a curious Irish–Polish lineage. He had one brother and two sisters who would later be scandalised by the activities of their sibling.

When the family moved to Kilgubbin in Chicago's North Side, the young George began to turn to crime to make a little money on the side. He would kidnap delivery horses and hold them hostage until the owner paid a ransom. Eventually, he was picked up for his horse theft as well as other petty crimes, and was incarcerated in Minnesota's infamous Red Wing Juvenile Correctional Facility. He escaped, however, changing his name to George Miller to avoid detection on the outside. He ended up in the North Side of Chicago but, when he was arrested in Bloomington, Illinois, for grand larceny in 1912, he gave the name George Moran in order to conceal his previous record. He had apparently tried on a few other names for size – George Heitl and George Cage amongst them, but Moran was the one that stuck and that is how he became known from then on. 'Bugs' is the gangster name for someone who is crazy or eccentric and in that name he has illustrious company – Bugsy Siegel and Bugs Bunny, to name but two. He was given it because of the volatility of his temper, but he was just as likely to burst into laughter as explode with anger.

By the time Moran was 21 he bore the battle scars of his tough criminal apprenticeship – a four-inch-long knife scar along the right side of his neck and a crooked middle finger from a broken bone that failed to heal properly. He had already been in prison three times, but had also formed friendships with several people who would influence the course of his murderous life – Dean O'Banion, the violent Irish gang leader and florist, who walked with a limp following a streetcar accident and was afraid of no one, skinny Polish mobster Earl Wojciechowski, known as Hymie Weiss, and a moody Italian robber and kidnapper, Vincent 'the Schemer' Drucci.

Their early activities were strictly small-time and gave no hint of the colourful lives they would later lead. They mugged drunk customers leaving the club at which O'Banion worked as a bouncer and they also busied themselves with pickpocketing, shoplifting, breaking and entering and, eventually, armed hold-up and safe-cracking. Moran was arrested in the process of robbing a warehouse and went to Joliet Prison for two years. But the gang were working their way up the gangster ladder, eliminating all their rival gangs and establishing the 42nd and 43rd Wards of Chicago's North Side as their territory. They began to socialise with politicians and judges, letting them know that they could help them out in whatever way they needed – delivering votes at election time, stopping people from voting for opponents and ending disputes. Moran, O'Banion and company had no objection to getting their hands dirty. The favours were returned. Once, when Moran was arrested after his fingerprints were found on the dial of a safe, the judge let him go after a tongue-lashing. As he left the courtroom, Bugs muttered to the amusement of the reporters: 'It was an oversight. Hymie was supposed to wipe off the prints and he forgot.' Soon, they had recruited more bootleggers, gamblers, safe-crackers and killers and had become the largest gang in Chicago.

Bugs could not bribe every judge, however, and in 1917 he was caught red-handed, carrying out an armed robbery in a department store. He went back to Joliet for a five-year stretch, emerging again in 1923.

When the Volstead Act introduced Prohibition in 1918, other gangs began to put their snouts in the trough that had been the North Side Mob's alone. Johnny Torrio and his lieutenant, Al Capone, moved into the Southside of Chicago, pushing out an Irish brothers' gang, the Southside O'Donnells, and any other gang that got in the way. Torrio tried to establish borders around each gang's territory and worked alongside O'Banion and his North Siders for a while. Trouble flared, however, when the Gennas, a band of Sicilian brothers who were allied to Torrio and Capone, started undercutting O'Banion and his men on sales of booze on North Sider territory. O'Banion started hijacking the Gennas' alcohol shipments.

When O'Banion started labelling the Italians as 'greaseballs' and 'dagos' and Moran used the words 'Scarface' or 'the behemoth' to the press to describe Capone, the situation started to get out of hand. It ended with the assassination of O'Banion. The Gennas owed him $30,000 for a gambling debt and O'Banion told them they had to pay it in a week 'or else'. He then set up Johnny Torrio, telling him that he wanted to get out and retire and inviting him to buy his Siben Brewery. When Torrio turned up the cops were waiting for him. It was his second offence and he went to jail for nine months while O'Banion just laughed and paid a paltry $7,500 fine. When Torrio found out that he had been set up, the order went out to kill the florist. Frank Yale, John Scalise and Alberto Anselmi obliged, gunning the Irishman down in his flower shop.

Following O'Banion's death, the leaders of the North Side gang, Weiss, Moran and Drucci, ran a brazen advert in the city's main newspapers, stating that they would be running the organisation as equals. They signed it 'Board of Governors'. Chicagoans were highly amused, but Chief of Police, Morgan Collins, was enraged by their nerve.

Hymie Weiss took over at the top and Bugs became underboss. Their names began to become regular features in the press, and Bugs would be photographed regularly, always immaculate in three-piece suit, cashmere coat and expensive fedora. He was loved by politicians because he gave them money and helped finance their affairs and their lifestyles, and ordinary Chicagoans loved him because he seemed a Robin Hood figure to them, taking on the authorities and ever-ready with a quip or a joke. They also loved the fact that he was beating the Sicilians at their own game. To them, even his violence was carried out with style.

The Capone mob and Weiss and Moran's gang now engaged in a massive turf war that would cost the lives of many men on each side, but would also, ultimately, cost Scarface his freedom.

Moran hated Capone. It was not just about fighting for power and wealth. It was personal. Like O'Banion, he was disgusted by the fact that Capone's business interests included prostitution. In spite of his violence and criminality, Moran was still a good Catholic, a better one, to his mind, than Capone. He refused to run brothels or pimp prostitutes, lucrative though these were. He set out to avenge O'Banion and kill his nemesis, Al Capone.

Their first attempt on Capone's life happened more by accident than by design. On a snowy night, 12 January 1925, Moran, Drucci and Weiss had been driving round town, hoping to find him. When they finally saw his black sedan parked outside Palermo's Restaurant on the South Side and 'the behemoth' climbing out of it, it was like all their Christmases rolled into one. They quickly took aim with three machine guns and opened fire, Capone and his men throwing themselves to the ground as bullets peppered the car. Only Capone's driver was injured and Scarface lived to fight another day. He took no chances though. From then on he drove round in a specially built armoured car.

They may have failed to nail Capone, but they came close to killing Torrio himself. He rarely carried a gun and refused a bodyguard, a stubbornness that he would live to regret. On 25 January 1925, Weiss and

Moran waited for him outside his house in a car driven by Vincent Drucci. As soon as Torrio pulled up and got out of his car, Moran and Weiss leapt out, guns blazing. Torrio's driver was wounded and fell to the ground. Torrio took off, running towards his house but as he reached the lawn, heard a blast and felt a sharp pain on his face. Blood began to spurt from where a bullet had blown away a part of his cheekbone. He was hit several times more and crumpled to the ground. Moran approached him, gun at arm's length, preparing to fire a shot into his skull to deliver the *coup de grâce*, but, pulling the trigger, all he heard was a click. He had run out of ammo. By now, people were looking out of their windows and cars were stopping at the top of the street to take a look. Moran cursed and jumped into the car, fleeing the scene, leaving the Italian still alive.

Torrio adhered to the strict Mafia code of *omerta* and would not divulge to the police who had tried to kill him. Moran was eventually arrested, but Torrio would not press charges and it was over. It was over for Torrio, too, however. He only just escaped with his life and decided to hang up his gun. He handed all his affairs over to his sidekick, Al Capone, and went into retirement.

Bugs decided that with Torrio out of the way, it was time to go after the Gennas. After all, they had caused all the trouble in the first place. Accompanied by Weiss and a few other associates, he ambushed Angelo Genna in May 1925, but he escaped and a frantic car chase ensued. Angelo lost control of his vehicle, crashed headlong into a lamppost and was trapped behind the wheel. Bugs's car pulled up and he got out, blasting away into the Sicilian's car, killing him.

Angelo's brother, Mike, tried to take revenge on the North Siders, engaging in a fierce but inconclusive shoot-out with them. Shortly after, however, he was shot to death by the police. Then Giuseppe 'The Cavalier' Nerone, a Genna ally, was added to the toll. In November of that same year, Vince Drucci wiped out Genna backer Samuzzo Amatuna in a shooting in a barbershop. That left only Tony Genna who was gunned down, although it is unclear whether he was shot by Bugs and his gang or by Al Capone, clearing up the last vestiges of the Gennas and grabbing the spoils.

Moran thought he could hurt Capone by taking out some of the heavy security presence around him. So he kidnapped one of his bodyguards, tortured him with wire and burned him with cigarettes, before executing him and dumping his body. It made no difference.

Capone, in his turn, ambushed the North Siders a number of times. One day, Moran and Drucci were intercepted as they drove along Congress Avenue.

Machine-gun bullets thudded into the car's upholstery as it jumped the kerb and crashed into a nearby building. They clambered out into the nearest doorway, firing backwards at their pursuers. They escaped through the building, and ran in the direction of the nearest friendly doctor.

In August, a passing car opened fire on Weiss and Drucci as they made their way to the Standard Oil building to pay off a politician. The two men jumped behind parked cars as passers-by screamed and hit the dirt.

Just five days later, Weiss and Drucci were again targets for Capone's goons. This time they shot back and the street became something like a scene from a Hollywood gangster movie, as Drucci jumped onto the running board of a car belonging to Capone soldier Louis Barko. The driver gunned the vehicle, hitting the pavement and throwing Drucci to the ground. He stood up and fired at the retreating car. When the cops arrived, Drucci said he was merely trying to stop some thieves who had tried to steal his wallet. He was charged with nothing more than creating a public disturbance.

In September 1926 Moran made another attempt on Capone's life. A fleet of six cars, machine guns poking out of curtained windows, drove into Cicero, the town on the outskirts of Chicago that was the base for Capone's operations. They drove down 22nd Street where Capone's hotel, the Hawthorne, was located, firing at every building. When they got to the hotel, a man dressed in overalls jumped out and began raking the lobby with machine-gun fire. Inside, Capone had been drinking with his personal bodyguard Frankie Rio. Rio threw Capone to the floor as the bullets shattered glass and furnishings around them. By the time the cars sped off, over 1,000 bullets had been fired, although the initial shots had been blanks, intended to scare people off the streets. Again Capone was left shaken but unhurt. In fact he was so shaken that he tried to call a truce with Moran and Weiss, but to no avail. The war continued and Capone again struck back, hitting the gang at its very heart.

The following month, as he was crossing State Street in Chicago with four of his men, Hymie Weiss was gunned down in a hail of shotgun and sub-machine-gun fire from a nearby second-storey window. Hymie died, aged 29, leaving $1.3 million. It was revealed that he suffered from arterial cancer, the symptoms of which were severe headaches, dizziness and fainting fits. He had not expected to live to an old age anyway, and had had little to fear when fighting Capone and his goons. Eventually, everyone decided enough was enough and, at a peace conference attended by Moran and the other bosses, it was decided to bring the shootings and bombings to an end and ensure that everyone got his fair share.

The peace held for a while but during it another of Moran's cohorts died. Vincent Drucci was killed in a fight with the police, not with other gangsters. Now, with everyone dead apart from himself, Bugs Moran assumed leadership of the gang at the age of 34.

Capone and Moran kept an uneasy distance from each other. Moran would hijack the odd shipment of bootleg liquor and Capone would retaliate by burning Bugs's dog track. Then Moran would burn Capone's Hawthorne racetrack. But Moran was still killing Capone's associates. It also scared him and he was now going everywhere with a retinue of 15 body-guards surrounding him.

Bugs made yet another attempt to assassinate him, this time by putting poison in his food. However, Capone's chef discovered the plot before it could happen. Even his own men were beginning to betray him – the Sheldon Gang, supposed to be his allies, were supplying hootch to Moran. Capone was getting edgy.

He became even edgier following the murders of a couple of close friends of his, successive leaders of the Unione Siciliano – Antonio Lombardo and Pasqualino 'Patsy' Lolordo. Lombardo was shot dead at a crowded intersection on 7 September 1928 and the killers are believed to have been Bugs and Frank Gusenberg, one of his men. Lolordo was shot in his own apartment. His wife reported that as the killers left, one of them gently placed a pillow under the dead man's head. Moran's regular bombings of his businesses did not help and Capone was beginning to unravel. There was only one thing to do and that was to undertake a massive strike against the North Siders. He missed Bugs who was late for a meeting at the S-M-C Cartage Company garage in North Clark Street which served as his headquarters, on 14 February 1929, but his men, dressed as cops, audaciously massacred seven North Siders in the Valentine's Day Massacre, one of the most infamous gangster hits in history.

The massacre was organised by Jack 'Machine Gun' McGurn, but, by 1936, seven years later, McGurn was broke. He had been abandoned by his former gangster associates and had even tried to make it as a professional golfer. One day he was at a bowling alley when two men carrying machine guns, walked in and shot him to death. Beside the body they placed a handwritten note containing a cruel rhyme. It read: 'You've lost your job/You've lost your dough/Your jewels and handsome houses/But things could be worse, you know/You haven't lost your trousers.' The date? Valentine's Day. Bugs had finally taken his revenge.

After the Valentine's Day killings, things started to go awry for Bugs and the North Siders. Capone began to move in and although he and what was left of the gang tried to regain their lost territory, it was all over and he was left with no option other than to get out of town.

He moved first of all to Wisconsin and then back home to Minnesota. His marriage broke up and he fell on hard times. Moving back to Illinois, he robbed a few banks and filling stations but by 1940 he was back in Ohio, a member of the Virgil Summers–Albert Fouts gang, a bunch of small-timers a million miles away from the hoods he used to run with. He was eventually arrested by the FBI in 1946 for robbing a bank messenger of $10,000, a sum he would not have crossed the road for in the good old days. Moran went to the Ohio Penitentiary for ten years, being released in 1956. However, he was immediately re-arrested for an earlier bank robbery that had brought him and his fellow robbers a measly $4,000. He went to Leavenworth Penitentiary for another ten years.

George 'Bugs' Moran died in Leavenworth of lung cancer on 25 February 1956, missing Valentine's Day by just 11 days.

VERNON C. MILLER

The body lay in a ditch by the side of the road outside Detroit. It was 29 November 1933 and Vernon C. Miller, known as Verne, had been tied up, savagely beaten and shot to death. It was surmised that he had been the victim of a gangland slaying, but the real reason was unclear. It had been an eventful few months, however. In October, he had been staying with New Jersey gangster Abner 'Longy' Zwillman in Orange, New Jersey, but an argument had ended in him killing one of Zwillman's henchmen. Then, on 1 November, while he was hiding out in the apartment of his girlfriend Vi Mathis, posing as an optical supplies salesman, the FBI had raided it. He had escaped but only just, shooting his way out.

It had all been so different back in 1916, when Verne Miller was 16. Tall and blond, he was born in Kimball in South Dakota to parents who divorced while he was still young. He went to live with his Uncle Clarendon, a county commissioner, treasurer and sheriff, in Bule County, South Dakota. He worked as a car mechanic and then left home aged 16, and convincing a recruiting officer that he was 21 enlisted in the National Guard, serving on the Mexican border when Mexican revolutionary Pancho Villa was active. In the First World War, he served in France with the 18th Infantry Regiment. He was gassed, wounded twice and, he claimed, was awarded the Croix de Guerre by the French for bravery. He reached the rank of colour sergeant before being honourably discharged at the cessation of hostilities.

He returned to America a war hero and spent his spare time fishing and boxing, although the latter activity was seriously hampered by the lung damage he had received in the war. He took a job as a policeman in the town of Huron, but resigned in 1920 to take the post of sheriff of Beadle County, South Dakota.

Prohibition had been voted in 1919 and Miller is reported to have raided at least ten stills making illicit whiskey in its first 18 months. In 1921, he displayed his own brand of justice when a young farm worker was shot dead by members of the Industrial Workers of the World, otherwise known as the Wobblies. He infiltrated the Wobbly ranks, disguised as a hobo, and although he never actually brought the killer to justice, he arrested a man for attempted murder. He disappeared at one point into what were known as the Badlands of South Dakota. It was believed that Sheriff

Miller had meted out his own justice to the boy's murderer.

Miller was considered after that to be a little too ready to use his gun to administer justice and is reported to have even fired warning shots at cars breaking the speed limit. However, he pursued lawbreakers relentlessly, even arresting a gang of his own friends who were running an illegal still.

Then suddenly, in July 1922, he disappeared. He had said he was going to a Washington hospital for treatment to his damaged lungs, but, when he failed to return, his deputies discovered that he had embezzled $6,000 from city funds. He was arrested in St Paul the following October, gave up without a struggle and pleaded not guilty. When it came to his trial, though, he changed his plea to guilty and was sentenced to two to ten years in prison and fined $5,200.

Miller kept his nose clean in the state penitentiary. He had none of the bad habits that most prisoners had, such as gambling or drinking, and the warden of the prison made him his personal chauffeur. He was released on parole in November 1924, after just 18 months, working as a farmhand for $70 a month until the conditions of his parole had been satisfied.

He was in trouble again in June 1925 when he was arrested for violating Prohibition. He skipped bail that had been put up by his father and brother and left town. The following summer, Miller met Vi Mathis, who had recent divorced her husband following his incarceration for first degree murder. When Miller met her, Vi was working at a carnival in Brainerd, Minnesota. When Miller spotted an antagonistic customer bothering the woman, he intervened and rescued her from a nasty situation. After that the couple were inseparable.

They prospered. Miller is thought to have been the getaway driver in a bank robbery in Huron, South Dakota and he was working as a bootlegger with a member of Al Capone's gang. But during the second half of the 1920s he was in the grip of syphilis and had been a heavy drug-user for years. He became unstable and prone to sudden violent outbursts. This was the case one night in February 1928, when he got into a fight at the Cotton Club in Mineapolis, in which two policemen were shot and wounded. His associates Kid Cann and Bob Kennedy were arrested, but released due to lack of evidence.

He was identified around this time as having taken part with another two men in a bank robbery in the small Minnesotan town of Good Thunder. Then, several months later, he was indicted for the shooting of a Prohibition agent.

By now he was a gun for hire, working on a freelance basis for Midwest mobsters and bootleggers.

In 1930, one of his associates was gunned down by Al Capone's men and Miller, incensed, tracked down three of them to a hotel in Fox Lake, Illinois, where he ruthlessly gunned them down. It was getting a little too hot and he and Vi quietly left town, heading for Montreal where, in partnership with a New Jersey mobster, they opened some casinos.

Returning to the States in 1932, Miller hooked up with the Holden–Keating Gang whose members included Harvey Bailey, the leader, known as the 'Dean of American Bank Robbers'; Tommy Holden; Francis 'Jimmy' Keating and accomplices Machine Gun Kelly and Frank 'Jelly' Nash. Their first bank robbery took place not long after Miller returned to American soil. They hit a bank in Wilmar, Minnesota, getting away with a $70,000 haul. One member of the gang was killed and two passers-by were wounded. However, there was an argument about the robbery, Miller believing that someone had double-crossed them. The outcome was the discovery by the police in the course of their investigation, of three men, shot to death and dumped at White Bear Lake. Miller had lost it and killed his three associates, Frank 'Weinie' Coleman, Sammy Stein and Mike Rusick.

The next three years consisted of little other than robbing banks and living the good life for Verne and Vi. Amongst these was a bank in Ottuma, Iowa, robbed in September 1930, netting them $40,000, and one in Sherman, Texas, in April the following year from which they got away with another $40,000.

Miller now retired from robbing banks and concentrated on being a hired gun, but he did not lose contact with the other members of the gang. Through them, he was hired as a shooter in one of the most notorious criminal attacks of the time, the incident known as the Kansas City Massacre.

Frank Nash, a member of the Holden–Keating gang, was a career criminal, sentenced to life in 1913 for murder, only to be pardoned. In 1920, he received a 25-year sentence for burglary with explosives, but again, astonishingly, he was pardoned. Twenty-five years was also the sentence handed down to him for assaulting a postman in 1924. This time he stayed inside for six years, escaping from the notorious Leavenworth penitentiary in October 1930. A huge manhunt was launched, but it was unsuccessful. In the meantime, Nash was thought to have helped in the escape of seven prisoners from Leavenworth.

The authorities knew that he had connections with the bank robbers Francis Keating and Tommy Holden, and when those two were arrested in 1932 they provided vital information as to where he was hiding out.

So in June 1933, two Federal agents, Frank Smith and F. Joseph Lackey, accompanied by Police Chief

Otto Reed of McAlester, Oklahoma, travelled to the Arkansas town of Hot Springs where they had been informed they would find Nash. After combing the town, they picked him up in a local store. They then drove him to the train station at Fort Smith, where they boarded a train bound for Kansas City. It would be arriving there next morning, at 7.15 on 17 June. In Kansas City they were to be met by R.E. Vetterli, the agent in command of the FBI's Kansas City office.

On the train were a number of agents apart from Lackey and Smith. Agent Raymond Caffrey and Kansas City detectives, W.J. Grooms and Frank Hermanson were also there as back-up.

Meanwhile, in Kansas City, Miller, Adam Richetti and Charles 'Pretty Boy' Floyd waited, machine guns at the ready.

Floyd and Richetti had already had an eventful couple of days. On the way to Kansas their car had broken down and while they were waiting in a garage for the work to be done on it, the local sheriff came in. Richetti, fearing he would be recognised, grabbed his machine gun and told the sheriff and the mechanics to stand against the wall. The two men then transferred the small arsenal they were carrying in their car into another, bundled the sheriff in and drove off in the direction of Deepwater, Missouri where they abandoned their vehicle and stole another. They released

157

the sheriff and drove on to Kansas City, arriving at 10.00 p.m. on the 16th. Again, they abandoned their car, replacing it with another, and went to meet Miller who took them to his house. There he outlined the plan to free Nash which had been given to him by the plan's originators, Chicago mobsters Richard Tallman Galatas, Herbert Farmer, 'Doc' Louis Stacci and Frank B. Mulloy.

Early on the morning of the 17th, they had driven to Kansas City's Union Station where they took up their positions and waited for the train from Fort Smith.

The agents were extremely cautious when they arrived. Lackey disembarked first to check that it was all clear, leaving Nash on the train with the other agents and police officers. Vetterli was waiting for them with two cars that were parked outside. The seven officers accompanied Nash off the train into the station. Lackey and Police Chief Reed were armed with shotguns, the other officers carrying pistols. At the entrance to the station, they stopped momentarily to check that there was nothing suspicious before moving towards the parked cars.

Agent Caffrey unlocked a door of one car, ordering Nash into the back seat. Lackey, however, insisted that Nash should get into the front seat, which he did. Lackey climbed in at the rear, on the driver's side, Smith sat in the middle and Reed on the right. As

Caffrey walked round to the driver's seat, he suddenly spied two men running from behind a car parked nearby. Both were armed with machine guns. Before he could shout a warning, one of the two men called out 'Let 'em have it!' The men opened fire and agents Grooms and Hermanson crumpled to the ground dead. Vetterli took a bullet in the arm and tried to crawl over to Caffrey, crouching down on the car's left side. As he did so, Caffrey took a bullet in the head and sprawled on the ground dead. Nash and Reed inside the car were also dead, but Lackey and Smith cowered in the back seat; Lackey was seriously wounded, but Smith was unscathed.

The gunmen ran to the car and, seeing that everyone was dead, turned and sped towards their own vehicle. At that moment there was gunfire from the direction of the station where a police officer had appeared, trying to see what the commotion was. One of his bullets hit Floyd, but he carried on running. They jumped in their car and took off, disappearing into the morning.

Floyd and Richetti headed for Toledo, Ohio and thence to Buffalo. Richetti was hanged for the murder of Frank E. Harmanson in October 1938. Charles 'Pretty Boy' Floyd died in a shootout with law officers at a farm near Clarkson, Ohio. The creators of the plan to free Frank Nash – 'Doc' Stacci, Herbert Farmer,

Richard Galatas and Frank Mulloy – were indicted by a Federal Grand Jury in October 1934. They were found guilty of conspiracy to cause the escape of a Federal prisoner from the custody of the United States. Each was sentenced to two years and fined the maximum amount of $10,000.

Whether Verne Miller was killed because of the killing at Zwillman's apartment, because of the failed attempt to free Frank Nash or because of the Fox Lake Massacre will probably never be known. But back in Huron, they chose to remember Vernon C. Miller the sheriff, and not Verne Miller the outlaw. The local newspaper, *The Evening Huronite,* reported that the citizens of Miller's hometown 'refused to remember his reputation of a life of crime and grieved the Verne Miller, fearless sheriff and valiant soldier they knew'. His wife Mildred, though legally separated since 1929, said that she didn't believe all the things that they were saying abour her husband, '. . . because he became involved in a few scrapes nearly every major crime in the country was laid to him. He was wonderful to me and I have nothing against him.'

As an army veteran and a member of the American Legion, Miller was entitled to full military rights at his funeral, but the local Legion prevented it. Instead, Verne Miller received his military rights at a service in his father's hometown, White Lake. His casket had a

Stars and Stripes flag draped over it and was escorted from White Lake to Huron by friends of his who were ex-servicemen. There, after a service in front of a huge crowd of onlookers, Verne Miller was buried in Huron's Riverside Cemetery

LOUIS 'TWO GUNS' ALTERIE

He would amble into a speakeasy, his large frame dominating the room, and throw his ten-gallon hat down on the bar, sending a loud cowboy whoop echoing off the rafters. He would then proceed to 'persuade' the proprietor that it would be in his best interests to sell the beer or whiskey that displayed the label of his boss, Dean O'Banion. They always knew it made sense. The alternative was a wrecked establishment, a beating, or a gutful of lead. Sometimes all three.

Louis Alterie was a complete one-off in the gangster world of the first four decades of the 20th century. He was a cowboy in the big city and photographs show him incongruously wearing a huge stetson and a double-breasted suit. He had a range of nicknames. Mostly he was known as 'Two Gun' but the names 'Three Gun', 'Diamond Jack' and 'Kid Hays' also attached themselves to him.

He was born Leland A. Varain, the son of a rancher in Northern California in 1886 and had been a shooter for the South Side's Terry Druggan gang, a union enforcer who loved to pretend to be a cowboy cleaning up the town like Wyatt Earp, although he was more like Jesse James. Alongside Hymie Weiss, Vincent Drucci and Bugs Moran, he became a member of Chicago's North Side gang, engaged in mortal combat with Al Capone's South Side gang throughout the 1920s.

Alterie's speciality for O'Banion was fixing union elections. He would threaten union leaders with violence in order to get him and his associates elected to the presidencies of their unions. This is reckoned to have netted him around $50,000 a month, after he had paid his dues to his boss, O'Banion.

He used his wealth to buy many things – restaurants, nightclubs, apartment buildings and theatres. He also fulfilled his cowboy dream when he purchased a 3,000-acre ranch in the vicinity of a town called Gypsum in Colorado. He would be seen walking around town in his huge white stetson, diamond-encrusted cufflinks and belt-buckle, and expensive, hand-made cowboy boots. His car had a massive pair of bullhorns fixed to the bumper. He always maintained that he made his living in the city, but his heart belonged to the West, claiming that he preferred wrestling unruly steers to fellow gangsters as the former endured mistreatment better.

His money also bought the support of judges, politicians, law enforcement officers and even the city's mayor, 'Big' Bill Thompson, as he joined with the rest of the O'Banion gang in battles against not just the Capone mob, but also the Druggan–Lake Valley gang, the O'Donnell Brothers and the Gennas.

When Capone's men gunned down Dean O'Banion in his flower shop in November 1924, Police Captain John Stege had Alterie hauled in for questioning. Alterie is reported to have vaingloriously boasted in full view of police officers and the gentlemen of the Chicago press: 'If those cowardly rats have any guts, they'll meet me at noon at State and Madison and we'll shoot it out.' Not Gunfight at the OK Corral; more like Gunfight at State and Madison, with Alterie as Wyatt Earp and all his brothers rolled into one. Needless to say, the good Captain Stege was far from amused with such inflammatory statements.

Neither did trying to stage a Western-style shoot-out on the world's busiest corner endear Alterie to the rest of the gang who did not need the unwanted attention Alterie's statement brought on them. Bugs Moran met him at the Friar Inn and ordered him to leave town. Alterie hightailed it to Colorado.

Alterie is often given credit for inventing the 'one-way ride' where someone is abducted, driven off and never seen again. It may actually have been Dean O'Banion who invented it, but it is probable that Alterie was there at the time. It happened after a North Side gang hanger-on, John Duffy, smothered his new bride after a violent, drunken argument. Waking next morning to find what he had done, Duffy panicked. He needed money and a car to get out of town quick and Dean O'Banion said he could help. They arranged to meet at a bar called the Four Deuces, a South Wabash drinking den run by the Johnny Torrio/Al Capone mob.

Witnesses saw Duffy being picked up by O'Banion in a Studebaker at around 8.00 p.m. with another man in the car. Duffy's body was later found in a snow-bank ouside Chicago with three bullets from a .38 pistol in his head. A witness claimed to have seen O'Banion and two unidentified men dump the body but later withdrew his statement.

This was all bad news for Capone as the last sighting of Duffy had been at his club. The last thing he needed was unwanted attention being focused on the club which was a haven for illegal gambling, prostitution and bootlegging.

O'Banion protested his innocence, telling reporters: 'The police don't have to look for me, I'll go and look for them. I'll be at the state's attorney's office at 2.30 p.m. Monday afternoon . . . I can tell the state's attorney anything he wants to know about me.

Whatever happened to Duffy is out of my line. I don't mix with that kind of riffraff.'

There was no need to go and look for them. They failed to get enough evidence to bring charges. They thought that what had happened was that O'Banion and two accomplices had driven the desperate Duffy out to a remote area. When he had got out to relieve himself, O'Banion or one of the others had approached him from behind and shot him in the back of the head, in classic gangland style. Another two bullets were then pumped into him to make sure he was dead before his body was dumped. O'Banion had obviously wanted to avoid the focus an investigation would bring to his organisation and he also sensed a chance to make things difficult for Capone, an opportunity he never missed.

If Alterie was not entirely responsible for the invention of the 'one-way ride', he was the progenitor of the ambush murder. This involved renting an apartment close to the home or office of the intended victim and then staging a surprise attack.

One other claim to fame that is unique to Alterie is that he was probably the only gangster to have carried out a hit on a horse. While Samuel 'Nails' Morton was riding it in 1923, it threw him. Morton died of his injuries and Alterie blamed the horse. After Morton's funeral, he rented the horse, rode it to a remote location and shot it. Jimmy Cagney later re-enacted the shooting in the film *Public Enemy*.

Alterie's ranch sometimes came in handy. In January 1925, the newspapers in Denver, Colorado, were agog with the news that notorious gangster and member of the Dean O'Banion gang, Louis Alterie, who was wanted by Chicago police in connection with a jewel robbery, was hiding out at a ranch near Castle Rock. When the local County Sheriff went to the ranch to investigate, he was welcomed by a six-foot tall man who introduced himself as Leland Varain. Varain told the sheriff that Alterie had been there but had left. A week later, the Chicago police removed Alterie from its wanted list and Alterie emerged from his alter ego and met reporters from the *Denver Post*. The sheriff was not pleased to find out he had been duped. In the *Post*, Alterie was described as 'Six feet tall, weighs around 200 pounds, extremely dark. From the carefully combed, jet-black pompadour to the spats encasing his shoes, he is a picture of sartorial splendor. . . . Deep chest, wide shoulders, and body mounted on slender legs, and his heavy arms and diamond-covered hands finish the picture.'

In 1935, Alterie was subpoenaed to appear as a government witness in the case against Ralph Capone, Al's brother, who had been indicted for tax evasion. He observed the usual Mob niceties by at first refusing to say anything in the dock, even to the detriment of a hated Capone. However, a threat of imprisonment for perjury loosened his tongue and he testified against Ralph.

Like every other member of the North Side gang, the end of Prohibition and the Depression hit Alterie hard. In 1932, he lost his beloved ranch as well as just about everything else – the diamonds, the flashy outfits and the expensive car.

When they arrested him on suspicion of the kidnapping of a Chicago bookmaker, Edward Dobkin, he pointed out to the authorities that he would not be as poor as he currently was if he was a kidnapper. He was acquitted when Dobkin refused to identify him.

A few months later, he wounded two travelling salesmen after a drunken brawl with an ex-boxer called Whitey Hutton, at the Denver Hotel in Glenwood Springs. He was fined and put on probation.

He moved to Santa Fe, but eventually returned to Chicago where he resumed his control of the Janitors' Union of which he had been president in the good old days. He responded to any resentment with threats of violence and maintained his position, once again improving his fortunes.

Louis 'Two Guns' Alterie was involved in some 20 gangster killings during his time as an O'Banion enforcer and was himself gunned down by a blast of machine-gun fire from a nearby first-floor apartment window on 18 July 1935 while walking to his car with his wife. She was walking behind him and escaped unharmed. As he lay on the pavement, fatally wounded, with nine bullets in him, he gasped to his wife: 'I can't help it, bambino, but I'm going.' He died shortly afterwards. His killer, who, ironically, had used the method that Alterie himself had invented, was never caught.

'Two Guns' was buried in an unmarked grave under the name of Leland Varain.

JAMES 'WHITEY' BULGER

It would have been sometime in the late 1950s or maybe early 1960s. Mist drifted in over San Francisco Bay, blurring the rocky island on which the forbidding outline of Alcatraz Federal Penitentiary stood. Not that it mattered in solitary confinement which consisted of windowless steel boxes, into which prisoners were thrown clad only in their underwear. If you slid open the viewing panel on the door of one particular box, you would have seen a strange sight – a man crouching, his weight resting on just his elbows, his knees and his toes, permitting only the smallest areas of his skin to touch the icy-cold steel floor. In this way, he could stop the seering cold from entering his body, sapping his energy. To him, it was a way of preserving some dignity.

The man was James 'Whitey' Bulger, although you would have been ill-advised to call him 'Whitey' to his face; it was a name he detested. Bulger was serving time for armed robbery following a series of bank robberies in Massachusetts, Rhode Island, and Indiana. He had already been in the federal penitentiary at Lewisburg, Pennsylvania, but when guards learned of an escape plan, he was transferred to Alcatraz, America's most famous, or infamous, maximum-security facility. It was Bulger's bad attitude there that got him thrown into the hole.

By the mid-1960s, however, Bulger was out, exercising his particular brand of mayhem across South Boston, and by the time the seventies came around he ruled the Boston underworld. His reign lasted until the mid-nineties.

Where is he now? That is a very good question. He could be sitting on a train next to you, quietly reading an evening paper, or he might be the guy you bought a drink for in the bar last night. Since he went on the run in 1995, the only place you would be certain of seeing Whitey Bulger would be on America's Most Wanted list in which he has featured a record 12 times and in whose top ten he lies second only to Osama Bin Laden himself.

Jimmy Bulger – the name he prefers to be known by – grew up in the Old Harbor housing projects in South Boston, the oldest of six children, another of whom, his brother William 'Billy' Bulger, would go on in later life to become President of the Massachusetts State Senate. Known as 'Whitey' from an early age because of the natural blond colour of his hair, Jimmy was a wild kid. He is reputed to have had a pet ocelot and, at one point, he ran away to join a circus. Later, while still a teenager, he dated an older woman, a burlesque dancer known as 'Tiger Lil'. In Southie, the locals' name for the area, he was always in trouble.

But no matter what, he remained a Southie boy all his life and is fondly remembered by numerous South Boston residents for spontaneous acts of kindness, such as purchasing groceries for widows and providing turkeys for the poor at Thanksgiving.

Paroled in 1965 after nine years and after taking LSD as part of a CIA experiment at Leavenworth Prison in Kansas, Bulger returned to Boston and worked as a janitor for a few years. It was not long, however, before he returned to a life of violent crime, working as an enforcer for South Boston gang boss Donald Killeen. When Killeen was murdered by the Mullen Gang, another Southie grouping, Howie Winter, boss of yet another South Boston mob, the Winter Hill Gang, mediated between Bulger and the Mullens and the remaining Killeens. Winter grew to like Bulger and his no-nonsense methods and made him his man in South Boston. Bulger hooked up with an old friend, Stephen 'the Rifleman' Flemmi, a former paratrooper in the Korean War. The two became Winter's enforcers and Bulger developed a reputation as a man with a fearsome and violent temper. People who owed the gang money tended to pay up when they were told that Whitey might come and pay them a visit.

Throughout his criminal career, Whitey Bulger had one distinct advantage over other Boston criminals; he had the FBI on his team. Both he and Flemmi acted as informants for the Boston FBI office for years, being looked after by a guardian angel, Special Agent John 'Zip' Connelly. Connolly had tried to get Whitey to become what was known as a Top Echelon Informant for a long time and Whitey had been reluctant at first, but Connolly persuaded him that he could trust him. After all, they were both Southie boys, were both of Irish descent and had even both attended the same church. Anyway, the Mafia, headed up by underboss Gennaro 'Jerry' Angiulo, who had controlled the Mob's activities in Boston for almost 40 years, already had the police in their pocket. If the Winter Hill Gang went to war with them, there was only one way it could end. So the deal was that if Whitey provided information contributing to Angiulo's downfall, he would be left alone to carry on his 'business'. Whitey agreed to do it. 'If the Mafia can play checkers,' he said, 'we'll play chess.'

In the next few years, Connolly repeatedly bailed Bulger out just when it seemed the force of the law was finally going to be brought down on him. In one instance, when one of Howie Winter's lieutenants, 'Fat Tony' Ciulla, was given six years for race-fixing, he made a deal with the police, testifying against the Winter Hill Gang in return for entry into witness protection. He fingered Whitey and Flemmi, amongst others, but when the indictments were handed out, the names of the two men were strangely missing.

Connolly and his superior John Morris argued that Bulger and Flemmi were helping the FBI to bring down the Mafia. Indicting them for race-fixing would have undone all their work.

Things got even better for Whitey, however, when Howie Winter was convicted and a gap appeared at the top of the Winter Hill Gang. Whitey grabbed the position with both hands. Boston's most vicious enforcer was now at the top of the tree and he had the FBI on his team.

Whitey's approach to running South Boston was adapted from the Mafia's methods. The Winter Hill Gang would not dirty its own hands by selling drugs, loan sharking or by running its own backroom betting shops. Rather, it charged rent to others to do it. It was a subscription fee for being in business. Fail to pay and the consequences were bad – a beating the first time and the wrong end of a gun barrel the next.

He set up headquarters in a garage, Lancaster Foreign Car Service, on Lancaster Street in Boston's North End near the Boston Garden, the arena that, before it was demolished in 1998, was home to two of Boston's sporting institutions, the Celtics and the Bruins. When police planted bugs in the garage, trying to capture some incriminating evidence from the parade of known bookies who came to pay Whitey his dues every day, they were surprised to come up with nothing. They would have been even more surprised if they'd known that Connolly had, of course, tipped Bulger off.

With the support of the FBI, Bulger felt invincible. Bookmaker Louis Latif had been playing up and one of Bulger's henchmen, Brian Halloran, escorted him to the Triple O Tavern on West Broadway in South Boston. Bulger wanted to have a chat. It was a brief one. Only minutes after going into the bar, Halloran, waiting outside, saw Bulger and another man carry out Latif's body, wrapped in plastic, throw it in the boot of Latif's car and drive off.

In 1981, Bulger organised the killing of Roger Wheeler, chairman of Telex Corp and owner of World Jai-Alai, an organisation that ran the obscure Basque sport of Jai-Alai, beloved of Latinos and Americans.

Importantly, it was a game that provided many gambling opportunities. Wheeler objected to the Winter Hill mob skimming money from his organisation in Connecticut and was threatening to go to the authorities. He was shot at his golf club. As a postscript, former World Jai-Alai president John Callahan's body was discovered in the trunk of his rented Cadillac parked in a garage at Miami International Airport a few months later.

Connolly now came into his own. Investigators working on the Wheeler case asked for photos of Bulger and Flemmi. Connolly refused to oblige saying that if his informants said they had not done it, that was good enough for him. The investigators asked that the two gangsters take polygraph – lie-detector – tests. Again Connolly prevented it from happening. He was eventually forced by his superiors to provide the pictures, but they proved nothing and Bulger and Flemmi got away with it.

By this time, Connolly was wearing expensive suits and John Gotti-style blow-dried hair. Other agents insultingly started calling him 'John Cannoli'. Meanwhile, his boss John Morris was taking money from Bulger in order to fund an affair he was having with his secretary.

Eventually, the FBI took down Jerry Angiulo, but it was no thanks to information provided by Bulger or

Flemmi. They did provide information, but nothing that the FBI did not already know. The really useful stuff was provided by a bookie who informed on Angiulo's gambling operation and about the building in which it took place. As a result, the Feds planted listening devices in the walls and the result was 23 convictions, including Jerry Angiulo and two of his brothers. Connolly and Morris, of course, skewed the reports to make it seem as if Whitey and Flemmi had played major roles in Angiulo's downfall, justifying their continued employment as informants.

With the Mafia out of the way, Whitey Bulger now had Boston all to himself. He linked up with disaffected Mafiosi and began to work closely with Angiulo's successor, 'Cadillac Frank' Salemme.

Whitey bought a liquor store – although he hated alcohol and loathed drunks – and the shop next door to it – Rotary Variety. When a Rotary Variety customer won $14.3 million on the state lottery with a ticket purchased from the store, Whitey thought it would be nice if he shared it with him. He and two of his associates took half the winnings, allowing Whitey to claim $89,000 a year in income and sort out his problems with the Internal Revenue Service (IRS) at the same time.

The FBI helped him out on yet another occasion. He told a South Boston estate agent, Raymond

Slinger, that he had been hired to kill him, a threat not to be taken lightly where Whitey was concerned. Cunningly, he told Slinger that he would not go through with it if Slinger paid him $50,000. When Slinger took the story to the FBI and offered to wear a wire to trap Whitey, the agent dealing with the case became very excited, convinced at last, he had a case against Whitey Bulger. Without warning or explanation, however, the case was dropped. The *Boston Globe* reports that a few days later Bulger told Slinger he was dropping the price to $25,000 and that 'there wasn't going to be an FBI investigation'. Someone had warned him.

Whitey Bulger is reckoned to have been responsible for at least 18 murders, if not directly then under his orders. However, it was ten-year-old tapes that brought him down. These tapes, recorded covertly in Heller's Café in Chelsea, a meeting place for bookies, provided police with unimpeachable evidence that Flemmi and Bulger were extortionists.

The bookies were rounded up and, instead of receiving a mere slap on the wrist for their bookmaking activities, they were threatened with far more serious money-laundering charges; it is reckoned that Heller's owner, Michael London, washed around $50 million a year for the bookies. They chose to make deals rather than face long prison sentences.

Then, in 1990, members of the Winter Hill Gang were arrested after a 15-month Drug Enforcement Administration (DEA) investigation into a South Boston cocaine ring. They did not inform on Bulger but the noose was tightening.

Others began to come forward and, finally, the authorities had enough on Bulger, Flemmi and Salemme to move. All three would be arrested simultaneously to prevent one of them from fleeing. Their plan did not altogether work, though. Flemmi was taken into custody without a hitch, but Salemme fled to Florida and was not arrested until seven months later. Jimmy Bulger, on the other hand, just vanished into thin air.

Connolly had warned him about the coming arrests and on 23 December Bulger had left Boston in a hurry accompanied by Theresa Stanley, the woman he had lived with for 30 years. He had prepared for this eventuality for a long time. As early as 1977 he had acquired documents in the name of Thomas F. Baxter and he had cash, jewellery and passports stashed in safety deposit boxes across North America and Europe. He is reckoned to have hidden at least $40 million.

Bulger and Stanley first went to Selden, New York, where they spent Christmas, and then travelled to New Oreleans for New Year. After commuting between New York, Los Angeles and San Francisco for the next three weeks, Stanley declared that this was not the life for her. Bulger drove back to Boston and dropped her off in a car park. He collected Catherine Greig, one of his favourite mistresses, and they went on the run together. When Kevin Weeks, shortly to take over the Winter Hill Gang, met him at the car park with Greig, Bulger is reported to have said: 'Every day out there is another day I beat them. Every good meal is a meal they can't take away from me.'

When Weeks himself was arrested in 1999, he was horrified to learn that Flemmi and Bulger had been informants. He returned the favour by revealing where all the money was hidden and where the bodies were buried.

Since 1996, Whitey Bulger has been spotted in Louisiana, Wyoming, Mississippi, California, New York and London. He is now 74 years old and Greig is 54. Investigators from the Massachusetts State Police, the FBI, the Boston Police, the Massachusetts Department of Correction and the state Parole Board are actively pursuing him and four members of this task force work full-time on his case.

John Connolly retired in 1990, but was arrested in 1999 on charges of racketeering, racketeering conspiracy, conspiracy to obstruct justice and obstruction of justice. He got eight years and one month to ten years and one month.

John Morris also retired, in 1995. In 1998, he was granted immunity from prosecution in exchange for the story of the relationship he and Connolly had enjoyed with Bulger.

Twelve years on, James 'Whitey' Bulger is still at large although recently released footage shows Bulger and his lover in the Sicilian resort of Taormina in 2007. FBI officers are now seeking help from Scotland yard in their hunt for Bulger, who has reportedly been sighted several times in London.

JAMES BURKE

Sometimes you can almost understand why some people turn to a life of crime. The hand dealt them by life is so bad that you can see why they would want to take revenge on everyone else. Jimmy 'The Gent' Burke is one such person, but there can be no excuse whatsoever for the carnage he wrought on the world.

Born in New York City in 1931, he was fostered at the age of two, never to see his natural parents again. As is often the case, his early years were turbulent and unstable as he spent time in numerous orphanages, children's homes and foster homes. Throughout, he was both physically and sexually abused by other inmates, as well as foster fathers and foster brothers. At the age of 13, Burke was in a car with his then foster parents, when his father turned round to hit him for some misdemeanour. His father lost control of the car and died in the subsequent crash. Burke's foster mother never forgave him for causing the accident and beat him relentlessly while he remained in her care.

As he got older, Burke became involved with the Upper West Manhattan's Hell's Kitchen Irish mob.

Gangster Hughie Mulligan taught him the ropes, and he was connected to Lucchese underboss Paul Vario. But he spent increasing amounts of time in prison, including a sentence of five years for forgery in 1949, when he was 18. It was the making of him, as he proved he could be trusted by fellow criminals and also came into contact with a number of Mafiosi who were incarcerated with him. They called him 'the Irish guinea', but he could never become a full, 'made' member of the Mafia because of his lack of Italian blood. However, the Mafia were always happy to work with people from other ethnic backgrounds, as their associations with killers of Jewish descent such as Meyer Lansky and Abe Reles proves.

Burke was a big man that you would not have wanted to be on the wrong side of. As his associate Henry Hill said: 'He was a big guy and knew how to handle himself. He looked like a fighter. He had a broken nose and had a lot of hands. If there was just the littlest amount of trouble, he'd be all over you in a second. He'd grab a guy's tie and slam his chin into the table before the guy knew he was in a war . . . Jimmy had a reputation for being wild. He'd whack you.'

Even being his friend could be problematic, as most of the people involved with him in the famous and lucrative Lufthansa heist in 1978 would attest. Hill said: 'Jimmy could plant you just as fast as shake your hand. It didn't matter to him. At dinner he could be the nicest guy in the world, but then he could blow you away for dessert.'

In 1962 he married and had a daughter, Catherine, who would go on to marry Anthony Indelicato, a member of the Bonanno Crime Family, and two sons, Frank James Burke and Jesse James Burke, named after the famous outlaws.

Around the time of his marriage, an ex-boyfriend of his wife's became a bit of a nuisance. Not a good idea around Jimmy 'the Gent'. He murdered him, dismembered him and left the body in pieces inside his car. All apart from the head. He gave that to his wife as a present.

Burke based himself in Ozone Park, Queens, and his main business was the hijacking of trucks leaving Kennedy Airport. He had a method all of his own. He would always take the driver's licence or union membership card to impress on the driver that he now knew where he lived and could take action if the police came looking for him. Sometimes Burke or a colleague would give the driver a punch, to add authenticity. Burke would always apologise for this, but soon the drivers just let him have the trucks anyway. These were called 'gimmes' and Burke would usually match the driver's weekly pay in the form of a bribe. It is from that that his nickname 'The Gent', arose. Part of his crew were Thomas 'Two Gun

Tommy' DeSimone, nephew of the Los Angeles Mob boss Frank DeSimone and the Irish–Italian Henry Hill, two young crooks on the make for whom Burke became something of a father figure.

All the time, Burke was keeping in touch with what was happening on the street, bribing corrupt cops who kept him up to speed with potential witnesses and informants. Every year, a dozen or so bodies would be found tied up, strangled and shot, in the boots of abandoned stolen cars in the car parks around Kennedy Airport. It did not pay to inform on Jimmy 'The Gent'.

Burke also owned a bar, Robert's Lounge Bar, in Ozone Park, where he could indulge his passion for loan sharking and bookmaking. Robert's became a hang-out for the area's low life.

He went to prison for ten years in 1972, after he and Henry Hill beat a man up in Tampa, Florida who owed a friend of theirs a large sum of money. Paroled after six years, he went into drug-trafficking in the company of Hill, who was released around the same time. The Mafia, of course, famously say that its members should not deal drugs. The truth is that its members should not *get caught* dealing drugs. The Crime Families were worried by drug-dealing principally because the sentences, if they were caught, were very long and that most people became informants in return for a reduction in their sentences. The Mafia probably began to use Jimmy Burke to carry out hits for them sometime in the 1950s and it is thought that, as well as selling untaxed cigarettes and whiskey, he also carrried out a number of hits for them at that time. The FBI reckons that he was involved in at least 50 murders and he had no hesitation in including the spouses and even the children of his victims in his mayhem. At one point he even kidnapped and threatened to kill Karen Hill, the wife of his partner Henry Hill, and their two children when he suspected Hill of being a grass.

One of his specialities was locking his victims, and more often their young children, in refrigerators. He would pick the child up in one arm, open the fridge and lock the child in there until he got his money or whatever it was he was after.

The Lufthansa Heist, the largest robbery in American history at the time, was a prelude to his most extraordinary killing spree.

The planning for it began when bookmaker and Lucchese Family associate Martin Krugman told Burke that millions of dollars in untraceable money was flown into Kennedy Airport from Germany once a month to be stored in a vault in the Lufthansa terminal. Burke sought permission from crime boss Paul Vario, whose Lucchese Family 'controlled' the airport.

While living in a halfway house after leaving prison, Burke and Hill put together an elite team consisting of Tommy DeSimone, Angelo Sepe, Louis 'The Whale' Cafora, Joseph 'Joe Buddha' Manri, Robert 'Frenchy' McMahon, a Lucchese mobster, and Paolo LiCastri. Frank James Burke drove a 'crash car' to prevent police from following the robbery van. Parnell Steven 'Stacks' Edwards was supposed to dispose of the van used in the robbery at a car-wrecker's in New Jersey where it was compacted. The robbery took place in the early hours of 11 December 1978 and they got away with $6 million in cash and jewels, very little of which has ever been recovered.

Burke personally walked away with $2 million. Another $2 million was kicked upstairs to Paul Vario, and the rest was split amongst the team, some getting as little as $10,000.

When he realized how much money was involved, Burke became wary of his fellow robbers. He realised that the authorities would pursue the perpetrators with a vengeance and the chances of his associates informing on him were great, especially as a number of them were complaining about their share of the proceeds. As far as he could see, there was only one thing he could do to safeguard his freedom – he launched a killing spree, which would knock off most of the members of the crew that had carried out the heist and a few others, just in case. Parnell Edwards was first to go. He was gunned down in December 1978 for getting high and forgetting to get rid of the van used to transfer the cash.

Tommy DeSimone was reported missing in January 1979. Henry Hill claims that when Burke killed DeSimone it was the only time that he saw him cry. It is possible that DeSimone was killed for his part in the killing of Gambino member William 'Willy Bats' DeVino, rather than anything to do with the heist.

Martin Krugman disappeared that same month and has never been seen again. Krugman stood to make $500,000 for providing the initial tip-off, but Burke was, of course, reluctant to cough up. Killing him meant that Burke got to keep Krugman's share.

Theresa Ferrera, cocaine-dealing daughter of Milwaukee Mob boss Joseph Ferrara and one-time mistress of both Tommy DeSimone and Paul Vario, had made the fatal mistake of becoming an informant. She was summoned to a meeting in February at a Long Island diner not far from her beauty salon. She never returned and her dismembered body was discovered on a beach in New Jersey in May 1979.

Louis Cafora went missing with his wife in March 1979 and has never been seen again. They were probably killed, dismembered and laid to rest in one of Burke's burial grounds – under the basement of

Robert's Lounge or in the basement of the now demolished South Side Inn located in South Ozone Park. When Henry Hill later told the FBI about these places, it is probable that Burke exhumed the bodies and re-buried them elsewhere.

Next up were Robert McMahon and 'Joe Buddah' Manri, shot dead in a Buick Riviera in May 1979. It is believed that Paolo LiCastri was paid $50,000 by Burke for the hit on the two men.

Paolo LiCastri's bullet-riddled, shirtless and shoeless body was found on a vacant lot on a smouldering rubbish dump in Flatlands, Brooklyn in June 1979. He was burned so badly that forensic scientists were unable to tell the body's age, race or even sex. He was later identified by dental records.

He also murdered a close friend, a Lucchese mobster known only as Remo, because he had become an informant and had contributed to Burke being arrested on a truck-hijacking charge. His body was buried under the bocce court behind Robert's Lounge. Whenever he played there, Burke would exclaim: 'Hey, Remo. How're you doing?'

Henry Hill became an FBI informant following his arrest for drug offences in 1980. And he was joined by Louis Werner, the man on the inside on the Lufthansa job and the only person actually prosecuted for it. He was hoping to knock some time off his 15-year sentence.

A judge issued a search warrant for Robert's Lounge, but Burke was one step ahead of them, already having re-located the bodies he had buried there – Remo and 16-year-old bartender Michael 'Spider' Gianco, who had been shot by DeSimone for insulting him and who had been buried beneath the basement floor.

However, the testimony of Hill and Werner was enough to have Burke arrested on 1 April 1980. In 1982, he was convicted of fixing college basketball games and was sent to prison for 20 years. The police did not have enough evidence to convict him of the Lufthansa job, but at least they had succeeded in getting him off the streets.

He was eventually only convicted of one of his 50 murders – Richard Eaton, a con artist. Burke had been careless in disposing of Eaton's body. After beating him and strangling him, he had dumped the body in an abandoned tractor trailor on a piece of waste ground in Brooklyn where it was found by some children a few days later. In a pocket sewn into the lining of his jacket, police found a small notebook containing Burke's name, address and telephone number. Henry Hill's evidence resulted in conviction for Burke. Hill told the court that Eaton had persuaded Burke to invest $250,000 in a cocaine deal, but Eaton had hung on to the money for his own use.

When Hill asked Burke where Eaton was, having not seen him for some time, Burke replied: 'Don't worry about him. I whacked the fucking swindler out.' Burke finally got life.

He was sent to Wende Correctional Facility in Alden, New York, where, a number of years into his sentence, he was found to have lung cancer. He died on 13 April 1996, aged 64. Had he lived, he would have been eligible for parole just eight years later, in 2004.

PART THREE

SICILIAN MAFIA KILLERS

MICHELE AND GIUSEPPE GRECO

Michele Greco could have carved out a career as a diplomat. His inate ability to mediate between warring Mafia Families led those who knew him to nickname him 'The Pope'. However, too often it was murder and not peace that was on his mind.

The Greco Mafia Family was made up of two separate warring factions in the first half of the 20th century. Grecos from Ciaculli fought Grecos from nearby Crocoverde Giardini. In the 1940s, however, the two sides amalgamated to become one Family.

Michele Greco was born in 1924 and gained control of the territory of the Crocoverde Giardini territory or *mandamento* on the death of his father Giuseppe Greco, also known as 'Piddu u tinenti'. On his estate, La Favarella, Michele would entertain politicians, financiers and public officials. At the same time, it served as a bolthole for fugitive Mafiosi as well as a heroin laboratory.

Money rolled in from various scams and rackets. European Union subsidies were earned from destroying crops that he had never grown; he, like many other Mafia Families, controlled the Sicilian water supply. They made sure that water was always in short supply and squeezed cash out of public coffers for use of their wells.

In 1978, The Pope was elected head of the Sicilian Mafia Commission, known as the *Cupola*, and when Stefano Bontade was murdered, he took control of his family and wiped out 11 of Bontade's allies in a massacre at La Favarella after inviting them there for a meeting.

The authorities learned of Michele Greco's status in the Mafia through a man who, wisely, chose not to attend the meeting. Salvatore Contorno went into hiding and started to write anonymously to the police, giving information about Mafia activities and personnel. He was almost caught in an ambush set by Michele's nephew, Pino, and was probably fortunate in that case to be arrested in 1983. He became a *pentito* and started to talk, apparently surprising police with the information that Michele Greco was a high-ranking Mafioso and not a wealthy landowner, as they had thought.

Greco, however, was on Totò Riina's pocket and did his bidding. *Pentito* Tommaso Buschetta described meetings where Greco merely agreed with everything Riina said, supporting him on every decision that was made.

Salvatore Contorno's information led to *carabinieri* chief Antonino Cassarà compiling a list of 162 men who were wanted in connection with Mafia activities. It was known as the 'Michele Greco + 161' report. Cassarà had made too much progress, however, and was assassinated along with one of his bodyguards in front of his wife by as many as 15 gunmen. His report laid the groundwork for the famous Maxi Trial of 1986/7 where hundreds of Mafia members were brought to justice.

Prosecutor Giovanni Falcone, later assassinated by a car bomb, indicted Michele Greco, and others, for the assassination of Police Chief General Carlo Alberto dalla Chiesa in 1982, but it took them four years to find him. In 1986, they learned that he was holed up in a farmhouse at Caccamo in Sicily. Four hundred *carabinieri* surrounded the building and a couple of police helicopters hovered overhead. At just after dawn, they burst into the farmhouse, finding two men inside. One of them said he was Giuseppe di Fresco when questioned, producing identity papers confirming this fact. The police, however, knew he was actually Michele Greco. After several hours of interrogation, he wilted, saying: 'You are behaving like gentlemen and I don't want to waste your time.'

He was charged on 78 counts of murder, including the killings of anti-Mafia magistrate Rocco Chinnici, two bodyguards and a passer-by in another car bomb in 1983.

Like all the defendants in the Maxi Trial, Greco denied all knowledge of something called the Mafia, insisting on his innocence. He listed all the influential people he had welcomed to La Favarella – the policemen, businessmen and even a former chief prosecutor. He described how he had entertained Mafia boss Stefano Bontade there just a few days before what he called his 'misfortune', or as others described it, a few days before he was ruthlessly machine-gunned in the face, very probably by Greco's killing machine of a nephew, Pino Greco.

Aged 63, The Pope was sentenced to life imprisonment, but released in February 1991 on appeal. In February 1992 he was re-arrested and sent to prison where he languishes to this day.

His friends said that Michele Greco's nephew, Giuseppe, must have been born with a gun in his hands and on 30 November 1982 he proved it when he was responsible for possibly the biggest massacre in Italian Mafia history, and that is quite a claim to fame.

As is often the case with the Mafia, death followed hospitality. Whether it was on the east coast of

America or in a tiny village in the rugged, sun-burnt land of Sicily, this was often the way it happened.

The venue was the hiding place of the Bruscas in the Sicilian village of San Guiseppe Jato and they enjoyed dinner before the bloodbath. The perpetrators were Greco's 'death team' – Mario Prestifilippo, Filippo Marchese, Gianbattista Pullarà, Giuseppe Lucchese, Giacomo Gambino and Nino Madonia. The victims were Rosario Riccobonno, boss of the Partanna Mondella Family and 20 'men of honour', his soldiers. To dispose of the corpses, they used the normal method of immersing them in a bath of acid. That way they would never be found, and, indeed, they never have. That same black day, in the province of Palermo, another 50 people were murdered. The Partanna Modello and Noce Families had been well and truly annihilated.

Giuseppe Greco may be the greatest individual killer in Mafia history. When arrested, he was charged with 85 murders, but estimates pile up more than 300 bodies at his door. Astonishingly, those estimates may be conservative.

Born in Palermo in January 1952, not a lot is known about either Greco's personal or family life. He was called 'Pino' which is a common abbreviation for the name Guiseppe and he joined the Mafia in the late 1970s. His nickname was 'Scarpuzzedda'. His father had been known as 'Scarpa', meaning 'Shoe'; consequently, Greco junior was called 'Scarpuzzedda', 'Little Shoe'. He came from a Mafia background – his father was a prominent Mafioso and he was a relative of the well-known Mafia boss, Salvatore 'Ciaschiteddu' Greco.

His Mafia Family was the Ciacullis run by Michele Greco, who was also known as 'The Pope'. In the first half of the 20th century, Greco had fought Greco when the Grecos from Ciaculli had fought the Grecos from nearby Crocoverde Giardini, but in the 1940s, they had joined together to become one Family. By the 1950s they were allied to the Corleonesi and they supported Totò Riina when he became Corleonesi godfather in 1974.

When Riina instigated what is called the Second Mafia War in 1981, the Ciacullis were at his side. Armed with his favourite weapon, the AK-47, Pino Greco personally killed dozens of their rivals. Amongst the men he shot to death were some big Mafia names – Stefano Bontade, Salvatore Inzerillo – and he was the man responsible for carrying out Totò Riina's orders to kill *carabinieri* General Carlo Alberto Dalla Chiesa.

After he killed Inzerillo, he heard that his victim's 15-year-old son had vowed to take revenge on his father's murderer, a threat not to be taken lightly in Sicily. He brutally tortured the boy, cutting off his arms, before killing him.

One of Greco's closest allies was Filippo Marchese who ran Palermo's Corso de Mille and who, like Greco, was closely linked to the Corleonesi. Marchese had a room in a squalid Palermo apartment, known as the 'room of death', which served as a killing factory, with an estimated 100 people having died there. Greco used it often and, according to *pentito* Vincenzo Sinagra, he and Marchese would sometimes garrotte victims together. That involved placing a loop of rope around the neck of the victim, who had usually already been tortured, and pulling together on each end. Sinagra confessed to holding on to the feet as the victim struggled for life. When the struggle was over, the body would be thrown into a bath of acid or dismembered and dumped in the Mediterranean. Sometimes, the remains were ground down and fed to pigs. Even Greco's friends were not safe, however, and when Riina concluded that Filippo Marchese was no further use to him, he ordered Greco to kill him. Around the end of 1982, like so many of his own victims, he was garrotted and dissolved in acid. By that time, Greco was underboss of the Ciaculli Family and was a member of the prestigious Sicilian Mafia Commission.

Then he suddenly vanished. It was towards the end of 1985 and, in the beginning, people said he had gone to America. But that was a rumour started by Totò Riina. Worried that Greco might be becoming just a bit too ambitious, he had, in fact, ordered that Greco be killed. A lot of the younger 'men of honour' had begun to look up to Greco and saw him as a future boss. Riina also believed that the Ciaculli Family was no longer any use to him, especially as boss Michele Greco, was languishing in prison, having been arrested in 1986. Some weeks before his murder, Riina ordered a massacre in Piazza Scaffa, which was situated in the district controlled by the Ciaculli. Eight people were shot dead, with the objective of demonstrating that Greco's control over his own territory was not effective.

Greco was shot to death in September 1985 in an upstairs room of his own house by two men he had considered friends, Vincenzo Puccio and Giuseppe Lucchese. Puccio would die in a prison cell in 1980 and Lucchese was captured in 1990 and sent to prison for murders which did not include that of Pino Greco. His body, inevitably, was never found.

At the famous Maxi Trial of 1986/87, Greco was found guilty of 58 counts of murder and given a life sentence *in absentia*. Of course, it was futile as, unknown to the court, he was dead by then. The informant, Francesco Marino Mannoia told the police of his death in 1988.

SALVATORE RIINA

At the end of the Second World War, the Corleone Mafia Family had almost become extinct. It was revived, however, by two men who had gone to seek their fortune in the United States in the 1920s – Angelo Di Carlo and Vincenzo Collura – who returned to rebuild the Family.

Di Carlo, who fought as a US marine during the war, was an influential man, with strong political connections and the ear of the most important Sicilian mobsters, men such as Calogero Vizzini from Villalba, Genco Russo from Mussomeli and Vanni Sacco from Camporeale. He gained their approval for his cousin Michele Navarra to become head of the Corleone Family. Collura would be underboss and Leoluca Leggio *consigliere*.

But it was not a decision welcomed by all of the Family, and it was particularly resented by Collura who had wanted the job for himself. There were also young Family members, such as Leoluca Leggio's nephew, Luciano, who had ambitions of his own.

It was around this time that Salvatore 'Totò' Riina

was introduced to the Mafia after committing a murder for them at the age of 18. Known as 'Shorty' due to his lack of height – he was five feet two inches in his stocking soles – but never, of course, to his face, Riina would become one of the Sicilian Mafia's most vicious and cold-blooded killers. He is thought to have been personally responsible for at least 40 murders and to have ordered many hundreds more.

His next murder, however, got him a jail sentence. In 1949, he shot dead Domenico Di Matteo during an argument, was convicted of manslaughter and sent to prison for six years. His sentence served, he returned to Corleone, working for Leggio as an enforcer. When Leggio finally made his bid for the top, Riina was one of the team that ambushed and killed boss Navarra in August 1958. During the next five years, 140 members of the two rival Corleonesi factions would die.

Riina became underboss to Leggio and the fugitive Bernardo Provenzano took the position of *consigliere*. Remarkably, all participants in the war, including Riina, Leggio and Provenzano, were absolved by the Italian state and were free to carry on with business as usual – extortion, corruption and heroin-trafficking. In 1969 Leggio and Totò were arrested for murder, but were acquitted after witnesses and jurors had presumably been intimidated. Later that same year, when he was indicted once again for murder, Riina had no option but to go on the run. He would remain a fugitive for 23 years. Nonetheless, in 1974, when Leggio was finally convicted of Navarra's murder, it was Riina's turn to be boss, fugitive or not.

In the 1970s it became obvious that the real money lay in the heroin trade and not in the traditional Mafia rackets of loan sharking and extortion. Riina set his sights on gaining control of the refining and exporting to America of heroin and went to war with the other Families to achieve his goal. He had a number of public officials assassinated – judges, prosecutors, policemen – ensuring that the blame fell firmly on his rivals. The fact that he and Provenzano and others were invisible, as they were in hiding, helped deflect state interest away from them and onto the more visible Mafia bosses who could often be seen socialising with mayors and public officials. The killings were more often than not also carried out on his rivals' territory, reinforcing the authorities' suspicions.

The Second Mafia War that started in 1981 was an attempt by Riina and the Corleonesi to destroy their rivals once and for all. The blood-letting was astonishing and before the end of 1983 almost 1,000 Mafiosi and members of their families lost their lives. Stafano Bontade and Salvatore Inzerillo, both bosses of powerful Palermo Mafia clans, were both killed and the Corleonesi, once a small and insignificant Family insultingly described as 'peasants' by their rivals, took control of the Sicilian Mafia. Riina reinforced his position by murdering Corleonesi allies such as Filippo Marchese, Guiseppe Greco and Rosario Riccobono. Meanwhile, in order to frighten the authorities there was a slaughter of judges, policemen and prosecutors, one of which was the killing of the carabinieri General Carlo Alberto Dalla Chiesa.

The tide began to turn in 1983, however, when Thomas Buscetta became the first Mafia *pentito* informant. He had lost many friends and members of his family in the Second Mafia War and wanted not only to save his own skin, but also wreak revenge on the man responsible for all the deaths – Totò Riina. The Maxi Trial, a huge Mafia trial in the mid-1980s, supervised by the prosecutor, Giovanni Falcone, saw Buscetta get his chance. Hundreds of Mafiosi went to prison and Riina collected another life sentence, but it was handed out *in absentia* as he was still a fugitive.

The life sentences were piling up, but they did not deter Riina. In 1989 he ordered the deaths of several more of his allies – Ciaculli boss Vincenzo Puccio and Puccio's two brothers who, he had learned, were plotting to overthrow him; never a wise move where Totò was concerned.

The prosecutors, Giovanni Falcone and Paolo Borsellino, were under no illusions that they were marked men. Their work was delivering results that were hurting the Mafia greatly and that was enough to force them to live under constant threat of death. Sometimes that was not the only problem. Their work was often held up by colleagues and even superiors who were on the Mafia payroll. Everywhere they or their families went, they were accompanied by a police escort, but even the added security did not save them. On 23 May 1992, there was revulsion in Italy when Falcone, his wife and three police bodyguards were killed by a car bomb on a road just outside Palermo. To add to the horror, just a few weeks later, Borsellino and five policemen were killed by another car bomb. The press and the public were naturally outraged that the state had failed to protect these men and the authorities were finally forced to take decisive action.

On 15 January 1993, the Palermo police intercepted a car waiting at a red light. Inside was a plump, quietly spoken 62-year-old man in a crumpled, badly fitting suit who, when asked what he did for a living, claimed to be an accountant. When asked for the name of the firm for whom he worked, he refused to say, for fear, he said, of causing damage to their reputation. When he was taken into custody, he claimed never to have even heard of the Mafia, let alone to have been the leader of it. As for being told that he had been Italy's most wanted man for more than 30 years, he expressed total surprise. But the game was finally up. Totò Riina had at last been captured, betrayed by his chauffeur, Balduccio di Maggio. Di Maggio would live to regret his action when a number of members of his family later were murdered as a result.

The media went crazy. News broadcasts were full of it and one newspaper pasted the words 'The Devil' across a photograph of Riina on its front page. Astonishingly, however, it emerged that he had been living in Palermo all the time he had been a fugitive from the law. He had received medical attention and his four children had all attended local schools under their own names. He had even enjoyed a honeymoon in Venice without being identified. Of course, there were many who claimed the Sicilian authorities, with their ambivalent attitude to the Mafia, had known where he had been all the time and had only finally taken action because of public and media pressure.

There was immediate and indiscriminate retaliation from Riina's men, however. Bombs went off in tourist locations and ten people lost their lives, amongst them an entire family. Giovanni Brusca, the man who had detonated the bomb that had killed Giovanni Falcone, claims that Riina gave instructions that the children of informants were now legitimate targets and Brusca confessed to torturing and killing the 11-year-old son of a man who was scheduled to give evidence against Riina.

Brusca turned *pentito* following his arrest in 1996 and provided an alternative version of Riina's arrest. He claimed that Mafia bosses had tired of Riina's leadership and that they had done a deal with the *carabinieri*. Bernardo Provenzano, himself a fugitive from the law, had been instrumental in his capture, exchanging Riina for a valuable collection of material incriminating him in many crimes, kept by Riina in his apartment in Palermo. Although this has never been confirmed, and in fact was flatly denied by the *carabinieri* commander General Mario Mori, many were puzzled by the fact that the apartment was not searched immediately and surveillance of it was halted only six hours after the arrest. It took the authorities 18 days to seal off the apartment and search it. The delay was said to have been caused by a 'misunderstanding'.

Riina had already been given two life sentences *in absentia*, but was tried and convicted of hundreds of others, including the sanctioning of the murders of Falcone and Borsellino. In 1998, he was back in court, charged with the 1992 murder of politician Salvo Lima. Lima had been suspected of Mafia connections and was shot dead for not preventing the Maxi Trial in the mid-1980s. In 2004 Riina had two heart attacks, but the convictions did not stop. April 2006 saw his conviction, 13 years after his arrest, for the 1970 murder of the journalist Mauro De Mauro.

In line with the new, harsh treatment of Mafia prisoners, Riina is held in a maximum security prison and, in order to prevent him from carrying on his business activities from behind bars, his only contact with the outside world is with his lawyer. More than $125,000,000 in assets was confiscated from him, his home in Corleone being turned into a school for local children by an anti-Mafia mayor.

When Riina was courting his wife-to-be Ninetta, it is said that her family were horrified at the thought of her being married to a man such as him. He is reported to have responded by telling friends: 'I don't want any woman other than my Ninetta, and if they don't let me marry her, I'll have to kill some people.' Needless to say, the wedding went ahead and their union produced four children. He is said to have been a dedicated family man. He must have been, as his two sons followed in the old man's footsteps. Twenty-four-year-old Giovanni was jailed in 2001 for four murders he committed in 1995. In 2004 Giuseppe Riina went to jail for 14 years for a variety of crimes amongst which were Mafia association, extortion and money laundering.

In 2006 the Corleone town council had T-shirts made with the legend 'I love Corleone' printed on them in an attempt to dissociate the town from its Mafia connections. However, a relative of Riina sued the mayor, claiming that the Corleone Family actually owned the copyright of that particular phrase.

BERNARDO 'THE TRACTOR' PROVENZANO

Italian news broadcasts on 11 April 2006 contained scarcely believable news. Firstly, the right-centre government of Silvio Berlusconi, the longest-serving Italian prime minister since the war, had lost the general election to a shaky leftist coalition led by Romano Prodi but, secondly – almost knocking the election off the front pages – Bernardo Provenzano, the 73-year-old Sicilian Mafia Godfather, the 'Ghost of Corleone', who had been a fugitive for a remarkable 43 years, had been captured.

It had begun two days previously, when the surveillance team that kept a constant watch on the Provenzano family home in the Sicilian hilltop village of Corleone saw a white plastic bag being carried from the house. An agent photographed the bag from a distance before it was followed on a tortuous route, passing through a dozen different pairs of hands to arrive, on 11 April, at its destination, a shepherd's hut only about a mile away from where it had begun its journey.

The authorities were certain they were finally onto something and early on the morning of the 11th, anti-Mafia prosecutor Marzia Sabella and others who had been involved in the hunt for Provenzano for years, waited at the high court in Palermo for news. Meanwhile, near Corleone, numerous pairs of powerful binoculars trained on the hut followed the shepherd who owned it, as he arrived carrying the bag. He went inside and a short while later came out without it.

For Renato Cortese it was the defining moment of his police career. For seven years he had led the team hunting Provenzano. Now, at last, the Sicilian Godfather was perhaps within their grasp. He ordered the van that he was in and which had been waiting at a distance, to be driven towards the hut, reminding the driver to move slowly in order to keep the noise of the engine down. Beside him was the woman officer known as 'The Cat' because of her grey-green eyes and because she possessed an extraordinary cat-like ability to take her targets by surprise. She had already used her talent for surprise to capture a number of important Mafiosi.

As the van approached the hut, Cortese watched carefully as the shepherd busied himself in the yard as if nothing was happening. But Cortese suddenly realised that the shepherd had become aware of the activity a short distance away and it would only be a matter of time before he shouted out a warning to their quarry inside the hut. It was now or never.

'Via!' (Go!) he shouted, leaping from the van, gun in hand, and running towards the hut's metal door which the man inside hurriedly tried to slam shut. But Cortese managed to catch it just before it closed, grazing his fingers. There was a brief struggle before Provenzano realised there was no escape. They held him, asking for his name. At first, he denied that he was the man they were looking for, but gradually began to understand that denial was futile.

Inside the building, they saw evidence of the pared-down, peasant existence that the fugitive had been living. The hut was sparsely and poorly furnished, chicory boiled in a saucepan on the cooker, and the fridge was stacked with meat and bread. The plastic bag that had finally led to his capture was located and found to contain clean underpants, vests and socks. Stashed in a cupboard was a pile of banknotes, a sum of 10,000 euros hidden amongst his underwear, and a pile of the sanitary towels he used due to incontinence resulting from an operation on his prostate some years earlier. On the desk in the shepherd's hut lay five copies of the Bible. The pious Provenzano had underlined several passages in them, including the words: 'Why do you call me Lord, Lord, and then you do not do as I say.'

They had finally captured the man who had been given the name 'The Tractor' because he mowed people down; the man of whom fellow Mafioso, Luciano Leggio once said: 'he has the brains of a chicken but shoots like an angel'.

It was said that the authorities had known for years where he was – Sicily is not a huge island, after all, and he had even been seen on occasion strolling through the streets of Corleone. In their defence, however, the police claimed not even to know what he looked like. The last known photograph of him was a passport-sized image snapped in 1950. Computer-enhancement, ageing the face in the photograph, greying the hair and beard and adding lines to the face, had helped, of course, but not much.

The third of seven brothers, Bernardo Provenzano had been born into a peasant family in 1933 and, after finishing his education at a very early age, he had been sent out to work in the fields. However, the life of a Mafioso was immeasurably preferable to that of a farmhand, and in his late teens he joined the local Mafia Family of Michele Navarra, working as an enforcer for Luciano Leggio, often in partnership with Totò Riina who would himself later become one of the most vicious of all Mafia bosses.

Back in the mid-1950s, however, it was Leggio who was after the top job and Provenzano took his side against Navarra. They made their move in September 1958. Provenzano and Riina were members of the team that peppered Navarra's car with 112 bullets, killing him and allowing Leggio to take over as head of the Family. With that, Provenzano rose through the ranks and was given the job of hunting down and liquidating as many of Navarra's men as he could.

He showed his true mettle and began to create a reputation for cold-blooded ruthlessness when on 18 September 1963 he and some associates wounded three members of a rival gang in Corleone. As the men lay in agony, The Tractor walked up to each in turn, delivering the *coup de grâce*, a bullet between the eyes. Chillingly, he smiled as he did so, as if this was what he had been put on this earth to do. He added to this reputation on another occasion, when he is reported to have killed a rival gangster by beating him to death with a stone.

He successfully dispatched a great many more of Leggio's rivals, but it was a failed hit in May 1963 that was to change his life. It was not the authorities who were creating problems for him, however. He found himself being pursued by other Mafiosi who had decided on a vendetta against him. A few months later, after the issue of an arrest warrant against him for the killing of one of Navarra's soldiers, he found himself being hunted by both sides of the law. He did the only thing guarnteed to maintain his life and his freedom. He became a fugitive, moving from safe house to safe house, protected by friends and family.

However, the killing did not end. In December 1969 The Tractor participated in a killing that bolstered his reputation as a hitman, the murder of Michele Cavataio. Cavataio was a target because he had betrayed the Corleonesi in what has become known as the First Mafia War. When the attack on him was launched, however, he succeeded in shooting to death one of his assassins. The situation was getting out of control and Provenzano averted what could have been a disaster by spraying bullets from his Beretta submachine gun and giving little thought to his own safety. Nonetheless, an eyewitness later claimed that it was actually Provenzano who caused the problem by opening fire too soon.

He remained a fugitive, but his status did not impede his progress in the organisation. When Leggio went to jail in 1974 for the murder of Navarra, Provenzano's associate, Totò Riina, took over as boss, Provenzano becoming his right-hand man. He was now second-in-command of the Corleonesi Family.

In 1981 Riina instigated the Second Mafia War in

which almost 1,000 people died, but following which the Corleonesi were installed as the principal Mafia Family in Sicily. To what extent Provenzano joined in the killing is unsure. His work took place behind the scenes and he dealt increasingly with the financial side of the business, taking control of a large percentage through the years of the publicly bid building and civil construction projects in western Sicily. He also took personal control of the Family's heroin trafficking. Meanwhile, he lived with his family in an opulent 18th-century villa in the Palermo suburb of Bagheria, often being driven to meetings in an ambulance to preserve his anonymity.

Riina, having himself been on the run for 20 years, was arrested in January 1993 and charged with dozens of killings, in many of which Provenzano had also been involved. Two of the most sensational were the murders of the prosecutors, Giovanni Falcone and Paolo Borsellino, murders that sickened not just Italy but the whole world. Provenzano was convicted of both murders *in absentia*.

It is presumed that, on Riina's incarceration, Provenzano became boss, but he had not been seen in public since 1963 and it was often suggested that he was actually dead. This suspicion seemed to be confirmed when his wife and two sons emerged from hiding in 1992. However, informants began to come forward, letting the police know that he was well and truly alive and that he had, indeed, become Godfather.

Police raids on a number of homes in Sicily in January 2005 resulted in the arrest of 46 people believed to have been helping Provenzano remain at large. But, still, they failed to unearth him and he was not among another 80 Mafiosi they picked up two months later.

As boss, Provenzano made a number of changes in the organisation, possibly sensing a change in society in general as a result of the high-profile killings of recent times. Following Riina's arrest, the Corleonesi carried out a series of bombings in tourist destinations on the Italian mainland. Bombs went off in Florence, Milan and Rome, killing ten people and injuring many. Important buildings such as the Uffizi gallery in Rome were damaged. The public were outraged and demanded that the authorities come down heavily on the perpetrators.

Provenzano immediately brought this kind of action to a halt. He rendered the organisation less blood-thirsty than it had been under Riina, helping to get the police off their backs. And he ensured greater efficiency. He is said to have arbitrated between rival Mafia factions who were wasting time and resources chasing the same business. He persuaded his associates that coexistence with state institutions and the infiltration of public finance was in their best interests. He made efforts to stop the flood of *pentiti*, men who turned state witness, by not targeting their families and trying to make the use of violence the final option. Finally, he re-established the old Mafia rules that Riina had done away with years before

In carrying out this overhaul, however, he remained elusive, even to his associates. He never used the telephone and all communication was carried out through small, handwritten notes, usually signed off with a religious blessing. Undetected at the time, he travelled to Marseille in France in 2002 where he underwent an operation for a prostate tumour, an operation for which, remarkably, he was reimbursed by the Italian health care system.

Provenzano did not say much when he was arrested and has said even less since. He went straight to jail, having been convicted already and given multiple life sentences for the murders of Falcone and Borsellino and many others. The man who was seen by very few people for years, of whose existence for so many years there was sparse photographic evidence, is now under constant video surveillance and is only allowed contact with his lawyer.

BENEDETTO
'THE HUNTER'
SANTAPAOLA AND
FAMILY

The harsh, industrial environment of the city of Catania on Sicily's east coast breeds similarly harsh individuals, tough men and women who grab what they can from life, because, as they well know, nothing is given willingly.

Benedetto Santapaola, known as 'The Hunter' because of his love of hunting, was born in 1938 and grew up in poverty in the San Cristoforo area of Catania, with his three brothers, Salvatore, Antonino and Natale. The extended family took in numerous cousins, members of the Ferrera, Ercolano and Romeo families, names that would provide a roll-call of Cosa Nostra in years to come.

Benedetto, or Nitto, as he was more familiarly known, was provided with an entrée into the largest

Mafia Family in the area in the early 1960s by his cousin Francesco 'Little Horse' Ferrera, at a time when its head was Giuseppe Calderone, a hugely influential figure who was the founder of the Sicilian Mafia Commission. Santapaolo spent the next few years supervising various gambling and extortion rackets before being promoted to *capodecina* at the beginning of the 1970s when he took over the family's heroin smuggling operation and became chief enforcer for the many businessmen associated with the Mafia. It was around this time that he made the useful acquaintance of Toto Riina, future head of the Sicilian Mafia, who was beginning his long period as a fugitive. The two would indulge their passion for hunting together in the forests and mountains around Catania. Riina liked Santapaola and lent him his support against Calderone whom Nitto was keen to replace.

Finally, in 1978, Calderone was murdered and Santapaola became head of what was now called the Santapaola Family, making Francesco Ferrera his underboss, another cousin, Franco Romeo *consigliere* and his brothers Salvatore and Antonino and cousin Aldo Ercolano *capodecina*. Riina promoted Nitto to the position of boss of the Catania province that same year and he was also given a position on the Regional Commission.

It was a busy time for The Hunter. He supported the Corleonesi in a war known as the Palermo War which lasted from 1981 until 1983, and at the same time he and his men were battling against another Family from Catania, the Cursoti, for control of the highly lucrative gambling and cigarette smuggling trade. Meanwhile, within his own Family, there was simmering discontent – fomented mainly by Alfi Ferlito – amongst some members over the murder of Calderone.

The discontent spilled over on 6 June 1981, when some of Ferlito's men, armed with Kalashnikovs and bombs, attacked and seriously wounded Benedetto Santapaola. He did not go down without a fight, however, and, during the attack shot dead the leader, Salvatore Lanzafame.

Nitto sought revenge and the war took to the streets of Catania, resulting in dozens of murders. Finally, in April 1982, when six of Santapaola's soldiers died in an explosion, he decided it was time to eradicate the cause of his problems. In June his men stopped the car transferring Alfi Ferlito from Enna to the prison in Trapani, following his arrest. Not only did they shoot Ferlito dead, they also murdered the four policemen accompanying him. The killers were from Palermo and members of the Corleonesi, allies of Santapaola.

He paid the Corleonesi back for their help shortly after. *Carabinieri* General Alberto Dalla Chiesa had been appointed prefect of Sicily at the beginning of the

1980s with the clear objective of bringing an end to the violence between rival Mafia Families. His last public interview made it clear that he was focusing particularly on the Catania Mafia. Santapaola sent a hit team to Palermo where they assassinated the General.

At the time, there was a great deal of suspicion about four entrepreneurs who were involved in property development in southern Italy – Carmelo Costanzo, Francesco Finocchiaro, Mario Rendo and Gaetano Graci. Rumours suggested that they operated with Mafia support and this was proved to be the case when Guiseppe Falcone, the magistrate investigating the Dalla Chiesa killing and himself a later victim of a bomb, discovered evidence linking one of the men, Carmelo Costanza, with payments that had been made to Nitto Santapaolo. In fact, Santapaola had even been a guest at the wedding of Costanza's nephew and had been hiding in a hotel belonging to Costanza. With his passion for hunting, he had been delighted to be permitted to use the private game reserve of another of the four. Added to that was the fact that Mario Rendo bought all his cars from a dealership owned by Santapaola and recordings were made of his men meeting with Mafiosi.

At that time, journalists risked their lives every time they put pen to paper to write about the Santapaola Family. Guiseppe Fava was one such, editor of the newspaper *I Siciliano*. In February 1984 he penned an article entitled *I quattro cavalieri dell'apocalisse mafiosa* (the Four Horseman of the Mafia Apocalypse), in which he exposed the links between the four businessmen and the Mafia. Nitto considered it to be one too many articles about him and his Family and sent a team consisting of Enzo Santapaola, Aldo Ercolano, Marcella D'Agata, Maurizio Avola and Franco Giamusso to make sure he would not be writing about them again.

Meanwhile, investigating magistrate Falcone brought in the Italian Finance and Customs Police who uncovered countless instances of political and business corruption involving the four businessmen, the local Mafia and political figures. There were even photographs of the Catania mayor and members of the council with Benedetto Santapaola. In one, Nitto was shown in a friendly embrace with Salvatore Lo Turco, all smiles and grins. This was even more astonishing given that Lo Turco was a member of the Sicilian parliament's Anti-Mafia Commission.

The Mafia were so embedded in local politics that they always had prior warning of arrest warrants being issued. They were even allowed to vet the warrants and have names added or taken away, if they wanted. The police also showed great leniency to men such as Santapaola. On one occasion they picked him up in his bullet-proof car at the scene of a violent gunfight in which there had been a number of fatalities. After a brief visit to the police station and the most perfunctory of questions, he was released without charge. Even more bizarre was the fact that they allowed this man with a long criminal record involving violence a licence to carry a gun.

By 18 May 1993, Benedetto Santapaola had been on the run for 11 years, but he was finally arrested in the farmhouse where he had been hiding out. Things were beginning to unravel.

In 1994 his nephew Maurizio Avola became a *pentito*, a witness for the state. Altogether, he confessed to 70 murders, amongst them the killing of the journalist Guiseppe Fava, in which he implicated his uncle, Nitto Santapaola.

Then, a year later, Santapaola's wife, Carmela Minniti, was shot dead by a gang of men pretending to be policemen. They pushed past Santapaola's daughter at the door, ran into the house and opened fire. It was said that she ran her husband's affairs for him and was far from innocent.

One of the killers was Giuseppe Ferone, whose father and son Santapaola had ordered to be killed. In court, Santapaola read out a letter forgiving Ferone for the killing of his wife.

In 1998 justice finally caught up with The Hunter.

He and his cousin, Aldo Ercolani, were sentenced to life imprisonment for the murders of Guiseppe Fava, General Carlo Alberto Dalla Chiesa, Giovanni Falcone and Paolo Borsellino.

Meanwhile, the wars continued and the Santapaola Family, headed by acting boss Umberto Di Fazio, underboss Vincenzo Santapaola and *consigliere*, Antonino Santapaola, fought a vicious war throughout the 1990s with the Cappello and Mazzeo Families. Hundreds died.

On 5 December 2007, Sicilian police arrested 38 Mafia suspects and hunted for nine others, another step towards terminating the grip that the gangsters have had on the island for hundreds of years. Amongst those arrested was Enzo Santapaola, Nitto's son. The suspects are being charged with an extensive menu of crimes, including extortion and drug-trafficking. This was just the latest in a series of sweeps.

PART FOUR

WILD WEST KILLERS

JESSE JAMES

Hero or villain? Robin Hood or cold-blooded killer? Which was Jesse Woodson James? Certainly only on a couple of occasions did he rob passengers on the trains he was holding up, and even then he only did it because the safes he and his gang were robbing, were almost empty. Added to that, before he robbed those passengers, he checked their hands to see if they were working men. If so, he left their wallets intact.

This handsome, dashing but utterly ruthless bank robber behaved more like a present-day rock star. Sometimes crowds would turn out to watch his robberies and newspapers treated him like a folk hero, taking revenge on an increasingly industrial society that was sweeping away the old ideas and ways of life. Or perhaps he did it because he was upholding the last vestiges of the old South, hanging on to the lost cause of secession from the Union. Whatever his motive, he and his various gangs carried out dozens of daring robberies during a 16-year period and he killed half a dozen or so men in the course of these actions before himself succumbing to the cowardly gun of Robert Ford at the age of 34.

Jesse had a good start in life. He was born in Clay County, Missouri, in 1847 but his father Robert, a farmer and Baptist minister, died when he was only three. His mother Zerelda remarried twice, the second time to Doctor Reuben Samuel in 1855.

The American Civil War that broke out in 1861 brought turbulent times to Missouri. Pro- and anti-slavery factions committed atrocities and fear stalked the territory. The James/Samuel family was caught up in it. Jesse's 18-year-old brother Frank joined the Confederate army, riding with Quantrill's raiders, while young Jesse, just 14 at the outbreak of hostilities, remained at home, itching to be old enough to join him.

One day, Federal troops rode into the farm and started to set fire to the barns and sheds. Their orders were to burn down the property of anyone fighting on the opposite side. When Jesse protested he was savagely beaten and one report suggests that they tried to hang his stepfather, but he survived.

In 1864, aged 17, Jesse finally got his chance to fight, joining the notorious guerrilla unit led by 'Bloody Bill' Anderson, the most feared Confederate guerrilla leader in the country. Anderson was a man who showed no mercy to his enemies. Once, discovering 25 Union soldiers on a train he was holding up, he lined them up outside and shot them dead. In the chaos of the end of the war, Jesse was shot and badly wounded as he tried to surrender. He was nursed back to health by his cousin Zerelda, who was named after his mother. He would later marry her after a nine-year courtship.

At the end of the Civil War, many men found it difficult to adjust once more to peaceful, civilian life. Jesse and his brother Frank joined up with a group of former Confederate guerrillas, led by Archie Clement, that was engaged in criminal activity. A year after the war ended, this gang carried out the first post-war bank robbery in America, robbing the Clay County Savings Association in Liberty. During the raid, Jesse shot and killed an innocent bystander but later claimed to have taken part merely in order to get back the deeds to his family's land. However, the Liberty bank job signalled the start of a wave of robberies and not long after, they hit the Aleksandr Mitchell Bank in Lexington.

More followed, but it was the December 1869 robbery of a bank in Gallatin, Missouri, that earned Jesse the notoriety that was to follow him for the rest of his life. A man called Samuel P. Cox had fired the bullet that had killed 'Bloody Bill' Anderson and Jesse mistakenly thought that the cashier at the bank was Cox. He shot him dead during the raid and became famous. The catalyst for this was the editor of the *Kansas City Times*, John Newman Edwards, a Confederate sympathiser, who published letters written by Jesse in his newspaper and wrote editorials supporting Jesse's rebellious political views and actions.

Frank and Jesse joined forces with the Younger Brothers – Cole, Bob and Jim – and some other former Confederate soldiers to form what became known as the James–Younger Gang. Cole Younger had become a Confederate after his father had been murdered by a detachment of Union troops whose captain was said to owe him money. He had joined Quantrill's men and taken part in the slaughter of 200 men and boys at Lawrence, Kansas. He also rode with Archie Clement after the war.

This gang robbed its way across the West, robbing banks, stagecoaches and, from 1873, trains, often in front of large crowds and often hamming it up for the delighted spectators. On 9 April 1874, when they robbed a stagecoach just across the Missouri River from the town of Lexington, hundreds of spectators follow the action from across the river.

Detective and spy Allan Pinkerton, who was born in Glasgow and emigrated to the New World in 1842, had established a private security and detective agency in 1850 to fight urban professional criminals as well as to break strikes and work against trade unions. The agency had made its name when it had foiled a plot to assassinate President-elect Abraham Lincoln, leading Lincoln to use Pinkerton's men for his personal security during the Civil War. It was to the Pinkerton National Detective Agency, with its proud motto, 'We Never Sleep', that the victims of the James–Younger Gang turned in 1874. However, even Pinkerton's could not tame the James and Younger boys. One agent sent in to infiltrate the gang was found dead shortly after he had arrived at Zerelda Samuel's farm. Two others posed as cattle-buyers as they followed the gang but met the same fate. One was killed by two of the Younger brothers in a gunfight, in which John Younger also died.

The deaths of the Pinkerton agents added to the embarrassment of the Missouri Governor Silas Woodson. He offered a massive $2,000 reward for their capture and persuaded the state legislature to provide $10,000 to fund the hunt for the outlaws. Jesse and the gang were undaunted, carrying out their most profitable robbery to date when they hit a train on the Kansas Pacific Railroad, near Muncie in Kansas, netting $30,000.

For Allan Pinkerton, meanwhile, it was getting

personal. In January 1875 he staged a raid on the James family farm, too late to catch the James boys who had left earlier. An iron incendiary device was thrown into the house, the explosion killing Jesse's nine-year-old half-brother Archie, and blowing off Zerelda's arm. A few months later, a neighbour, Daniel Askew, who had provided a base for the Pinkerton's men who took part in the raid on the farm, was shot dead by an unknown gunman.

The raid, however, persuaded Jesse and Frank to move to Nashville to safeguard their mother. From his base there, Jesse wrote numerous letters to the press, making his political views known.

Possibly the most famous raid in the gang's history, the attack on the bank at Northfield, Minnesota, also set the scene for the demise of Jesse and the gang. It was selected, according to Bob Younger, speaking later, because it had connections with two prominent Union generals and politicians – Benjamin Butler and Adelbert Ames. Ames, a former Minnesota Governor, had moved to Northfield where his family owned a mill and had a large amount of stock in the bank.

Frank and Jesse, accompanied by Cole, Jim and Bob Younger, Charlie Pitts, Clell Miller and Bill Chadwell, took the train to St Paul and Minneapolis at the beginning of September 1876. On arrival, they split into two groups, one going to the town of Mankato on one side of Northfield, the other heading for Red Wing on the other side. They bought horses and began to plan the robbery, scouting out the land around the town.

At two in the afternoon on 7 September, they made their move, three of them entering the bank, the remaining five standing guard on the street outside. Word spread that a robbery was in progress and a number of armed men opened fire on the men in the street, immediately killing Miller and Chadwell and wounding the Youngers. A local man was also shot dead. Meanwhile, the mayhem continued inside the bank when cashier Joseph Lee Haywood refused to open the safe and was gunned down.

The remnants of the gang fled, hiding themselves in nearby woods. After several days of dodging posses and road blocks, they had only succeeded in getting a few miles away from Northfield and decided to split up. The Younger brothers were eventually captured near Madelia, Minnesota, while Jesse and Frank made it back to Missouri. The Northfield raid had signalled the end of the road for the James–Younger Gang.

Frank and Jesse spent the next three years living quietly in Nashville, but while Frank seems to have taken to the quiet life, Jesse could not adapt. By 1879 he had assembled a new gang and began a wave of robberies over the next few years in Alabama,

Kentucky and Missouri. In October of 1879 they held up the Chicago and Alton Railroad, getting away with $40,000. In September 1880 they robbed a Wells Fargo Stagecoach in Kentucky and, shortly afterwards, a paymaster's office in Muscle Shoals, Alabama. The Seton Bank in Riverton, Iowa, brought them a $5,000 haul. Jesse was well and truly back in business. Dime novels told fantastic stories about him and newspapers raved about his audacity. He grew a beard to enhance his image.

When he hit the Chicago and Alton train again in 1881, the safe did not yield much more than $1,500. So, for only the second time in his career, Jesse ordered the gang to rob the passengers. He walked through the train, the only member of the gang not wearing a mask, introducing himself to the incredulous passengers. It would be his last robbery.

Missouri's new Governor, Thomas T. Crittendon, was determined to bring down the James Gang, persuading the state's railroad and express executives to fund a huge reward – $10,000 – for the capture, dead or alive, of the James brothers. Things slowly began to unravel and gang members began to be arrested or killed.

Robert and Charley Ford had been fringe members of the gang for a short while and by 1882 they were the only remaining members apart from Jesse.

Unknown to Jesse, however, Robert Ford had recently met with Governor Crittendon and had made a deal to kill the great outlaw and claim the reward.

On 3 April of that year, the Ford brothers were visiting Jesse at his house; Zerelda, Jesse's wife, was busy in the kitchen and his children were playing outside. It was breakfast time and they were discussing plans for their next job, the robbery of the Platte County Bank. Bob Ford played along, delighted to see that Jesse was not wearing his gunbelt.

Suddenly Jesse spotted something and stood up. He stared at a picture on the wall, saying that it was crooked. He walked over to it, pulled up a small stool and climbed up, reaching out to adjust the angle of the picture.

It was the perfect moment for Ford. Jesse was unarmed and had his back to him, preoccupied with the picture. Ford jumped out of his seat, pulled his revolver from under his coat, took aim and fired from a distance of about four feet. Jesse jerked and grabbed his neck, the bullet having entered his head just below his ear. Another three shots rang out in quick succession as Ford made certain. The stool beneath Jesse's feet fell over and he crashed to the floor, dead before he reached it.

Five months later, a worn-out Frank James surrendered to Governor Crittendon, declaring: 'I have been hunted for 21 years, have literally lived in the saddle, have never known a day of perfect peace. It was one long, anxious, inexorable, eternal vigil.' They tried him, but he was found not guilty and walked free. For the next 40 years, Frank worked in a variety of jobs. He was a shoe salesman and then a theatre guard in St Louis. He was an AT&T Telegraph operator in St Joseph, Missouri, and he worked the lecture circuit with his old comrade, Cole Younger. In 1902 he became betting commissioner at the Fair Grounds Race Track in New Orleans. Towards the end of his life he lived on the James Farm, giving tours for just 25 cents. He died in 1915, aged 72.

The reward money did not bring happiness to the Ford brothers. Charley shot himself a few years later and Bob bought a saloon in Colorado. However, his life was filled with people who wanted to see, as the popular song went, 'The dirty little coward who shot Mister Howard'; Howard being the identity Jesse had adopted towards the end. Eventually, a customer shot him dead in 1892.

BILLY THE KID

Billy the Kid's entry into life was as enigmatic as his departure from it.

His childhood is shrouded in mystery and even the birth date usually attributed to him – 23 November 1859 – cannot be confirmed absolutely. There is also confusion about the names of his parents. They appear to have been of Irish Catholic descent and may have been Catherine McCarty and a man called either William Bonny or Patrick Henry McCarty and Billy may have been born as Henry McLarty in Manhattan's Lower East Side. Whatever is the case, his father appears to have died around the end of the American Civil War, in 1865, and his mother, having met a man called William Antrim, definitely remarried in Silver City, New Mexico, in 1873 after travelling around the country with him. Sadly, she died of tuberculosis just a year later and 14-year-old Henry was taken in by a neighbouring family who ran a hotel where he washed dishes and waited on tables to pay for his board and lodgings.

The young Henry was reported by schoolteachers and by those for whom he worked to be a willing and well-behaved boy, but in 1875 that all changed when he made the acquaintance of a young thief, drunk and gambler known as Sombrero Jack. One day, Jack stole a bundle of clothing from a Chinese laundryman and gave it to Henry who had no decent clothes to wear. It was discovered in Henry's room and he was thrown in jail. After a couple of days, he escaped by climbing up the jailhouse chimney, becoming a fugitive. He would remain a fugitive until his death.

Henry made his way to south-east Arizona where he had hoped to move in with his stepfather, whose name he had taken, but when Antrim learned why he had fled Silver City, he threw him out. Henry, on his own and still only 16, hooked up with a man named John Mackie and together the pair made a living from stealing saddles and horses from the army in the Fort Grant area. They were caught and thrown in jail, but, not for the last time, Henry escaped.

Around this time, now known by his famous nickname 'the Kid' because he looked so young, he found work as a ranch-hand. Then in 1877 he took a job driving a wagon hauling logs from a timber camp to a sawmill at Fort Grant. A blacksmith called Frank 'Windy' Cahill, who was working in the camp, liked nothing better than to bully and humiliate the Kid in front of the other men. One day Cahill attacked Henry during an argument and the young man pulled his gun and shot Cahill. He died the next day and 'the Kid' found himself in prison once again. Before the local marshal could arrive to deal with the case, however, he again escaped.

Heading back to New Mexico, he joined one of the most ruthless bands of killers and cattle-rustlers in the south-west, a gang known as 'The Boys', led by Jesse Evans. The gang rustled and killed its way towards Lincoln County, New Mexico, with the law breathing down its neck.

They arrived in Lincoln County in 1877, just at the right time. The region was being torn apart by a war between a faction led by wealthy ranchers and another led by the wealthy owners of the mono-polistic general store in Lincoln County. In the midst of this, the most acrimonious and bloody feud was between the English cattle rancher, banker and merchant John Tunstall, and the Irishman, James Dolan. Henry and his crew went to work for Dolan, but he fell out with Jesse Evans and 'The Boys' and was offered employment by Tunstall.

This move seemed to McLarty to represent a new beginning and what better way to celebrate than to adopt a new identity. From that day on, he went by the name of William H. Bonney. He was welcomed and liked by his new colleagues. One of the other men who worked for Tunstall recalled that: 'He was the centre of interest everywhere he went, and though heavily armed, he seemed as gentlemanly as a college-bred youth. He quickly became acquainted with everyone, and because of his humorous and pleasing personality grew to be a community favourite.'

One day, not long after the Kid had been hired, John Tunstall was caught unarmed out on the range while herding cattle and was shot dead in cold blood. Tunstall's murder outraged Billy and his fellow ranch-hands so much that they formed their own gang, the Regulators, with Dick Brewer as leader, and went out in search of the killers. On 6 March they caught up with Bill Morton and Frank Baker and killed them. Then as they made their way back to the ranch, they killed one of their own number whom they suspected of being a traitor.

Sheriff William J. Brady was next, gunned down on Lincoln's High Street by a number of Regulators, including Billy who was wounded in the attack. On 4 April the killing continued when an old buffalo hunter, Buckshot Roberts, who had been involved in Tunstall's murder, was killed, but not before he had killed Brewer. Bonney took over as leader and the gang was now wanted for several killings but especially for Sheriff Brady's. He went into hiding at the house of Aleksandr

McSween, a lawyer and former associate of Tunstall. News got out and an alliance of Dolan's and Brady's men set fire to the house with the Regulators trapped inside. When McSween was shot dead fleeing the fire, the Lincoln County War was effectively over.

In 1878 when Lew Wallace became Governor of New Mexico, he declared an amnesty for any man involved in the Lincoln County War who was not already under indictment on other charges. Billy was one such, still under indictment for Cahill's murder the previous year. So, he now had enemies on both sides of the law, a dangerous situation that was likely to result only in his being gunned down sometime soon.

He decided to call a truce with James Dolan and Jesse Evans. The two sides met and agreed to lay off each other. Afterwards, they went to the saloon to celebrate, getting extremely drunk as the evening wore on. As the townspeople hid indoors, they staggered down the street, bumping into McSween's attorney, Huston Chapman. Billy claimed that he could see trouble brewing and wanted no part of it, trying to get away, but he was blocked by one of the other men. Bill Campbell and James Dolan pulled their guns and shot the lawyer in the chest, killing him. They then suggested, in their drunken stupour, that they should all go to a restaurant and eat oysters as if nothing had happened. Billy had no choice but to tag along.

When Dolan suggested in the restaurant that some-one go and place a gun in Chapman's hand to suggest that the killing was in fact an act of self-defence, Billy immediately volunteered. Stepping outside, he jumped on his horse and hightailed it out of town.

Governor Wallace was furious when he heard about Chapman's murder and issued warrants for the arrest of everyone present. The Kid realised that this might be a chance for him to get on the right side of the law once and for all and he wrote to the Governor from Texas offering to testify against Dolan and Campbell if he was granted an amnesty. The two met in March 1879 in Lincoln County, Billy turning up at the meeting with a revolver in one hand and a Winchester rifle in the other. He agreed to testify.

The deal was that he would be arrested and put in jail and be freed after testifying. However, neither Wallace nor prosecutor William Rynerson had any intention of letting Billy go. Rynerson insisted that before Dolan was tried, Billy should stand trial for the murder of Sheriff Brady. Billy knew he had no chance and grabbed the opportunity to escape, yet again, when his guard was looking the other way.

He spent the next 18 months rustling cattle and killing where necessary. In January 1880 he shot dead Joe Grant in a saloon in Fort Sumner. Grant was boasting that he would kill Billy the Kid on sight, not realising that the man sitting across the table from him was Billy. The Kid asked Grant at one point if he could have a look at the ivory-handled pistol he was carrying. In those days it was common for men to only put five bullets into a gun, leaving one chamber empty for safety as there were often accidents and mishaps. Billy made sure when he returned the pistol to Grant that the hammer would fall on the empty chamber. He then calmly informed the other man that he was actually seated across from Billy the Kid. Grant pulled his gun and fired but, of course, nothing happened. Billy raised his own gun and shot him. When asked about it later, Billy replied: 'It was a game for two and I got there first.'

Pat Garrett was elected sheriff of Lincoln County in November 1880 on a promise to rid the area of cattle-rustlers. He was a former bartender and buffalo hunter who had befriended Billy back in his saloon days. Now, he had to go out and try to collect the $500 bounty that had been placed on his friend's head.

Garrett and the posse he had put together came close to capturing the Kid, ambushing him one night at Fort Sumner and fatally wounding one of Billy's men. Then on 23rd December they tracked down the Kid and his gang to a stone building at a place called Stinking Springs. The posse surrounded the building and waited for daylight. At dawn a figure stepped out of the building to feed his horse. The posse opened fire, thinking it was Billy, and the man fell to the ground dead. It was the wrong man, though. The posse cooked breakfast, waiting for the cornered men to make a move and Billy and Garrett engaged in a conversation, Garrett inviting Billy to breakfast and Billy laughing and telling him to 'Go to hell'. He knew, however, that there was no hope of escape and later that day he surrendered. By this time, Billy the Kid was just 21 years old and had killed 21 men.

He was jailed in the nearby town of Mesila awaiting trial, and while he waited he gave newspaper interviews, adding to his notoriety. He was thrilled by the crowds who gathered outside the jailhouse hoping to catch a glimpse of the famous outlaw. When they did catch sight of him, they were surprised by his youthfulness. Meanwhile, he inundated the Governor with letters asking for clemency. Wallace remained aloof, however, and Billy was sentenced to hang on 13 May by Judge Warren Bristol.

He was taken to Lincoln and locked up on the top floor of the town's courthouse, but escaped yet again, killing his two guards while Garrett was out of town. It is thought that the townspeople had some sympathy with Billy due to his work with the Regulators and that they allowed him an hour to remove his leg irons and get away. He borrowed a horse and, apparently, rode out of town singing, returning the horse a couple of days later.

Foolishly, he did not travel far from Fort Sumner and was still hovering in the vicinity of the town several months later when Pat Garrett and some of his men rode out to question Pete Maxwell, a friend of the Kid.

When they arrived at the Maxwell property, they unsaddled their horses, had some coffee and then went into an orchard which ran down to a row of old buildings, some 60 yards from Maxwell's house. Approaching these buildings, they could hear people inside speaking in Spanish. After a short while, a man stood up. He was wearing a broad-brimmed hat, dark waistcoat and trousers and shirt sleeves. He spoke a few words, left the house, jumped the fence and walked towards a nearby house. Unknown to Garrett and his deputies, this man was the Kid.

Billy walked into the house, took off his hat and boots and threw himself down on a bed to read a newspaper. After a short while, he woke up a friend who was asleep in the same room and told him to get up and make some coffee. He also said he was hungry and asked for a butcher's knife so that he could go over to the Maxwell house to get some beef. The Mexican gave him a knife and the Kid, hatless and in stocking soles, set off on the short journey to the other house.

Garrett still did not recognise the Kid as he left the orchard. He and his men retreated a short distance and, in an effort to avoid the houses, approached from the opposite direction. Arriving at the porch of the Maxwell house, Garrett told two of his men to wait there and went into the house.

It was close to midnight and Maxwell was already in bed. Garrett walked up to the bed in which he was lying, sat down on it and quietly asked him if he knew where Billy the Kid was. Maxwell whispered that the Kid had been there but he had no idea if he still was. Just then, a man sprang quickly into the doorway and exclaimed in Spanish: 'Quién es? Quién es?' (Who is it?) When there was no reply he took a step into the room, holding a gun in his right hand and a knife in the other, peering into the darkness.

As he approached the bed, Garrett leant down and whispered: 'Who is it, Pete?' Maxwell did not answer. For a moment, Garrett thought it might be Maxwell's brother-in-law, Manuel Abreu. Perhaps he had seen the men outside and wanted to know what was going on. The intruder came close and leaned down, both hands on the bed, his right hand almost touching Garrett's knee. He asked in a low voice: 'Who are they, Pete?' At that moment, Maxwell hissed to Garrett: 'That's him!' The Kid, realising there was another man present, raised his pistol about 12 inches away from the sheriff's chest. He then retraced his steps back across the room, shouting in Spanish: 'Quién es?' Garrett wasted no time. He drew his revolver rapidly and fired into the darkness in the direction of the words. He then threw his body to one side and fired again. There was no point to the second shot. Billy the Kid was already dead as he hit the ground.

Henry McLarty, alias Henry Antrim, alias William H. Bonney, alias Billy the Kid, was buried the next day in Fort Sumner's old military cemetery. On either side lay his fallen companions Tom O'Folliard and Charlie Bowdre. A single tombstone was later erected over the graves. On it are written the three outlaws' names and the word 'Pals' is carved into it. The tombstone has been stolen and recovered three times since being placed there in the 1940s.

PART FIVE

GREATEST
HITS

THE COLLINGWOOD MANSION MASSACRE

It was autumn 1931, and the city of Detroit was gearing up for the American Legion Convention when thousands of legionnaires would hit town. For bootleggers that meant only one thing, they would also be hitting the speakeasies and blind pigs of Detroit and downing thousands of gallons of illicit booze. Huge orders were being placed across town in readiness and bootleggers were licking their lips at the thought of how much money would soon be rolling into their coffers. Enormous amounts of supplies were being brought into town and shipments were being hijacked and then re-hijacked while the federal authorities ran around like headless chickens trying to clamp down on the illegal alcohol trade. Tensions were running high.

Meanwhile three out-of-towners, Hymie Paul, Joe 'Nigger Joe' Lebowitz, both 31, and 28-year-old Joe 'Izzy' Sutker had been brought to Detroit by the

Oakland Sugar House Gang, run by Harry Shorr and Charles Leiter. Schorr and Leiter were affiliated to the Purple Gang and employed the three as hired guns to provide armed protection for their booze shipments. Hymie, Joe and Izzy were men of ambition, however, not content to merely play the role of hired guns. They wanted to elbow in on the big money and what better way to do that than to add illegal gambling to their existing bootlegging business. They opened a bookie's and started to coin it in.

They hooked up with a gang who were known as the Third Avenue Navy because their headquarters, where they unloaded crates of Canadian Whisky, smuggled in over the border, was in some railway yards close to Detroit's Third Avenue. But for Hymie, Joe and Izzy rules were made to be broken. However, even gangsters have a code which you breach at your peril and when the trio started to hijack other hoods' shipments, double-crossing customers and suppliers and reneging on deals, they became an irritant to the movers and shakers who ran the Detroit underworld.

The trio made a smart move in taking on an experienced mobster named Solomon 'Solly' Levine to work with them. Levine was well connected in Detroit, having grown up in the same neighbourhood as the Bernstein brothers, Abe and Ray, two of the leading lights of the Purple Gang.

251

All seemed to be going well until, suddenly, their bookmaking business was hit for a payout of several hundred thousand dollars to the East Side Mafia. They were broke and unable to pay out, which was obviously not a good position to be in. Nonetheless, they devised a scheme to raise some money quickly. Purchasing some whisky from the Purple Gang on credit, they watered it down and sold it at a low price, undercutting the market and making a healthy profit.

No sooner had they done that, however, than the East Side gang came back looking for another big payout on a race that had been fixed. Izzy, Joe and Paul bought another 50 gallons on credit from the Purples, diluted it and sold it again.

By now they were in deep trouble and there was usually only one way that trouble of that kind ended. Still, they were optimistic that the Legionnaires Convention would reverse their fortunes and they would be able to pay their now considerable debts. So they spoke to Ray Bernstein, one of the leaders of the Purple Gang, about the money they owed for the whisky they had bought, asking him to give them some more time, at least until after the convention. Bernstein came back to them, suggesting a meeting at which they could thrash out a plan. He hinted that they could work for the Purple Gang again once everything seemed to be sorted out. The trio jumped at the chance to get things back on an even keel and relaxed a little.

The night before the meeting, Izzy and Hymie took some time off. Izzy sent for his 18-year-old girlfriend, Virginia White, who lived in Port Huron. They went to a club and drank the night away, listening to a band. Hymie went carousing in town and went to bed with the beginnings of a crushing hangover. Joe stayed at the bookmaking joint, working.

It was there, next day, 16 September, that he received a phone call giving him an address for the meeting. It would be at three in the afternoon at 1740 Collingwood, Apartment 211. The three, accompanied by Levine, left for the meeting at quarter to three, deciding to leave their guns behind. It was, after all, a peace conference and it would be bad form to turn up armed to the teeth.

They arrived at the Collingwood Mansion apartment house, located in a quiet, residential area on the West Side of the city, at precisely three o'clock, to be met at the door by Ray Bernstein. A gramophone playing inside was switched off abruptly as they entered the apartment, the needle left in the middle of the record on the turntable. The men exchanged pleasantries with Bernstein and another three seasoned Purple Gang veterans who were present – Irving Milberg, Harry Keywell and Harry Fleischer. Although he had a cast-iron alibi for the day, Keywell was thought to have acted as lookout on the notorious St Valentine's Day Massacre in 1929, while Fleischer was at the time a fugitive from the law, having gone on the run a short time before. At 29 he was a killer whose crimes included assault with intent to kill, armed robbery, kidnapping and receiving stolen property. As for Milberg, he was a crack shot who had, in the past ten years, committed every crime in the book. They were no lightweights these guys.

Hymie Paul, Joe Lebowitz and Solly Levine sat down on a sofa in the living room, while Izzy perched on an arm. They talked about nothing for a few minutes before Fleischer enquired of Bernstein: 'Where is that guy with the books?' They claimed they were waiting for their accountant who would take them through the money that Izzy, Joe and Hymie owed. Bernstein said he would go and look for him and left the room and went outside. Out in the street, he climbed into their car, switched on the engine and gunned it at the kerb, sounding the horn at the same time. Curtains twitched in the neighbourhood windows as people looked out to find out who was making all the noise.

It was a signal, however, as well as an attempt to cover the noise. As soon as he heard the engine roaring, Fleischer pulled out a gun and fired it straight at Lebowitz. Meanwhile, Milberg and Keywell had pulled out their weapons and opened fire on Izzy and Hymie.

The three victims were taken completely by surprise, but from where their bodies were later discovered it was evident that they had tried to escape the gunfire. Hymie Paul was found slumped against the side of the couch, eight bullets in his back and head, a cigar still dangling from his fingers. In a corridor leading to the bedroom, Joe Lebowitz was found sprawled on the floor, cigar stub fixed grimly between his teeth. Izzy Sutker lay in the bedroom, a couple of bullet holes in his forehead, close together. Crack shot Irving Milberg had taken care of him.

They never did make it to the riches they so desired. Izzy had just 11 cents on him, Hymie had $2 and Joe was comparatively rich, with all of $92 in his pocket.

When the shooting started, Levine was certain he was next, but what he did not realise was that they had him lined up to take the rap for the shooting. Therefore they did not want him to die in the apartment. Perhaps somewhere else, though. The plan was to take him for a ride and dump his body somewhere later. They would then spread the word that he had been taken care of for the hit on the three.

They ran to the kitchen with Levine where they threw their 38s, serial numbers already filed down, into a bucket of green paint, rendering it impossible for the cops to trace them back to them. They then ran downstairs, climbing into a black 1930 Chrysler, Fleischer arriving a minute or so after them, having pumped another couple of bullets into 'Nigger Joe' who had seemed to be still breathing. They sped out of the alleyway at the rear of the house, leaving rubber on the road as the tyres spun and drove fast for a few blocks before jumping out of the car and splitting up. Bernstein handed Levine $400, saying to him he was his pal and telling him to go back to the bookie's. He would see him later, he said.

Within an hour, however, Solly had been picked up by the police. He had prepared a story that the three dead men had been kidnapped while en route to a meeting with a well-known bootlegger named Harry Klein, but the police were not convinced, especially as he seemed to change his story each time he told it.

A massive police hunt was launched and Wayne County prosecutor Harry S. Toy, ordered the round-up of every member of the Purple Gang, even though they offered to surrender. He said he was not interested in doing any deals and he wanted these killers 'dead or alive'. Phones turned red-hot as people called in with information, most likely members of other gangs who sensed an opportunity to get rid of the Purple Gang once and for all.

One anonymous tip-off pointed them in the direction of a house owned by Charlie 'The Professor'

Al Capone (1899–1947), circa 1931. With his smooth suits, silk ties, fedora and gruesomely scarred face, he was the embodiment of the American gangster.

8 February 1990: American reputed Mafia boss John Gotti (1940–2002) leaves court with his laywers in New York City during a recess in his trial for the jury's deliberation.

Circa 1928: American Mafia boss George 'Bugs' Moran (1893–1957), leader of the North Siders and Al Capone's main rival in the Chicago Mafia.

The dead bodies of gangsters from George 'Bugs' Moran's gang, murdered at the garage at 2122 North Clark, Chicago, by Al Capone's gang led by 'Machine Gun Jack' McGurn, in what was known as the St Valentine's Day Massacre, 14 February 1929.

Portrait of William 'Billy the Kid' Bonney (1859–1881) posing with his rifle, circa 1880.

James 'Jimmy' Hoffa (left), former president of the Teamsters union, with his son James P. Hoffa en route to the federal prison in Lewisburg, Pennsylvania after visiting Jimmy's wife at a hospital in San Francisco in April 1971.

Austrian Nazi war criminal Karl Adolf Eichmann (1906–1962) standing trial in Jerusalem in 1961.

Property baron Nicholas van Hoogstraten leaving the High Court in London on 29 March 2004. Hoogstraten – a man who is quite happy to be detested – has described his tenants as 'filth', people living in council houses as 'worthless and lazy' and ramblers as 'nosy perverts', and once paid for a hand-grenade attack on a business rival.

Auerbach. Auerbach, who listed his profession as jewellery salesman, was nicknamed 'The Professor' on account of his refinement and polished appearance. But he was a major criminal and was, in fact, the first gangster to be convicted under the Public Enemy Law in 1931. Police stormed the house and discovered Ray Bernstein and Harry Keywell along with Auerbach, his wife and an 18-year-old cabaret entertainer called Elsie Carroll, whom Ray Bernstein had been seeing. Police found guns and tear gas in the house and the women had $9,000 in their possession.

The following day, they picked up Irving Milberg. While they were raiding his house on West Chicago Boulevard, his wife made the mistake of telephoning to enquire about the welfare of her children from the maid who was looking after them. The call was traced to the house of Eddie Fletcher, another Purple Gang gunman, a few blocks away. Police charged round there and burst in on a card game being played by Fletcher, Abe Axler, another of the Purples, and Irving Milberg. They had a small armoury at the ready – a rifle and five pistols – but they never got a chance to use them and all were arrested.

Harry Fleischer was never convicted for the murders. He went on the run until 1932.

The trial was huge. People crowded into the

courtroom to see the famous gangsters. The Purple Gang spared no expense in putting their defence together, levying a special tax on local bookmakers of $2 a day that went straight into the defence fund.

Solly Levine was the main witness for the prosecution and it was an open and shut case, the jury taking a mere 90 minutes to return guilty verdicts on all three. As soon as it was announced, there was a riot in the courtroom as relatives, friends and fellow mobsters screamed hysterically and scuffled with court attendants.

A week later, all three received mandatory life sentences without parole and took a train to the maximum security prison in Marquette to begin their sentences.

Irving Milberg served the least time. He died in prison seven years later. Harry Keywell was a model prisoner for 34 years, at which point his life sentence was commuted. He was released in 1965, married, got a job and disappeared. In 1963 Ray Bernstein had a stroke in prison that left him paralysed on his left side and with impaired speech. He had, like Keywell, been a model prisoner and had taught other inmates after he had gained his own high school diploma. The parole board took pity on him and released him in 1964. He died two years later.

As for Solly Levine, he became a hunted man. The remaining Purple Gang members wanted revenge.

So the police put him on a boat to France. Unfortunately, however, the French did not want him and sent him back. He then tried to go to Ireland, but while he was trying to get it organised, he disappeared.

ALBERT ANASTASIA

Tropea spills down into the Gulf of Euphemia on the west coast of Calabria in Italy. It was there that Albert Anastasia, or Umberto Anastasio as he was then known, was born in 1902 and where he spent the early years of his life. In his mid-teens, he left Tropea and went to sea with his younger brother Tony, never to return.

In 1917 as America was about to enter the First World War, the 15-year-old Umberto jumped ship in New York harbour. Shoeless, and without a single possession, he lost himself, with his brother, in the slums of Brooklyn. They had the address of a relative who had already established himself in the new world and they stayed with him until they could find work and earn some money. Eventually Umberto and his brother found work on the New York docks and, at the age of 16, Umberto was a longshoreman, doing the physically demanding work of loading and unloading ships.

Albert was famous throughout his life for his short temper, and when he lost it death was often the result. His first murder resulted from it. In the early 1920s he became involved in a heated dispute with another longshoreman of Italian origin, Joe Torino. The argument was over who had the right to unload ships with precious cargoes. This could be lucrative work for a longshoreman on the make. Anastasia, now a powerful physical specimen, stabbed and strangled the unfortunate Torino as their dispute escalated and was arrested. Unfortunately for him, there were several witnesses to the incident and he was convicted and sentenced to death. For 18 months he languished in the death house at the notorious Sing Sing Correctional Facility in Ossining, New York, awaiting his turn in Old Sparky, Sing Sing's famous electric chair.

Shortly before the execution date, however, strange things began to happen. The witnesses changed their statements. They were no longer sure if they had seen Anastasia kill Torino; their memories became blurred. A retrial had to be scheduled and Anastasia was released. Then, coincidentally, four of the prosecution's most important witnesses disappeared. The retrial never took place and the charges were quietly dropped.

Anastasia began to drift into organised crime in the 1920s, starting out in bootlegging once Prohibition had been introduced and then working as a bodyguard for crime boss Joe Masseria. Around this time, too, he changed his name from Umberto Anastasio to Albert Anastasia, apparently to prevent shame falling on his family if and when his name appeared in the newspapers in relation to his criminal activities. His brother decided to retain the family name and was known as 'Tough Tony' Anastasio. He would run the New York docks for the Mob 20 years later.

Albert ended up working for Vincent Mangano, head of the Mangano Crime Family, following the Castellamarese War, in which the future direction of the Mafia was fought for. The ultimate winner of that war was Charles 'Lucky' Luciano, and Albert Anastasia played a major part in Lucky's rise to the top of the heap.

Until then, the Mafia had been run by old-fashioned mobsters, known as Mustache Petes. They were members of the Sicilian Mafia who had come to New York as adults in the early 1900s. They ran organised crime according to the old ways and were resented for it by the younger soldiers. When Luciano informed Anastasia that he intended to deal with the old Mustache Petes once and for all, Anastasia was delighted. He had been waiting for more than eight years for Lucky to take control and is reported to have claimed that he would kill anybody who got in Lucky's way. Naturally, Luciano made Anastasia a major part of his bid for power. As for Albert, he knew that once Lucky was head of the National Crime Syndicate, he would get his reward.

So it was that when Bugsy Siegel led four men with guns blazing into Scarpato's Italian restaurant on Coney Island in 1931 to kill Joe 'The Boss' Masseria, Albert Anastasia was one of them and it is rumoured to have been Anastasia who delivered the *coup de grâce*, the bullet in the head to ensure that Masseria had eaten his last supper.

When Luciano founded the National Crime Syndicate, a grouping of the five Crime Families of America, he turned to his man Anastasia for an important job. By this time, Anastasia was renowned for his ruthless brutality; so he was perfect for the job as operating head of the syndicate's enforcement arm, Murder Inc., working alongside another legendary sociopath, Louis 'Lepke' Buchalter.

The idea of Murder Inc. was that if you were connected to the Mafia you could approach Anastasia to take a contract out on someone. If it was acceptable, one of the killers on Murder Inc.'s books would be assigned the job. Those books contained some formidable names – killers such as Frank 'Dasher' Abbandando, Louis Capone, Martin 'Buggsy' Goldstein, Harry 'Happy' Maione, Harry 'Pittsburgh Phil' Strauss, Allie Tannenbaum, Seymour 'Blue Jaw'

Magoon, Mendy Weiss and Charles 'Charlie the Bug' Workman. The organisation set up its headquarters in a small Brownsville candy store named Midnight Rose's on the corner of Saratoga and Livonia Avenues. To his nickname the 'Mad Hatter' Anastasia could now add a new one – the 'Lord High Executioner'.

One of Murder Inc.'s top killers, Abe 'Kid Twist' Reles, claimed the organisation was responsible for more than 63 murders on the direct orders of Albert Anastasia. It is reckoned, however, that Murder Inc. was actually responsible for some 800 deaths.

At the start of World War Two, Anastasia signed up – perhaps he fancied a bit of legitimate killing. Then, after his military service he moved to New Jersey where he controlled the waterfront as capo, reporting to Vincent Mangano. Mangano was the last of the old-school Mafiosi and, as with the Mustache Petes, he was hated by the men working under him, including Anastasia who was still hanging out with other crime bosses such as Luciano, Frank Costello and Lepke Buchalter. This did not help their relationship and Mangano began to distrust Anastasia. There were many arguments between the two, even fist fights when they had to be separated by others, although Mangano, getting on in years, would never have been a match for the younger, fitter Anastasia.

Anastasia made his play in 1951, after, it is believed,

hearing that Mangano was going to kill him. Firstly, on 19 April 1951 the body of Philip Mangano, Vincent's right-hand man, was found near Sheepshead Bay, Brooklyn. On the same day, Vincent vanished and not a trace of him has been seen since.

Naturally, Anastasia put himself forward to fill the gap at the top of the Family. He convinced the other bosses of the syndicate that Mangano had been plotting to kill him and that he had acted in self-defence, being supported in his claim by Luciano Family boss, Frank Costello. They believed him and the man who had arrived in New York shoeless and penniless 34 years previously, found himself at the top of the heap as head of what was to become known as the Gambino Family, with the young Carlo Gambino as his underboss.

Anastasia ruled the Family with characteristic ruthlessness and extreme violence. Once, it is reported, he was infuriated by a television interview with Arnold Schuster, a young man who had been witness to a robbery by a man called Willie Sutton. He ordered his men to hit the young man. 'I can't stand squealers!' he is reported to have screamed. 'Hit that guy!'

With Frank Costello he controlled the National Crime Syndicate, but this killing of an 'outsider' caused consternation within the organised crime world. It had been Bugsy Siegel who had said 'we only kill each other' and Anastasia had stepped over the line. Vito Genovese, a rival of Costello for the leadership of the Luciano family, began to spread rumours of Anastasia's instability, undermining his position as head of a Family. He won sympathy from Anastasia's underboss, Carlo Gambino, and Joe Profaci another Family head, both of whom had turned against Anastasia.

Genovese launched an all-out campaign against Costello and Anastasia, trying to convince the other bosses in the crime commission that Anastasia was breaking Family rules by selling membership of his Family. A boss could not be killed without the agreement of all the other bosses and Costello stood in the way of a hit on Anastasia. So they went after Costello and on the night of 14 May 1957, a bullet grazed his head as he entered his Manhattan apartment building. Just before squeezing the trigger and fleeing the scene, the man who had accepted the contract, Vincent 'The Chin' Gigante, shouted out: 'This is for you, Frank!'

Word spread that Anastasia had hired Gigante to hit Costello and Gigante had screwed up. Of course, it was actually Genovese who had hired Gigante and the miss was deliberate. He had wanted Costello to go after Anastasia and that was exactly what happened. The bosses all agreed that Anastasia should be hit and the contract was handed to Joe Profaci who did the hiring.

The momentum was building against Anastasia and on 25 October 1957 the antipathy towards him was given full expression.

If Albert Anastasia was one thing, he was a creature of habit. Every day would start for him with a haircut in the barbershop at the New York Park Sheraton Hotel. Joe Bocchino had been cutting Anastasia's short curly hair for years and as he sat down in the leather chair, Bocchino, as usual, threw a candy-striped barber's cloth around him. On a chair next to Anastasia sat a manicurist and Jimmy, the shoeshine boy, sat at his feet, working on his wing-tipped shoes. It was relaxing and Anastasia sat quietly dozing as everyone worked on him.

Suddenly, two men – thought to be Larry and Joe Gallo – wearing fedoras and dark glasses entered the barbershop, pulling out .38 revolvers and silently waving the people away from the chair. They opened fire on Anastasia who immediately raised his left hand, shielding his head. The first bullet ripped through his palm. Another couple of bullets shattered his left wrist and entered his hip.

Anastasia no longer carried a gun, believing himself to be immune to attack, but he is said to have instinctively reached for the one he used to wear. There was mayhem as the bottles of hair unctions were smashed by the fusillade of shots. Anastasia was hit again, in the back this time, as he stood up, dazed and reaching towards the figures, but not realising that he was reaching towards their reflections in the mirror in front of him.

The barber's cloth still wrapped around his large body, he sank to the floor. One of the men calmly walked up to his prone figure and fired a bullet into the back of his head, just as Anastasia himself had done to Joe Masseria all those years before.

JIMMY HOFFA

He tapped his watch impatiently and squinted into the distance, down Telegraph Road towards the affluent Detroit suburb of Bloomfield Hills. It was 30 July 1975 and he was standing in the car park of the Machus Red Fox Restaurant. Inside, the plush red velvet, English country, hunt-club style restaurant awaited with its dimly lit booths, but his lunch companions were already 15 minutes late and Jimmy Hoffa hated people being late. He was a stickler for punctuality.

There was a payphone nearby. He walked over to it and called Josephine, his wife, telling her it looked like he had been stood up and might be home early. Leaving the booth, he scanned the street again and began pacing up and down outside the restaurant, a smartly dressed stocky man in a dark blue short-sleeved shirt, blue pants, white socks and black Gucci loafers, angry and edgy.

He had been strangely on edge earlier that morning before setting out for the restaurant, according to Josephine, and when he had dropped into the offices of a friend's limousine service in Pontiac en route to the restaurant, his nervousness was apparent to one of the employees.

The reason for his edginess was simple. He was supposed to be meeting Anthony 'Tony Jack' Giacolone, the go-between for Hoffa and Vincent Meli, the Detroit Mob's union specialist, and Anthony 'Tony Pro' Provenzano. Provenzano was a capo in the Genovese Crime Family who had been vice-president of Hoffa's Teamsters Union and who had gone to prison with Hoffa in 1964 for tax evasion. Hoffa and Provenzano had once been close friends, but were now sworn enemies. Hoffa was annoyed that Provenzano had taken up his old union role and Provenzano, for his part, was refusing to back Hoffa's attempt to gain re-election to the presidency of the Teamsters. They had recently bumped into each other by chance at an airport and had a stand-up fight during which Hoffa broke a bottle over Tony Pro's head. Provenzano had declared he would take revenge on Hoffa's grandchildren screaming: 'I'll tear your heart out!'

The Machus Red meeting had been called to discuss his re-election but the Mafia, with whom Hoffa had worked well in the past, were not sure they wanted him back. His handpicked successor as president, Frank Fitzimmons, was much more malleable than Jimmy had ever been and he was also liked by US

President Richard Nixon, which was a major plus. And since Nixon had granted Hoffa clemency in 1971 a lot had changed. The Mob were happy with things the way they were.

They must have arrived shortly after Hoffa's call home, because a few minutes later a maroon 1975 Mercury Marquis Brougham sped out of the restaurant car park, almost hitting a passing delivery truck. The driver, pulling up alongside the car, peered in and recognised Jimmy Hoffa in the back seat behind the driver, another passenger whom he did not recognise, seated alongside him. Between them, on the seat, he noticed a long object wrapped in a grey blanket. He later said its shape suggested to him a rifle or a shotgun.

The next day, Jimmy Hoffa's green 1974 Pontiac Grand Ville was still sitting in the restaurant car park and when the FBI checked on the whereabouts of the two men he was supposed to meet, Tony Jack Giacalone said he had been at the gym. Witnesses placed him, just as he claimed, at the Southfield Athletic Club around two. Tony Pro said he was playing cards in New Jersey with friends and was unaware of any meeting with Hoffa.

Charles 'Chuckie' O'Brien was an associate of Hoffa and he claimed he had not seen him on the day in question. He said he had delivered a 40 pound salmon to the home of the Teamsters' vice president in the Mercury and had helped the man's wife to cut it up. He had then been with Giacalone at the gym, he said, before taking the Mercury to a car wash, although no one at the gym or the car wash could corroborate his alibi.

Eight days after Hoffa's disappearance, the police brought in sniffer dogs that picked up Hoffa's scent in the back seat and boot of Giacalone's Mercury. In 2001, a DNA match was made between a hair found in the car and a hair taken from a hairbrush belonging to Hoffa.

James Riddle Hoffa was born in Brazil, Indiana, on US Route 40, a highway that used to run all the way from New Jersey to San Francisco. His father, a coal miner, died when he was still young, and the family moved to Lake Orion, Michigan, where, unable to remain in school because he had to earn money for his family, he went to work in a warehouse.

He showed an early interest in labour relations, gaining a reputation as a tough street fighter who always stood up for the rights of his fellow workers. This tendency lost him his warehouse job, but it got him another as a union organiser for Local 299 of the International Brotherhood of Teamsters, working in the Detroit area.

Hoffa began, in the course of his work, to develop organised crime connections. The Mob had always seen unions as a means of making money and it was inevitable that he would have to work with them. His first criminal conviction, a fine, came as a result of his use of them against an association of small grocery stores. It did not prevent him, however, from continuing to use his contacts as a threat when he was promoted to a senior union position.

He was a natural leader of men and was genuinely passionate about the mistreatment of workers by management and government. At the age of just 20, he organised his first strike involving workers known as 'swampers' who loaded and unloaded strawberries and other products on and off delivery trucks.

The International Brotherhood Teamsters had originally been a craft union when founded in 1903, a teamster being someone who drove a team of oxen, a horse-drawn, or mule-drawn wagon or a mule train. By the 1950s, it represented truckers and firefighters. It was good at using strikes and secondary boycotts to win its demands. It was sometimes known also to use less lawful methods. Jimmy Hoffa won the presidency of the Teamsters in 1957, following the conviction and imprisonment of the previous president, Dave Beck, on charges of bribery. Hoffa himself was not averse to the odd kickback. The McClellan Committee which investigated union activity in the 1960s, found evidence that he had received a payment, disguised as a loan, for averting a potentially disastrous strike in the Detroit laundry industry.

But he went from strength to strength, expanding the reach of the union and, by 1964, he had signed up virtually every truck driver in the United States. He also attempted to bring in airline employees and other transport employees. This led to concern in government circles that were the Teamsters to call a strike, the entire US transport system could be brought to a halt, with devastating consequences for the economy.

Hoffa had a good relationship with the mobsters who controlled union activities in areas such as the garment industry. They had, after all, thrown their muscle behind his efforts to get elected president. But the Teamsters pension fund was used as a bank by hoods such as former Purple Gang member and bootlegger Moe Dalitz, and Allen Dorfman to pay for the construction of hotels, casinos and other projects. The Desert Inn and the Stardust Hotel in Las Vegas were built with money 'loaned' from the pension fund. Dorfman would eventually be charged with future Chicago Mafia boss, Joey 'The Clown' Lombardo, for embezzling £1.4 million from the fund. The case failed to make it to court as the main witness was killed two days before his court appearance.

When John F. Kennedy became President of the

United States and he appointed his brother Robert as Attorney General, pressure built on Hoffa and the Teamsters. The Kennedys were convinced that Hoffa and his cronies were pocketing union money and launched an investigation.

In 1964 they finally caught up with him when he was convicted of attempted bribery of a grand juror and jailed for 15 years.

Hoffa's disappearance was to America what Lord Lucan's was to Britain. Every killer in the United States claimed that he had done it, from Richard 'the Iceman' Kuklinski to Tony the Greek.

The claims and rumours as to what happened to his corpse are legion. It is variously claimed that his body was buried in concrete on the Straits of Mackinac Bridge connecting the strip of water between two of the Great Lakes, Lake Michigan and Lake Huron; it was taken to New Jersey and put into the concrete used in the building of the New York Giants' Stadium; it was buried in a residential area in Hamilton, New Jersey; it was shipped across the border and buried at the Mondo Condo in Toronto, Canada; it was buried in the concrete foundation of the Renaissance Center in Detroit; it was cremated in the animal crematorium at the Wayne State University Medical School in Detroit; it is being held in the United States Bullion

Depository at Fort Knox; it was encased in the foundation of a public works garage in Cadillac, Michigan; it was buried at the bottom of a swimming pool behind a mansion in Bloomfield Hills, Michigan; it was ground up and dumped in a Florida swamp; it was crushed in an automobile compactor at Central Sanitation Services in Hamtramck, Michigan; it was buried in a field in Waterford Township, Michigan; it was weighted down and dumped in Michigan's Au Sable River; it was ground to mush at a fat-rendering plant; it was buried under the helipad at the Sheraton Savannah Resort Hotel, owned, at the time, by the Teamsters; it was put in a steel drum and buried on the grounds of Brother Moscato's garbage dump, a toxic waste site in Jersey City, New Jersey.

It seems the truth of what happened to Jimmy Hoffa may actually lie in a series of confessions made by a man by the name of Frank Sheeran. Before he died in 2003, Sheeran claimed that he used his friendship with Hoffa to lure him to a house in north-western Detroit where Teamster business agent Thomas Andretta, Salvatore Briguglio and his brother Gabriel were waiting. Sheeran claimed he fired two shots into the back of Hoffa's head before fleeing. He said that Hoffa's body was then driven the short distance to Grand Lawn Cemetery where it was cremated within an hour of the murder. The hit had been ordered by

Pennsylvania Mob boss Russell Bufalino and handed to Provenzano. Bufalino's cousin, William, had had a serious disagreement with Hoffa some years previously, which, added to the fact that the Mafia did not want him to become Teamster president again, led to his murder.

Speculation continued, however, and in May 2006 land at the Hidden Dreams Farm in Michigan was dug up by the FBI following information received from a marijuana smuggler called Donovan Wells, incarcerated in Lexington, about a group of men who had met there 30 years previously. Nothing was found.

Jimmy Hoffa was declared legally dead in 1982. His case is still open, however, with an agent working on it full time at Detroit's FBI field office. The investigation has generated more than 16,000 pages of documents gathered from interviews, wiretaps, and surveillance, but a question mark remains as to what the Mob did with his remains.

The authorities may not have been able to charge anyone with the disappearance and murder of Jimmy Hoffa, but the principals all got their come-uppance in one way or another over the following years.

Tony Pro's Local 560 branch of the Teamsters came under investigation and his activities were seriously curtailed. In 1978, he was found guilty of the murder of Anthony Castellito some 17 years after Castellito's body was put through a tree shredder. He died in prison in 1988, aged 81.

Tony Jack Giacalone was arrested for tax evasion and went to jail for ten years. In 1996 he was charged with racketeering but died before the case reached the courts.

Chuckie O'Brien who, in all likelihood, drove Hoffa from the restaurant to his death, worked in Florida for the Teamsters, but was kicked out of the union in 1990 because of his Mafia links. He has survived cancer and four heart bypass operations and now lives in Boca Raton. He resolutely sticks to his story that the government, not the Mob, killed Jimmy Hoffa.

Salvatore Briguglio, who was waiting in the house for Hoffa with the others, was murdered in Little Italy in New York when two gunmen fired a number of bullets into his chest and head. He had been talking to prosecutors about testifying against Provenzano in the Castellito case.

Only Frank Sheeran got to die peacefully, in a Philadelphia nursing home in 2003, aged 83.

ROBERTO CALVI

It was a postman passing at 7.30 in the morning who spotted it – a body dangling on the end of an orange rope tied to some scaffolding under Blackfriars Bridge in London. The body's feet were submerged in the murky waters of the Thames and in his pockets and the flies of his trousers were stuffed a number of building bricks to weigh the body down. His expensive Patek Philippe watch was still on his wrist and his wallet still contained around 8,000 or so pounds in three different currencies – Swiss francs, Italian lire and sterling. So it seemed that he had not been the victim of a robbery or mugging. In his pockets police also found four pairs of spectacles and a passport in the name of Gian Roberto Calvini.

It was 18 June 1982, and the dead man, as the police quickly ascertained when they cut him down early next morning, was Roberto Calvi, chairman of the Italian Banco Ambrosiano. He had disappeared with a bag of documents from his Rome apartment ten days previously, had shaved off his distinctive moustache and travelled to Venice. There, he had hired a private plane that took him to London, using his false passport. Now the bag of papers had vanished, as well as £1.2 million from the Banco Ambrosiano's subsidiaries in the Bahamas, Peru, Luxemburg and the Vatican.

An inquest held in London shortly after the body was discovered found that Calvi had committed suicide, raising eyebrows around the world. A second inquest, one year later, delivered an open verdict.

Nonetheless, it was a mystery and, to some extent, remains a mystery some 25 years later, in spite of countless books, films and theories about what actually happened to the man who, due to Banco Ambrosiano's links with the Vatican, came to be known as God's Banker.

A post-mortem examination was carried out by one of England's most experienced pathologists, Professor Frederick Keith Simpson. He reported that there was no river water in Calvi's lungs and that death had resulted from asphyxia by hanging. However, he deduced that the banker had dropped on the end of the noose only about two feet. Apart from the fact that the dead man had a noose around his neck, there was no evidence of foul play, nothing to indicate he had been restrained or involved in a struggle, no puncture marks to indicate that he might have been sedated by drugs and no chemicals in his stomach, other than some sleeping pills which Calvi was known to take.

Professor Simpson established the time of death to have been between one and two-thirty in the morning and further surmised that the time made suicide all the more unlikely. Calvi was 62 years old when he died. He was overweight and he suffered from vertigo. However, if he had in fact killed himself, he would have had to find the scaffolding, which was difficult to see from the walkway by the Thames, load up with bricks and clamber over the parapet onto the bridge. There was then a 12-foot-long vertical ladder and a 30-inch gap to negotiate to get onto the scaffolding. Once there, he would have had to edge his way along the rusty scaffolding poles, about eight feet, and tie the rope onto them. As there was no neck damage, however, he could not have leapt from there. He would have climbed down to the next row of scaffolding. All of this achieved while carrying the bricks and the rope.

It could be done, of course, but making it more unlikely was the lack of rust from the poles on his fingers, or under his fingernails, no scrapes or marks on his hands and the pristine state of his suit. When the bricks were examined, it also transpired that there was no evidence that Calvi had ever touched them.

The police could find no one who had seen Calvi that night. In fact, they could not even find out what he had been doing during the previous three days that he had spent in London. His personal effects were found in his suite at the Chelsea Cloisters Hotel, but he had been invisible during his time in London and no one at the hotel could even recall him leaving that night.

His journey to London had been extraordinarily complex, involving three false identities, eight separate private plane journeys in Europe, a speed boat, four cars and 14 different temporary residences in Zurich, Amsterdam, Edinburgh and London. This amazing escape was planned by, amongst others, Flavio Carboni, a contractor from Sardinia, Silvano Vittor, a cigarette smuggler and two Austrian sisters, Manuela and Michaela Klienzig.

After his flight to Venice, via Rome, he had been taken by road to Trieste and thence by speedboat to an abandoned pier in Yugoslavia. He was then driven to a chalet in Austria, followed by a car journey to Innsbruck Airport from where, disguised as a Fiat executive, he flew in a private jet to Britain.

When Calvi was settled in London the conspirators all left for various European destinations, Carboni to Switzerland to count the $11 million he had been paid for his trouble. However, by the night of 17 June they had all left England and they all denied having seen him that fatal night or knowing what might have happened to him.

Founded in 1896, and named after Saint Ambrose, the fourth-century archbishop of the city, the Catholic Banco Ambrosiano had originally been created as an alternative to Italy's 'lay' banks and was supposed to have moral goals, to help pious works and religious bodies. In the 1960s it had begun to expand into business and consequently had become Italy's second-biggest bank. Its collapse in 1982 sent shockwaves around Italy and the banking world.

Four years previously, the Bank of Italy had claimed in a report on Banco Ambrosiano that several billion lire had been exported, contravening financial regulations. This resulted in the bank's chairman, Roberto Calvi, being tried in 1981. Found guilty, he was given a four-year suspended sentence and fined almost £10 million for taking £13 million out of the country. Calvi was under a great deal of stress and while imprisoned for a short while awaiting trial, he attempted to kill himself. However, released on bail pending his appeal hearing, he was allowed to retain his position at the bank.

This was not the first time the Roman Catholic Church had been embroiled in a financial scandal. When bad loans and foreign currency transactions had brought about the collapse of the Franklin National Bank in 1974, the Vatican had taken a bath to the tune of around £15 million. That bank had been owned by Michele Sindonna, a Sicilian-born financier. Sindonna later died in prison after drinking a cup of coffee containing cyanide.

Just a few weeks before the collapse of Banco Ambrosiano, Calvi had written to the Pope, John Paul II, warning of the danger to the Church the bank's collapse would pose. And, sure enough, when it all came tumbling down in June 1982, debts emerged of somewhere between £350 million and £1.5 billion. Much of this money had been syphoned off via the Istituto per le Opere Religiose, the Vatican Bank, Banco Ambrosiano's principal shareholder.

Two years later, the Vatican Bank acknowledged its 'moral involvement' in the bank's collapse by making a payment to creditors of around £120 million.

The mostly likely cause of Calvi's death was that he just knew too much about too many things.

For instance, he knew a lot about the vexed question of Italian political funding. While being held in the prison at Lodi, he had provided magistrates with information about a loan of around £10 million to the Italian Socialist Party, hinting that he knew a great deal more. Indeed, he did. He knew the details of how major state-owned companies channelled funds in to the bank accounts of Italian politicians and political parties.

Or it could have been something to do with the mysterious Propogande Due – more commonly known as P2 – Masonic lodge in Rome. This lodge, run by Italian financier Licio Gelli, listed amongst its 900 members, 43 members of parliament, 48 generals, the heads of the Italian secret service, the top magistrates in the judiciary system, civil servants in charge of various state-owned enterprises, key bank regulators and leading businessmen. It was later described by a Parliamentary Commission as a 'state within a state'. Unlike other lodges, P2 never held meetings or conducted the normal business of a Masonic lodge. In reality, by 1980, the year that Calvi joined, it had become a means by which businessmen could buy political favours from government officials. Licio Gelli was the go-between for many of these arrangements.

One of these was a move to take control of Rizzoli, the Italian publishing house. Gelli and other P2 members fashioned a deal involving the Rothschild Bank and Calvi's bank which meant that Calvi lent £70 million to a Panamanian company called Bellatrix which deposited that money at the Rothschild Bank to buy the shares in Rizzoli. What made it worthwhile for all involved was that Bellatrix paid an artificially high price for Rizzoli's shares – a staggering ten times what they were worth – and the P2 members involved made a small fortune. However, the Rothschild principals became frightened of the deal and decided to try to hide the money coming in from Bellatrix by putting it into two different accounts at the bank – Zirka and Reciota. Before too long, the money was flooding into accounts held by Gelli and other P2 members. Calvi's £70 million had disappeared.

Unfortunately, though, Calvi had never received permission from the Italian financial authorities for Banco Ambrosiano to take control of the publishing house. This meant that the money that was now in P2 bank accounts was still technically cash that belonged to Banco Ambrosiano. This money was what brought the bank to its knees in June 1982.

Not long after Calvi's body had been found Juerg Heer, executive director of the credit section of Zurich's Rothschild Bank was given some secret instructions. Around £2.5 million, drawn from Licio Gelli's account in Geneva – part of the Bellatrix money – was delivered to him in a suitcase. He also received half of a $100 bill. His instructions told him that two men would arrive with the other half of the $100 bill. He was to give them the suitcase and later discovered that the money was payment for the murder of Roberto Calvi.

Gelli was later arrested while making a withdrawal of £25 million from his account in Geneva. He was sentenced to 18 years and six months for fraudulently contributing to the bankruptcy of the Banco Ambrosiano. This was reduced on appeal to 12 years, but on the eve of his imprisonment, he escaped and was recaptured on the French Riviera.

Or perhaps it was the Mafia who killed God's Banker. Rumours suggest that Calvi was laundering money for the Mafia and was about to spill the beans. Then again, the Mafia lost a great deal of money when the bank collapsed and somebody had to pay. Mafia *pentito*, Francesco Mannoia suggested that Calvi had been killed by Mafioso Franco di Carlo, who had been living in London at the time of the murder. Di Carlo, eventually given a 25-year sentence in Britain for narcotics smuggling, denied it, but it emerged that £50,000 had gone into his bank account the day before Calvi disappeared.

The Vatican is also in the frame. During a police raid against a gang of hashish and heroin importers in 1988, police discovered correspondence addressed to a high-ranking Vatican official, Cardinal Agostino Casaroli. The letters asked for around half a million pounds which the drug smuggler had given to Flavio Carboni to obtain documents written by Roberto Calvi. These were the documents that Calvi had taken on his tortuous journey to London. The documents had been delivered to a Vatican bishop who had paid him with cheques drawn from his personal account at the Vatican Bank. Carboni had received almost a million pounds for them.

In April 1986 the bag surfaced when Carboni and Silvano Vittor, Calvi's bodyguard, showed it off on Italian television. The documents were filled with opportunities to blackmail. One letter from Calvi to Pope John Paul II said: 'It was I who took on the heavy burden of remedying the errors and mistakes made by the present and former representatives of the IOR . . . providing financial aid to many countries and politico-religious associations on the instructions of authoritative representatives of the Vatican.'

Given the fact that more than half a billion pounds had gone missing from the Banco Ambrosiano, this was bad news for Archbishop Paul Marcinkus who had been a director of the bank's overseas business and had forged greater links between the Vatican Bank and Banco Ambrosiano. The Vatican's status as a sovereign state allowed Calvi to transfer money abroad.

Eventually, it was concluded that a number of people were guilty, but the judge presiding over the inquiry recommended that Franco di Carlo and Pippo Calò, the two Mafiosi allegedly contracted for the murder, be prosecuted alongside Flavio Carboni who got Calvi to London, and Licio Gelli who provided payment for the hit.

In 1998 Calvi's body was exhumed and in 2002 it was confirmed that he had been murdered.

In June 2007, in a specially fortified courtroom in

Rome, Giuseppe Calò, alleged to be cashier for the Sicilian Mafia, Flavio Carboni, businessman Ernesto Diotavelli, Silvano Vittor, Calvi's former bodyguard, and Manuela Kleinszig were cleared of the murder of Roberto Calvi. The charges had claimed that they had arranged his death to prevent him blackmailing 'his political and institutional sponsors from the world of Masonry, belonging to the P2 lodge, or to the Institute for Religious Works (the Vatican Bank) with whom he had managed investments and financing with conspicuous sums of money, some of it coming from Cosa Nostra and public agencies'.

As for Licio Gelli, he was not indicted for the murder. He has denied involvement, but has acknowledged that Calvi was murdered. In a statement before the court, he claimed the killing was commissioned in Poland, a reference to Calvi's alleged involvement in financing the Solidarity trade union movement at the request of the late Pope John Paul II, allegedly on behalf of the Vatican.

Calò, who gave evidence from his high security prison, denied the charges. 'I had no interest in killing Calvi. I didn't have the time, nor the inclination. Besides, if I had wanted him dead do you not think I would have picked my own people to do the job?' His lawyers argued there were plenty of people who had wanted Calvi silenced.

A private investigator, hired by Calvi's family in 1991, claimed it was likely that senior figures in the Italian establishment had been involved in his murder. 'The problem is that the people who probably actually ordered the death of Calvi are not in the dock,' he said. 'But to get to those people might be very difficult indeed.' He said it was 'probably true' that the Mafia had carried out the killing but that the gangsters suspected of the crime were either dead or missing.

The prosecutor's office in Rome had opened a second investigation implicating, among others, Licio Gelli. Meanwhile, Giuseppe Calò is serving a life sentence on unrelated Mafia charges.

PART SIX

KILLING
ALL OVER
THE WORLD

AUSTRALIA
CHRISTOPHER DALE FLANNERY

Melbourne, Australia, could never have been said to be crime-central. It purports to be the country's arts and culture capital and lacks the healthy anti-authority attitude of Sydney with its history of transported criminals and centuries of political and police corruption.

All the stranger, then, that Australia's first contract killer, the hitman known as 'Rentakill', should have been born there, in Brunswick, an inner suburb of the city and home, since the war, to thousands of émigrés from southern Europe, Greece, Italy and Turkey.

It was against such a background that Christopher Dale Flannery was born, in 1949. He was always trouble, getting into scrapes from an early age and leaving school at 14. It was in that same year that he first came to the attention of the authorities with his first conviction and, by the age of 17, he was a fully fledged criminal; there was really only one direction his life was going to take. He was arrested and convicted of a whole litany of crimes – housebreaking, car theft, police assault, carrying firearms and rape. As a criminal, he was becoming something of a jack-of-all-trades. No one thanked him for it, however, and he was sentenced to seven years in prison.

In 1974, a few years after being released, Flannery was in trouble again. He was arrested along with two other men for an armed robbery on a David Jones department store in Perth. The arresting officer was Detective Sergeant Roger Caleb Rogerson, one of the New South Wales Police Force's most decorated officers. Rogerson had received awards for bravery, outstanding work and devotion to duty. His awards included the Peter Mitchell Trophy, New South Wales's highest annual police award.

Following his arrest, Flannery was extradited to Perth from Melbourne, but he was acquitted on the robbery charge. It has been alleged that he had paid a bribe to Rogerson to help him escape conviction. The fact that a few years later Rogerson spent time in jail for perverting the course of justice in relation to AU$110,000 deposited by him in bank accounts under a false name, lends credence to the view that he helped Flannery on this occasion. However, Flannery did not get to savour the taste of freedom. On his release, he was rearrested on a charge of rape for which he was wanted in the state of Victoria and he went to jail for that anyway.

Released from prison at the end of the 1970s, Flannery took the route of many ex-cons who possessed a physical presence and a certain attitude – he became a bouncer at a club called Mickey's Disco in Melbourne's red-light district, St Kilda. The disco was a front and Mickey's was, in reality, a massage parlour. It had a need, therefore, for a bit of conspicuous muscle and Flannery could provide that, in spades.

Christopher Dale Flannery was, however, a man easily bored. He craved some excitement and some decent money for a change. The nightly drudge of throwing out drunks and sorting out punks who thought they were something they were not was never going to satisfy those needs. He decided, therefore, on a complete change of career, made some enquiries and managed to convince the right people that he was capable of being a hitman.

One of the first contracts Flannery undertook was the murder of a barrister, Roger Anthony Wilson. He had two accomplices – Mark Clarkson and John Williams. They followed Wilson's car and forced it off the road, abducting him and driving him to

Pakenham, a satellite suburb of Melbourne. Stopping next to wooded land, Flannery pushed the terrified Wilson out of the car and into the bush to shoot him. He failed to kill him with his first shot, however, and Wilson, with blood gushing from a head wound, attempted to escape into the bush. It is reported that Flannery, a man not renowned for his patience, 'went mad' at this point, emptying his gun into Wilson's head and back. Police never did find the barrister's body but Flannery was still arrested and charged with the murder. In October 1981 he was unexpectedly acquitted, but he only got as far as the courthouse steps where he was surrounded by New South Wales detectives who arrested him for an earlier murder, that of the Sydney brothel owner who rejoiced in the exotic name of Raymond Francis 'Lizard' Locksley. 'Lizard' Locksley had been done away with on 11 May 1979, in Menai, a suburb 29 kilometres south of Sydney's commercial centre.

Lady Luck was still batting for Flannery, however. In 1982 the trial jury failed to reach a verdict and then, at the retrial in April 1984, Flannery was yet again acquitted of murder.

He decided it was time to get out of Melbourne and bought a place in the southern Sydney residential suburb of Arncliffe, a pleasant, quiet place with detached and semi-detached townhouses and not too much commercial development; a good place to raise a family. He brought his wife and kids over from Melbourne and went to work as a bodyguard for George Freeman, one of the leading lights of the Sydney underworld.

Since Sydney's earliest days as a prison colony, crime has been part of the city's make-up. Organised crime had been around since the 1790s and arriving from England were a new breed of officers – the New South Wales Corps. Nicknamed the Rum Corps, its ranks were composed of officers on half pay, troublemakers, soldiers paroled from military prisons and those who saw no future in England and were gambling on an improvement in their prospects in the New World. They began to operate more like the Mafia than a police force, smuggling rum and carving up the new territories.

As time passed, political and police corruption became endemic in Sydney and by the 20th century organised crime was well established in the city. Illegal gambling houses, brothels and illegal alcohol outlets proliferated throughout the century, while the police turned a blind eye or, more likely, accepted money to ignore them.

By late 1984, when Christopher Flannery arrived on the scene, rival gang leaders were engaged in a war for control of Sydney's crime industry. This led to a number of high profile killings and rumours of corruption in high places. Flannery sided with Sydney gang leader Neddy Smith. Smith has claimed that Flannery was paranoid, and shot at anyone he suspected of having anything to do with Sydney gangsters Tom Domican or Barry McCann. Smith recounts how, when police officers tried to mediate in the gang wars and negotiate a cessation of hostilities, Flannery threatened a high-ranking policeman with the words: 'You're not a protected species, you know – you're not a fucking koala bear!'

The truth of his words was confirmed in 1986. Mick Drury was a Sydney Drug Squad detective who had been an undercover agent in an operation mounted against Melbourne drug dealer Alan Williams, a close friend of Christopher Flannery. The operation was successful and charges of heroin-trafficking were brought against Williams. Flannery repeatedly tried to bribe Drury, using his old friend Roger Rogerson, who had recently been kicked out of the police force, but Drury rejected all his advances. Williams then claims to have agreed to pay Rogerson and Flannery AU$50,000 to kill Drury, and on 6 June the detective was shot twice through his kitchen window as he sat feeding his three-year-old daughter Belinda. He survived the bullets, but on what he thought was going to be his deathbed, he said he was convinced that the shooting had taken place because of his involvement in 'the Melbourne job'.

Flannery was a hated man now, loathed in equal parts by both sides of the law. Some seven months after the Drury shooting, on 27 January 1985, as he and his wife walked towards the door to their house, shots rang out. Someone fired off 30 rounds at the couple using an Armalite rifle. He and his wife threw themselves to the ground and he received a bullet through his hand as he pushed his wife's head down. But, miraculously, neither received any other injury.

Flannery was understandably furious, blaming Sydney hood Tom Domican, whose people he had been shooting at for months. Domican was arrested and convicted of attempted murder but the conviction was later overturned on appeal. Interestingly, Roger Rogerson was picked up by police a few days later in the area of Flannery's house. When they interviewed him, he told them he was there because he was just curious to see the kind of damage an Armalite could do. They released him without charge. They also interviewed Mick Drury, in case he had been tempted to take revenge on Flannery, but he was never a serious suspect.

Flannery carried on with business as usual. On the early evening of 23 April 1985, two children returning home from sports training found a man called Tony

Eustace lying in a pool of blood but still breathing, beside his gold Mercedes. He had been shot six times in the back and the attack had all the makings of a professional hit. Eustace had been an associate of Flannery's boss, George Freeman, and he and Freeman had had a falling out. Freeman had sent his man Flannery to take care of him. However, when police at Eustace's bedside asked him who had shot him, Eustace, close to death, hissed hoarsely: 'Fuck off!' He died shortly after.

Following the attack on him and his wife, Flannery was concerned for himself and his family. He figured it might be safer to move into an apartment. Even safer if it was in close proximity to the Criminal Investigation Branch of the New South Wales Police. So he rented an apartment at the 30-storey Connaught Building, a recently built luxury apartment block in the centre of Sydney, home of celebrities and the well-to-do.

Not long after moving in on 9 May 1985, he received a phone call from George Freeman instructing him to attend a meeting with him. When Flannery went to the car park, though, his car would not start. Knowing Freeman was not a man who liked to be kept waiting, Flannery hurried back up to his apartment to call him. Freeman was in a hurry and told Flannery to forget his car and jump in a cab.

Flannery left the Connaught, presumably to do just that, and that was the last anyone ever saw of him.

Neddy Smith claims that while Flannery was waiting for a taxi in the busy Sydney traffic, two police officers he knew well drove past. They stopped, asked where he was headed and offered him a lift. Flannery thought nothing of it, considered how impatient George Freeman could be and gratefully accepted their offer. He climbed into the back seat. At the next set of traffic lights, however, the car stopped and another two police officers climbed in on each side of the hitman. Before Flannery could even smell a rat, the officer in the front passenger seat turned round with a revolver in his hand and shot Flannery.

His body was never found, but on 6 June 1997 the New South Wales Coroner Greg Glass found that Christopher Dale Flannery was murdered on or about 9 May 1985. Interestingly, Glass also found that the key to his murder lay with the former highly honoured detective, Roger Rogerson.

Rogerson, on the other hand, denied any involvement. In February 1994 he told an Australian TV show: 'Flannery was a complete pest. The guys up here in Sydney tried to settle him down. They tried to look after him as best they could, but he was, I believe, out of control. Maybe it was the Melbourne instinct coming out of him. He didn't want to do as he was told, he was out of control, and having overstepped that line, well, I suppose they said he had to go but I can assure you I had nothing to do with it.'

Was he telling the truth? Perhaps it is worth knowing that on 17 February 2005 Rogerson went to prison again for two and a half years. His crime? Lying to the 1999 Police Integrity Commission.

Australia
Carl Williams
and Family

The Australian city of Melbourne is a pretty safe town by world standards, with the lowest per capita rate of violent crime of any Australian city. Like any city, anywhere in the world, however, it has its trouble; gangs competing for more than their share of what's available. Melbourne's ugly underbelly became highly visible in 1999 when two drug-dealing families embarked on the city's bloodiest underworld war.

It kicked off on 13 October in the city's Barrington Crescent Park, located in the tidy, residential suburb of Gladstone Park. Drug dealers Jason Moran and his half-brother Mark had arranged to meet amphetamine manufacturer Carl Williams there.

The Williams and Moran families were two of Melbourne's leading drug-dealing factions and, as such, they had business matters to chew over. But Williams, always cautious, insisted on holding his meetings in public places in order to minimise the chance of being overheard by police listening devices. So the park seemed like a good spot for the meeting.

Although they remained deeply suspicious of each other, the Williamses and the Morans often worked together when it was mutually beneficial. As they met that day, they did so against a background of escalating demand for amphetamines; business was excellent and sales had recently increased by around 1,000 per cent. It was a good time to be a drug dealer.

Still, there were some undercurrents. The Morans were annoyed with Williams because, they claimed, he was selling his pills too cheaply, undercutting them. They were also irritated by a supply of crumbling pills that they had bought from Williams in which insufficient binding material had been used. There was also the little matter of AU$400,000 that the Morans claimed was owed to them by Williams for the purchase of a pill press. Moreover, in the background was a more personal issue. Williams' wife, Roberta, had previously been married to Dean Stephens, a close friend of the Morans.

The Morans were a particularly violent bunch, especially Jason, a hothead who thought nothing of using a gun to settle disagreements. He had had enough of Williams and reckoned it was time to make a point. As they greeted each other, he suddenly pulled out a .22 Derringer, firing a single shot into the other man's abdomen. Stupidly, however, he did not finish the job as he so easily could have, claiming when his brother urged him to do it that if Williams were dead they would have no chance of ever seeing their $400,000. It was the worst decision he ever made and resulted not only in the destruction of his immediate family but the loss of many other lives because, as Carl Williams lay on the ground in a pool of blood, he resolved to kill everyone in the Moran family as well as anyone associated with it.

Rushed to hospital and found not to be in danger of losing his life, Williams was interviewed by detectives keen to find out who had pulled the trigger. He was having none of it, though. He resolutely refused to cooperate, acting as if the bullet had been a complete surprise to him as he went for a stroll in the park. He was going to settle this matter his way. He had always done things his way.

He had been raised in the Broadmeadows suburb of Melbourne and lived at home with his parents until he met and married Roberta at the age of 31. He settled down, but stacking shelves at a supermarket paled for him as soon as he discovered that there was a lot more money to be earned working for bookies at the racetrack.

His brother was a junkie and Williams's mother maintains that on account of this her other son was always being harassed by the police. Or perhaps it was just because he was an inveterate crook. At the age of 20 he was convicted of handling stolen goods and then in 1994 he went to jail for six months on amphetamine charges. As time went on, though, his criminal standing rapidly increased, much to the surprise of the police. Soon, from a standing start, this suburban drug dealer had become Australia's most dangerous criminal, heading up a network of reckless young dealers in search of big paydays.

Following his shooting, Williams became a cold-blooded killer, driven by hatred and an overwhelming desire for revenge. He is connected to at least ten murders, and yet it could all so easily have been prevented.

A Broadmeadows family had been involved in a credit card scam and on a November morning in 1999, police arrived to arrest them. No one was home, but when one of the policemen drove past the house again later that same day, he noticed two cars parked outside. The team was reassembled and when they broke the door down, they discovered a pill press, 30,000 tablets and seven kilos of speed, valued at AU$20 million. They also found Carl Williams and his father George hiding upstairs.

Williams was lucky this time, however. While he was awaiting trial, two of the detectives who had been involved in his case, were arrested on corruption charges and it was decided that the Williams case should be delayed until the prosecution of the corrupt policemen had taken place. So, instead of being locked up, Williams was released on bail and was free to wage war on the Morans.

Revenge on the Morans became much easier when Jason Moran was charged with affray and sentenced to 20 months behind bars, leaving his brother Mark isolated. It took Williams five months to get him. Mark Moran was shot dead getting out of his car after driving home. The guman was Carl Williams.

The Morans' father, Lewis, a man said to still have the first dollar that he ever stole, called a family meeting to decide on a response and, bizarrely, they still did not realise that Williams had declared war on them and their associates. A pity, really, because of the seven men in attendance at that meeting, five were later killed. Some time later, Lewis would take out a contract on Williams, but the $40,000 he offered was not enough to persuade anyone to take what would be a hit filled with danger.

Nonetheless, Williams was the number one suspect for the murder of Mark Moran and his house was raided by police the day after the murder. However, the drug squad, who had been investigating the Morans for years, withheld information from homicide detectives, believing that their investigation was far more important than a murder case that they thought could not be successfully prosecuted.

When Jason Moran was released from prison on parole, in September 2001, it was inevitable that he would go after Williams, but by then Williams himself was back in prison on remand following another drug-trafficking charge: 8,000 ecstasy pills this time. The parole board, fearing for Moran's life, sent him overseas. Meanwhile, in Port Philip Prison Williams continued his recruitment campaign.

One recruit was a ruthless armed robber, Victor Brincat, who was known as the Runner. He had staged around 40 armed robberies across Australia over a period of seven years and had earned his nickname because he would run away to a parked car after each robbery. Williams recruited him to kill Jason Moran when he got out of prison. Moran, by this time, had somewhat recklessly decided to come home.

Incredibly, given his previous record, Williams was again bailed in July 2002, his case still being held up while the drug detectives' case was pending. In December of that year, Victor Brincat was released and Moran sent him after Jason. Once he was found,

Williams would kill him. As Brincat has been reported as saying: 'Carl developed a deep-seated hatred of the Moran family . . . it was an obsession with him. Carl told me on numerous occasions that he wanted everyone connected with the Moran family dead.'

Williams and Brincat dreamed up numerous hair-brained schemes for the murder of Moran. They would remove the lock from the boot of his silver BMW and jump out and shoot him. Or Williams would hide in the rubbish bin outside the house where he was thought to be staying. Maddest of all, was to lure him to a park where Brincat, disguised as a woman pushing a pram, would shoot him as he pushed the pram past him. They even went so far as to buy a shoulder-length brown wig.

But Moran was not easy to find. He kept a low profile, employed a bodyguard and kept on the move.

In February they finally spotted him at a fast food outlet in Gladstone Park, but Williams was not carrying a weapon. Nevertheless, they followed his car which was being driven by a woman not known to them. However, Williams drove too close and when he spotted them, Jason fired a volley of shots at them from the back of his car. Williams decided to call it quits on that occasion.

Once again, Jason vanished and Williams began to get desperate. He ordered Brincat to keep an eye on his target's friends, but still to no avail. Finally, he offered Brincat and gunman and former kickboxer Andrew 'Benjy' Veniamin, a massive bounty of AU$100,000 each to find and kill Moran. They approached the task with renewed vigour. They waited outside the school Moran's children attended – coincidentally, the same one that Williams's kids went to. Still no sign. They even persuaded Roberta Williams to start a fight with Moran's wife at the school gates in the hope that he would turn up to support her, but still he did not show.

Then they found the perfect opportunity. They learned that Moran regularly took his children to an Australian Rules football clinic every Saturday morning in the Melbourne suburb of Essendon North. By this time, Brincat had a new partner, Thomas Hentschell, and he and Hentschell practised the hit at the football oval for a week before the designated date. Meanwhile, Williams arranged to have a blood test that morning, providing himself with a watertight alibi.

On the Saturday morning they waited at the oval and, before too long, spotted Jason. They waited until he made his way back to the car park at the end of the game and climbed into a blue van. Brincat and Hentschell drove to the rear of the car park, Brincat pulled a balaclava over his head and jumped out of their vehicle with a shotgun as well as two revolvers stuffed into a belt around his waist. He ran to the window of Jason's car, raised the shotgun and let off a round through the closed window, killing Moran instantly. He then dropped the shotgun, pulled out one of the revolvers and fired a further three shots into Moran's slumped body behind the shattered glass. Unknown to him, another man was in the front seat of the van, a small-time crook, employed by Moran, called Pasquale Barbaro. He, too, was dead. Brincat then ran over a footbridge to Hentschell in the waiting van; he wasn't known as Brincat for nothing.

The simple phone message 'that horse has been scratched' told Williams that the hit had been carried out. Brincat was paid $2,500 and was supposed to be given, in addition, a unit in the nearby city of Frankston. The unit never materialised, however, an oversight Williams would live to bitterly regret.

There had now been 11 unsolved underworld-related killings in two years and police were frustrated by the lack of progress. In Moran's case, Carl Williams was an obvious suspect, but his alibi placed him somewhere else at the time of the hit.

Senior homicide detective Phil Swindells lobbied for a taskforce to tackle these crimes and the Purana taskgroup was formed in May 2003 with Swindells in command. In the beginning they were at a disadvantage due to their lack of intelligence on the leading players. So they doggedly began to compile dossiers on their targets and even called on the Essendon Aussie Rules coach, Kevin Sheedy, to help boost morale.

In October they enlarged the taskforce to 53, with Detective Inspector Andrew Allen in charge. Of course, they knew that Williams was behind the killings, but there was as yet no hard evidence.

They did get one break after months of work, however. Checking calls made from a public phone box near where Moran was shot, they discovered that on the day before the shooting, someone rang Carl Williams from this phone. They found out from other calls made around the same time that it had been Hentschell, already known to them as a thief, drug dealer and friend of Carl Williams. Then, in Hentschell's driveway, they found a white van of the kind that had been spotted by a closed-circuit camera at the scene of the crime.

It would be 14 months before they could press charges, however, and in the meantime the killing continued.

Another victim of Williams was drug dealer Mark Mallia, 37, whose body was found in a burning wheelie bin in Sunshine in August 2003. Williams had lured

Mallia to a meeting and had then bound and gagged him before torturing him with a soldering iron. He was then strangled and put in the bin which was set on fire.

Williams's team was becoming overconfident, though. In October 2003 a bug was placed in a car Hentschell was using in a hit. When he discovered it, he wanted to abandon the hit but Brincat insisted on carrying on with it. This view was supported by Williams when they met him later that evening. Williams, by now calling himself 'The Premier', as he believed he was controlling the entire state of Victoria, ordered them to continue with the job. Stupidly, Hentschell then used his own car to drive to the location. This car was also bugged and he and Brincat were heard discussing guns and getaways. However, the tracker that police had placed on the car failed and they had no idea where the action was going to take place.

Then, in their earphones, they heard what sounded like gunshots and, shortly after, received calls that a man had been shot in South Yarra. Michael Marshall, a drug dealer and hot-dog salesman, had climbed out of his four-wheel drive, in which his five-year-old son was sitting, and had been shot four times. Police overheard Hentschell asking: 'Shall I ring the Big Fella?' Williams shortly afterwards received the same message as before: 'That horse has been scratched.'

Within a few hours, Hentschell and Brincat had been arrested and the clock began to tick for Carl Williams.

The war continued and, not long after, Andrew Veniamin was killed by known criminal Mick Gatto, whose close friend Graham Kinnisburgh had been a recent victim of Williams's vendetta. Veniamin had advised Williams to take out Gatto, in effect sentencing himself to death when Gatto heard of it. Gatto shot him in a Carlton restaurant but was acquitted in June 2005 on grounds of self-defence.

Kinnisburgh's murder also resonated with Lewis Moran. As if it were not bad enough losing his two sons, Lewis was destroyed by the loss of Kinnisburgh who was his best friend. He did not seem to care about anything any more and made no effort to protect himself. On 31 March 2004 he was gunned down by two contract killers at his favourite haunt, the Brunswick Club. They were paid AU$140,000 for the hit by millionaire drug dealer Tony Mokbel and Carl Williams.

In May 2004 the police finally nailed Williams when two of his associates were overheard carelessly discussing a hit in a car they wrongly thought to be clean of bugs. Four men were arrested, including Williams who had been implicated by the men's conversation. This time there would be no bail.

However, Williams was confident his men would stay loyal, especially Brincat. After all, following the Marshall killing, forensic officers had tried to take a swab from his mouth and had found a brown 'substance' there. It was never properly identified, but it compromised any evidence. And it smelled terrible.

Nonetheless, the case against Brincat was unimpeachable. Marshall's blood was found on his trousers, and the taped conversations as well as positive identifications, provided police with a solid case against him for the murder. The Runner realised that the game was up, and, anyway, he now also bore grudges against Williams who had failed to pay him in full for the hits he had carried out. He caved in and, over the course of 30 days of interviews, told police everything he knew, linking Williams comprehensively to Melbourne's gangland murders.

In quick succession, five more of Williams's lieutenants turned on him. Police learned that he had armed robber George Peirce killed by Veniamin because he reneged on a contract to kill Moran. Mark Anthony Smith was shot after he, too, agreed to kill Moran and didn't go through with it. Smith survived and fled to Queensland.

Police realised that if they were to get anywhere near putting Williams away for good, they would have to make some deals. Consequently, they offered the criminals they had rounded up the chance of freedom if they cooperated. Men who faced decades in prison suddenly saw an opportunity to taste freedom once again.

Hentschell did a deal, but the star witness was Brincat who implicated Carl Williams in at least six murders. He also fingered Tony Mokbel for one killing. Mokbel saw the writing on the wall and disappeared. The police dismantled his financial empire, and finally caught up with him in June 2007, arresting him in a Greek café.

Williams, too, knew it was all over once Brincat started to talk. He was convicted of the murder of Michael Marshall and was sentenced to a minimum of 21 years for that. Many other trials are pending forthe murders of, amongst others, Mark and Jason Moran and Pasquale Barbaro.

Recently, he pleaded guilty to the murders of Lewis and Jason Moran and another man whose name has not been released. He refused to include Barbaro because, he says, that death was an accident. As a result, he will never be charged with the other six murders he is believed to have committed. Carl Williams still hopes that one day he will be free again.

COLOMBIA
PABLO ESCOBAR

In 1989 *Forbes Magazine* listed ruthless Colombian drug dealer, Pablo Escobar, as the seventh richest man in the world. He owned a multi-million dollar home, ranches, farms and horses. He had beautiful fixtures in his home and an antique car collection. At the time, his Medellín drug cartel was raking in around $30 billion a year and controlling 80 per cent of the cocaine market. Who says crime doesn't pay?

Escobar was born Pablo Emilio Escobar Gaviria in 1949, the son of a peasant farmer and a teacher, in humble surroundings in Medellín, a city in the Antioquia region of central Colombia. Medellín is not a quiet town – in 1991 it recorded a murder rate 11 times that of Chicago – and Escobar's criminal career began when he was a teenager, after he was expelled from school – stealing cars on the city's streets. Allegedly, he also did a good trade in stolen headstones, selling them in other towns and villages of the region. It was during the 1970s that he saw the vast potential in cocaine-trafficking and began building his enormous empire. But he began his life in drugs as a courier, transporting coca paste from the Andes to the laboratories in Medellín.

There was a lot at stake and that meant that life was pretty cheap. Escobar bolstered his own reputation and his bank balance in 1975 when he murdered a well-known drug dealer by the name of Fabio Restrepo, from whom he had purchased a quantity of cocaine. Restrepo's men were instructed that they had to work for Escobar now.

In March 1976 Pablo married Maria Victoria and they had two children: Juan Pablo and Manuela. However, he is known to have had affairs with several women and towards the end of his life he seemed to have shifted his sexual preferences to underage girls. For him and his new family, however, he built a luxurious estate called *Hacienda Napoles* (Spanish for Naples Ranch), complete with private zoo, and had planned to construct a Greek-style citadel which was started but never finished. He hired a professional cameraman to shoot his home movies. He and his men posed in front of his proudest possession, a car that had once belonged to the gangster Al Capone, and he saw himself as a future Al Capone. The ranch, the zoo and the citadel were expropriated by the government and given to low-income families in the 1990s under a law called *extinción de dominio* (domain extinction).

In May of the same year that Pablo got married, his luck ran out temporarily when he and a number of his associates were arrested following a drug run to Ecquador. In response, Pablo introduced what was to become his customary tactic when dealing with intransigent authorities, a tactic he called *plata o plomo*, Spanish for 'money or lead'. He tried to bribe the judge and, when that failed, and months of legal wrangling passed without a satisfactory outcome for him, he had the two arresting officers killed. The official documents disappeared from the courthouse and nine judges refused to try the case after receiving death threats. The case was dropped.

Escobar's genius was in realising that the smugglers were stronger together than individually. So he persuaded his rivals to share shipments, no matter whom it belonged to. They constructed a massive processing plant deep in the Colombian jungle. It was called Tranquilandia and consisted of an entire complex of airstrips and laboratories capable of refining and shipping cocaine on an industrial scale. When it was located by the authorities, Colombia's head of anti-narcotics, Colonel Jaime Ramirez, was visited by Escobar's people who offered him a multi-million dollar bribe to cease all operations in Tranquilandia. He refused and ordered his troops to torch the place.

Escobar's reputation grew further when he succeeded in getting elected to the Chamber of Representatives of the Colombian Congress – his election brought the additional benefit of giving him immunity from prosecution. But it was his drugs network which garnered international interest, especially in the United States. The Medellín cartel came to control a huge proportion of the cocaine that entered the States, Mexico, Puerto Rico and the Dominican Republic. But Colombian cocaine was of poor quality. Therefore Escobar would buy coca paste in Peru and Bolivia, and have it processed and shipped to warehouses in the Bahamas and Mexico. From there it would enter the United States. And his tentacles are alleged to have reached into many other parts of the world, even beyond the Americas and into Asia. In his last years, it is reported that he distanced himself from direct involvement in drug-trafficking, instead syphoning off profits from cocaine dealers through a kind of taxation system he imposed on other criminals operating within his area of influence. He considered this to be compensation for his contribution to the development of the Colombian cocaine industry and his efforts to have the American–Colombian extradition treaty of 1979 nullified.

Hundreds died as Pablo Escobar went about his business, often killed personally by Escobar himself – anyone who failed to cooperate with him or who presented any kind of threat was ruthlessly disposed of. He was also responsible for the deaths of three presidential candidates, all taking part in the same election, and numerous government officials, judges and politicians were accepting bribes from him.

On 6 November 1985, 35 armed rebel commandos of the left-wing M-19 guerrilla group took hostage 300 lawyers, judges and Supreme Court magistrates at the Palace of Justice in Bogota, where the Colombian Supreme Court sits. They demanded that the Colombian President Belisario Betancur be tried for allegedly betraying the country's desire for peace. The army surrounded the court and negotiations began. With no resolution in sight, it was decided to let the army take the Palace by force, but in the ensuing gun battle and fire, some 100 people died and vital records were destroyed.

Debate rages to this day about the correctness of the government's approach, but it is also said that Pablo Escobar may have instigated M-19's operation in order to destroy documents relating to several criminal investigations into his activities. It is also worth noting that at the time of the siege, the

Colombian Supreme Court was studying the constitutionality of Colombia's extradition treaty with the US, a matter of some importance to Escobar.

In late 2006 a Truth Commission, comprising three judges of the current Supreme Court, presented a document which argued that the M-19 met with Escobar, received money from the cartel and executed some joint actions, although some M-19 members disagreed with that course of action. It also mentioned a claim made by former Escobar associate John Jairo Velásquez Vásquez, known as 'Popeye', implicating the druglord in the events, allegedly through the payment of some $2 million to the rebel group.

Then, in 1989, Escobar was responsible for an even greater atrocity. On 27 November the worst single criminal attack in Colombia's violent history occurred when a Boeing 727 of Avianca Airlines, en route from the Colombian capital Bogota to Cali in the west of the country, was ripped apart five minutes after take-off by an explosive device. All 107 passengers and crew on board died and a further three were killed on the ground by falling debris. Escobar and the Medellín cartel immediately claimed responsibility for the bomb, saying they were targeting César Gaviria Trujillo, a candidate in the forthcoming presidential elections. Trujillo never made it onto the plane, though, and the assassination attempt was in vain.

Dandeny Munoz-Mosquera, Escobar's chief enforcer, was convicted in the United States for the bombing and was given ten consecutive life sentences.

In spite of these dreadful actions, the people of Medellín worshipped Pablo Escobar. He bought their love by building hospitals and football stadiums and by sponsoring football teams. He won over the Catholic Church by using his vast wealth to build a number of churches in the city. He even distributed large sums of money to the poor and built houses for them. They, in turn, watched out for him, informing him if the authorities were closing in on him and they did not give information to the police.

By 1991, however, things were getting too hot and, in order to avoid his inevitable extradition to the USA and incarceration for the rest of his days in a federal penitentiary, or death at the hands of one of his rivals, Escobar tried to win public support by calling a halt to his violent terrorist acts and handed himself over to the Colombian government. He was put in prison, but it was no ordinary jail. Amazingly, he was allowed to build his own luxurious private prison, called La Catedral. He had a suite with a living room, a kitchen, a master bedroom and an office. The bathroom had its own jacuzzi. The prison itself contained its own discotheque as well as its own bar where parties were held on a weekly basis. He was known to have visits from family, but additionally, outside his personal room at the prison, he had a very powerful telescope set up which pointed at the building where his wife, son and daughter lived. He would talk on his cell phone to his daughter while looking at her through the telescope. He negotiated a five-year jail sentence and a guarantee that he would not be extradited to the United States in exchange for the cessation of his drug-dealing activities.

Even in his country club prison, Escobar's violent nature was given full vent and a report that he had murdered two business associates, the Moncada brothers, at La Catedral, coupled with pictures in the media of his lavish prison, incensed public opinion. The government was forced to make plans to move him to another prison. However, fearing that he was about to be extradited, Pablo did the only thing he could. He escaped.

A huge manhunt was launched. Operatives of the United States Delta Force, a special operations group, joined in, supported later by United States Navy SEALS, who engaged in training and advising the special Colombian task force that was created and which became known as the Search Bloc. Later, a Colombian vigilante force, known as Los Pepes (People Persecuted by Pablo Escobar), added their weight to the search. Los Pepes were given financial support by Escobar's rivals, the Cali cartel, and by Carlos Castaño, founder of the Peasant Self-Defense Forces of Cordoba and Uraba (ACCU), an extreme right paramilitary organisation. Castaño was also a drug-trafficker. Their campaign against Escobar was bloody and ruthless – more than 300 of his family and associates were killed and large parts of the Medellín cartel's property were destroyed. It has been insinuated that the Search Bloc and the American forces helped the Los Pepes death squads in their campaign, either through sharing intelligence or even by participating in actions.

Pablo Escobar remained a fugitive for 499 days. But on 2 December 1993 the Search Bloc finally caught up with him. Using radio triangulation technology loaned by the United States, an electronic surveillance team located him in a middle-class barrio in Medellín. A prolonged gunfight took place on the rooftops of Medellín and Escobar was finally dispatched with gunshots to his leg, back and the fatal one behind the ear. That final wound may have been sustained during the gunfight, but, more likely, he was simply executed as he lay wounded.

The Medellín cartel was no more and the Cali cartel dominated the cocaine market until it, too, was brought down in the mid-nineties.

FRANCE
JACQUES 'JACKY LE MAT' IMBERT

Marseille has long enjoyed a reputation as one of Europe's harder cities and Jacky Imbert, known to all as Jacky 'le Mat' (Mad Jacky), was one of the hardest criminals the city ever produced. He was also one of its great survivors. Against the odds, when his associates and rivals were dropping all around him, either as victims of gangland shootings or being arrested, Jacky would be left standing, defeating the assassins and duping generations of policemen.

Little is known of Jacky's early years and the first time he appeared in any official records was in 1963 when he was a suspect in the murder of a gangster, Andreani Baptiste, outside a gaming room in Paris. In the document he is described as 'a very dangerous individual; a veritable contract killer', but the police failed to back up their suspicions and he was never prosecuted for the murder.

Neither did the charges stick five years later when he was implicated in the drive-by killing of another Marseille godfather, Antoine Guerini. Guerini had associated with gangsters in his youth, but had became a hero of the Resistance in the Second World War, smuggling arms into Marseille to be used against the Germans. However, at the end of the war he returned to his old ways, rising to become the dominant crime boss in the city and, according to one of the many conspiracy theories surrounding the death of US President John F. Kennedy, the organiser of his assassination. According to this theory, it was not carried out by Lee Harvey Oswald, but by members of the Marseille mob. However, by June 1967 Guerini's grip on the city's criminal underworld was faltering and on the 23rd of that month, two hired assassins pumped 11 bullets into him while he sat in his car at a petrol station.

With Guerini dead, everything was up for grabs and Imbert tried to take control of the city's highly lucrative heroin trade, as well as prostitution and protection rackets, joining forces with the Corsican mobster Gaetan 'Tony' Zampa. Zampa, a pimp and the son of a pimp, had begun his career as an enforcer for a small but violent Paris syndicate, the Trois Canards. He had been a major force in the Marseille underworld for 20 years. Imbert and Zampa worked the French Connection – made famous by the 1971 William Friedkin film starring Gene Hackman – whereby heroin was imported from Turkey to France and then sent onwards to the Mafia in the United States. They became immensely wealthy from the drug trade, although they eventually fell out over their shares of the money they earned from extortion.

A few years after their split, in February 1977, Imbert was driving his classic Alfa Romeo onto the driveway of his home at Cassis, a commune to the east of Marseille, when he was ambushed by three gunmen who fired no less than 22 bullets into him. Miraculously, Jacky survived the attack which, police presumed, was organised by Zampa, a fact confirmed by an interview with one of the hitmen in the newspaper, *Liberation*. He confessed that Zampa gave them the contract and, himself, took part in the hit. As Imbert lay on the ground, blood seeping from his wounds, Zampa is reported to have ripped off his mask to let him see who had shot him. He then barked to the other men: 'Don't finish him off. Leave him whimpering like a dog.'

However, Imbert's only lasting injury was a partial paralysis of the right arm. The newspaper *Le Monde* knew Jacky well. 'Small matter,' it reported. 'He will learn to shoot with the left.'

All-out war now erupted between Imbert and

Zampa and Zampa lost 11 men before things calmed down. Meanwhile, the police detained Jackie for six months, trying and failing to prove a case against him for the killings. Once again, they were unable to bring charges and he walked free. On the other hand, in 1983 Zampa was arrested and sent to prison for tax evasion and fraud relating to nightclubs he owned. On 23 July 1984, he was found hanged in his cell.

Jacky was now free to get on with his life and he lived it to the full, becoming something of a folk anti-hero. He became a champion trotting driver and an accomplished yachtsman. He earned a pilot's licence and became a friend of the stars, most notably film star Alain Delon, the great French actor who played glamorous gangsters in fantastically popular films such as *Borsalino*.

He travelled to his properties in the Caribbean and Italy, purchased with the profits from the French Connection. In the 1980s, he described himself as a PR man for a Paris disco that was owned by a Russian businessman, Richard Erman. At this time, he was described in *Le Figaro* newspaper as 'looking as though he just stepped off a cinema set ... larger than life'.

The police tried to get him again in 1993. Aged 63 and known now as 'The Boss', he was arrested along with a dozen others in a police clampdown in Marseille. They were arrested on suspicion of armed robbery, protection, slot-machine rackets and money laundering. Meanwhile, Francis Vanverberghe, Imbert's partner in crime, was also picked up in Paris. They were believed to be behind a dozen deaths as yet another long-running feud had raged along the Mediterranean coast over control of nightclubs. Both Imbert and Vanverberghe denied any involvement, both claiming to have retired from such activities long before.

Yet again, the authorities failed to make a case against Mad Jacky and, before long, he was back on the streets of Marseille.

It seemed as if Mad Jacky had retired. However, French police found it hard to believe and it hurt that they had been trying to nail him for decades, without success. So while they were investigating a criminal operation run by the Russian Mafia which was going to build a clandestine cigarette factory in a warehouse in one of Marseille's suburbs, they were overjoyed when they overheard, on a tapped phone line, a conversation between Imbert and Erman that seemed to implicate Imbert in the operation. In October 2003 they raided his house and placed him under arrest.

When he appeared in court with seven other accused in November 2004, astonishingly, it was with a completely clean record. His previous convictions had all been expunged by the passing of time and various presidential amnesties. Nonetheless, the state was asking for a five-year prison term, more than for any other of the accused. Prosecutor, Marc Gouton said: 'Everyone here has testified that without Imbert's authorisation nothing could be done. He has a very strong character. He is not a man who takes orders. He gives orders and others carry them out.' Gradually, however, the testimonies he spoke of were withdrawn by prosecution witnesses, leaving as the only evidence of Jacky's involvement the telephone call with Erman in which all he said was: 'Look, all these ups and downs, they are beginning to cause me problems, you get it?'

Imbert's lawyers claimed the words were open to interpretation but they failed to persuade the jury and he was found guilty and sentenced to four years in prison for masterminding the operation. At last, they had him . . . or did they? He appealed and on 8 April 2005 the appeal court decided that the telephone evidence was not convincing, finding in his favour and clearing him of taking part in the manufacture of contraband cigarettes.

The authorities were smarting but it did not take them long to come up with another set of charges to try to bring him down. This time, he was charged with extorting £57,000 from a Parisian property developer, Pierre Ossana, and from various Marseille and Paris nightclubs during the early 1990s. He had been up to his old tricks, it seemed, even in 'retirement'. Naturally, he denied all charges, telling a courtroom ringed by commandos from the French army: 'It's unthinkable I extorted money from Mr Ossuna, because he's a friend.' Suddenly, Mr Ossuna agreed, stating that the £57,000 was, in fact, a simple loan. 'I knew Mr Imbert in Saint-Tropez,' he testified. 'He never threatened or mistreated me, nothing like that. The 540,000 francs I lent him did not disturb my lifestyle.' Nevertheless, the judge, Domique Bréjoux, disagreed, dismissing Ossuna's testimony as untrue.

Imbert was convicted on 6 June 2006 and sentenced to four years in prison. Defence attorney Sophie Bottai had earlier said: 'Certainly, my client has a past, but he wants to be judged as Jacques Imbert, not as Jacky le Mat.' Now she condemned the trial and the sentence as a sham and said she would be lodging an appeal.

So, at the age of 76, Jacky le Mat at last went to prison, after five decades of avoiding it. However, at least he was still alive and, what's more, he had a 35-year-old wife and an 18-month-old son to prove it.

CHARLES SOBRAJ

Charles Sobraj is not just an extraordinary killer. He is an extraordinary man. Like Charles Manson, this charismatic, half-Indian, half-Vietnamese psychopath is the possessor of a strange power over people – the ability to bend them to do his will and to follow him blindly.

In an early instance of this, Sobraj, aged ten, persuaded his stepbrother to rob a shopkeeper. He explained to his mother how he could 'always find an idiot to do what I wanted' and throughout his life he did just that. Along the way, he probably killed around 30 people, mostly unsuspecting young backpackers and pilgrims who had travelled to India and the Far East in search of spiritual enlightenment and met Charles Sobraj and death.

Murder for him was no more than a means to an end. He killed in order to obtain a fresh passport, or jewels or money, in order to fund and maintain an adventurous lifestyle which took him all over Europe and the Far East for many years. 'If I have ever killed, or have ordered killings, then it was purely for reasons of business,' he once said. 'Just a job, like a general in the army.'

Needless, to say, Sobraj's childhood was unpleasant and difficult. He was born Gurhmuk Sobhraj in Saigon, in 1944, to a Vietnamese mother, Song, and an Indian tailor father. The father left shortly after Sobraj came into the world and Song never really forgave the young Guhrmak for her abandonment.

Gurhmak, however, never really gave up on his father, even after his mother married Lieutenant Alphonse Darreau, a French officer stationed in Vietnam. Instead, his father took on a heroic status in his mind and he determined to link up with him. By now, the family was living in Marseille in France and, with easy access to ocean-going ships, the young Charles would stow away on them, hoping to get to his father in the Far East. Several times he was discovered at sea and sent home to arguments, especially when his fare for the journey had to be paid by his family. Furthermore, Darreau, his stepfather, had been invalided out of the army and saw his step-son as nothing more than a drain on what little income the family brought in.

Meanwhile, in school, he was a handful. He was intelligent but intensely disobedient, and often absent from lessons. The older he got, the worse he became and his family grew tired of bailing him out of trouble until he was eventually arrested for a burglary in Paris and sent to prison for three years. It was 1963.

Life was brutal in Poissy prison and Sobraj had to learn to look after himself. It had been built in the 16th century as a convent and had cells so small that prisoners could not spend the day in them, being herded, instead, into pens. His knowledge of karate helped him get out of scrapes and his natural charm enabled him to obtain favours no one else enjoyed. He befriended a wealthy young prison visitor, Felix D'Escoigne, who provided Sobraj with emotional support and reading materials.

Paroled, Sobraj moved into D'Escoigne's apartment and, unknown to his flatmate, started to return to the life of the underworld he had left behind when he went to prison.

He met a girl, Chantal, in Paris and to the dismay of her wealthy parents, it looked like they would marry. On the night that he was going to propose, however, he drove her to a casino in a car he had stolen earlier. Later, having lost a lot of money at the casino, he was followed by a police car because he was driving too fast. He responded by driving even faster, but crashed the car, was arrested and sent back to prison for another eight months. Chantal told everyone he had been called up to do national service.

When released again, Sobraj took up with Chantal

once more. He had managed to make a lot of money from various scams while in prison and the girl's parents, seeing that he seemed relatively wealthy, began to come round to the idea of Chantal marrying him. They married in a civil ceremony.

Chantal quickly became pregnant, but things were getting too hot for Sobraj in France. He had been bouncing cheques everywhere and it would not be too long before the police linked him to a series of burglaries from large houses, especially as he had recently visited each one of them.

So he borrowed a car from his friend Felix and he and the pregnant Chantal set out for the East, leaving a trail of bounced cheques, robberies and victims of cons in their wake. When they arrived in Bombay, Chantal gave birth to a daughter.

They began to integrate into life in India, Sobraj using his charm and intelligence to smooth his way into society. Soon they were hobnobbing with some of the wealthiest and most influential people in town and he was finding it easy to carry on with business as usual in this new environment where he was unknown and the pickings were easy.

It was 1970 and his main source of income was a stolen car racket. He would steal or fence cars in the neighbouring countries of Pakistan or Iran and bring them over the border into India, bribing border guards en route. He would then hand them over to the authorities as stolen and buy them back cheaply at auction. He then sold them for a profit to wealthy Indians or Westerners who wanted to drive a Western car.

Gambling was always Sobraj's weakness. He had already lost large sums of money in the casinos of Paris and in India it got him into trouble once again. He lost badly at the casino in Macoa and had to sell a lot of the expensive jewellery he had acquired for Chantal over the years they had been together. What he would be able to raise would not be quite enough, however, to satisfy the casino owners which, given their capacity for violence where unpaid debts were concerned, could have been bad news. Sobraj met a man who had a plan to rob a jewellery store in the Hotel Ashoka in Delhi. The plan was to hire a room above the store, drill a hole through the roof and drop into the store below. However, the drilling was unsuccessful and they had to get in another way. They told the manager that there was a wealthy potential customer in the room and when he entered the room, they took the keys from him at gunpoint and cleaned out the store.

When Sobraj fled to the airport to make his escape, he found it to be surrounded by the police and he had to abandon the jewels as well as $10,000 in cash that he had taken from the store. He flew back to Bombay empty-handed.

Unfortunately, there had been a witness to the robbery and Sobraj fitted the description he gave. He was arrested and taken to Bombay's notorious Tihar prison. However, as Charles Sobraj proved several times in his long criminal career, escaping from prison was not a problem and before long he was writhing in agony, pretending to have a bleeding ulcer. They took him to hospital where they announced that it was not an ulcer but appendicitis. Amazingly, they removed his appendix and he went back to his room to recuperate from the unnecessary surgery. There, he persuaded Chantal, who was visiting him, to drug a guard for him. He told her to breathe in some chloroform to make it look like he had drugged her, too.

He escaped, but was soon picked up again and Chantal was lucky to get away with her phoney drugging. Sobraj managed to get out on bail, with borrowed money, and fled to India, heading now for Kabul in Afghanistan.

There were even easier pickings to be had in Kabul. Wealthy Westerners, mostly naive hippies who had taken the hippy trail east in search of enlightenment and, to Sobraj, conning them was like taking candy from a baby. He, Chantal and their baby lived well for a while. However, bored with life there, he decided to leave, but was arrested at the airport for unpaid hotel bills.

Imprisoned again, he dreamed up an even more dramatic escape than the one in India. He obtained a syringe with which he drew a quantity of blood from his body. He drank the blood to make it seem as if he had an ulcer and was, once again, taken to hospital for treatment. Once again, he managed to drug a guard and make his escape. He fled to Iran.

For a year, he travelled a great deal, using as many as ten different passports. From 1972 to 1973 he lived in Karachi, Pakistan, Teheran, Kabul, Yugoslavia, Bulgaria and Denmark. But the life had proved too much for Chantal, abandoned in Kabul, and the marriage had run its course. Chantal returned to France and never saw her husband again.

Now Sobraj had another partner in crime. His younger brother André, whom he had persuaded to rob the shopkeeper all those years ago, joined him in Istanbul and they decided to work together, carrying out some robberies there before heading for Greece. After a minor jewel robbery in Athens, however, they were arrested. Charles pulled his usual stunt, feigning illness. However, as he was being transported from hospital back to prison, he escaped and disappeared. Meanwhile, the unlucky André was handed over to the Turkish authorities and sentenced to 18 years' hard labour.

Charles Sobraj made his fraudulent way across the Near East and India, fleecing people everywhere he went. He would befriend French- or English-speaking tourist couples and either use them to courier jewels for him or just steal whatever he could from them – passports, money or tickets. Around this time, he met another woman, Marie LeClerc, a French Canadian, who had travelled east in search of adventure. He persuaded her to return with him to Bangkok where he had made his base and she became his new partner, both in bed and in crime, although that did not prevent him from enjoying the odd dalliance with other women.

He began to surround himself now with acolytes, creating a family. A French teenager named Dominique became part of the family but only after Charles had drugged him and made him believe he was suffering from dysentery. Dominique's 'illness' made him dependent on Sobraj. Two other men joined up with them. Yannick and Jacques had been police officers in the French colonies touring the East. After he met them, Sobraj sent them for a night out with Marie and while they were gone, stole their passports and money. He then encouraged them to stay with him while they obtained new passports from the French embassy in Bangkok.

His final recruit was Ajay Chowdhury, a young Indian whom Charles quickly made his lieutenant.

It was around this time that the killings are said to

have begun, although some say he had already become a murderer. His first known victim was Jennie Bollivar, an American Buddhist. It is presumed that Sobraj made efforts to recruit her into his 'family' or to become a smuggler for him, but she refused and he killed her. He was not the type to take rejection easily and she was found face down in the sea in the Gulf of Thailand. It took some weeks to establish that her head had been held under water until she drowned.

Next was Vitali Hakim, a young Sephardic Jew. He stayed with the Sobraj family for several days before going on a trip with Sobraj and Ajay to a resort by the sea. He never returned, even though he had handed over his traveller's cheques and passport to Sobraj. Sobraj said that he had decided to stay with friends. A few days later, a badly burnt body was discovered near the resort. He had been savagely beaten and then, while still alive, had had petrol poured over him and set alight. The police put it down to Thai bandits.

Meanwhile, Charmayne Carrou, a friend of Vitali Hakim, had arrived and started asking questions about his whereabouts. She traced him to Sobraj's enclave and was strangled by Sobraj so violently that he shattered the bones in her neck.

Henk Bitanja and his fiancée Cornelia 'Cocky' Hemker, two Dutch students, encountered Sobraj in Hong Kong. He told them he was a gem dealer and called himself Alain Dupuis. He invited them to his villa in Bangkok, telling them to let him know when they arrived so that he could send a driver to pick them up. Needless to say, when they arrived they fell victim to a mystery illness and remained at his apartment and Sobraj locked up their passports and valuables in his safe. A few nights later, the bodies of a man and a woman were discovered. They had been beaten and strangled before being set on fire.

Then it was the turn of Laddie DuParr and Annabella Tremont. Laddie was a Canadian in Katmandu with the intention of climbing Mount Everest, and Annabella was a Californian looking for the meaning of life, like all the rest. Before too long, Laddie was found in a field; he had been stabbed and burned. Annabella, found a short distance away, had been stabbed to death.

When the police discovered that Laddie DuParr had flown out of the country shortly after the murders, it was surmised that he had killed Annabella and fled, although they were at a loss as to who the other body was. Of course, it had been Sobraj leaving the country, using Laddie's passport. Back in Bangkok, he sold jewels he had stolen from Laddie and then, using Henk Bitanja's passport, returned to Kathmandu next day.

The police succeeded in working out the whereabouts of Laddie and Annabella in the last days of their lives, investigations which led to Sobraj, and he, Ajay and Marie were hauled in for questioning. As ever, though, Sobraj talked his way out of it and they were released.

The other members of the 'family' had, by now, realised what was going on. They had discovered dozens of passports in Sobraj's office and informed Thai police before fleeing back to Paris. But Sobraj, Ajay and Marie, being pursued again by the Nepalese police, were now in Calcutta where Sobraj killed Israeli scholar Avoni Jacob for his passport and about $300. He was drugged and strangled.

The three fled onwards to Singapore before returning to Bangkok, where Sobraj drugged and robbed a wealthy American tourist before being picked up with Ajay and Marie by police for questioning based on their former friends' information about what were becoming known as 'The Bikini Murders'. The Thai police were, however, not keen on a scandalous murder trial that might damage the lucrative tourist trade and did not pursue their enquiries with any great rigour. Sobraj had always maintained that he could bribe his way out of anything in the Far East and $18,000 was all it took to get them out of this situation.

Their next stop was Malaysia where Sobraj killed Ajay after the Indian had procured around $40,000 of gems for him. It seemed that he had simply outlived his usefulness, or perhaps he just knew too much, literally where the bodies were buried.

Word was beginning to spread now that there was a serial killer on the loose in Thailand and this tended to focus the minds of the authorities somewhat. So far, the press screamed, two American women, two Canadians, a Turk, two Dutch citizens, a French woman and an Israeli scholar had all died mysteriously and no one had been arrested for any of the murders.

Sobraj and Marie were now back in Bombay, drugging people and stealing from them. A Frenchman, Jean-Luc Solomon, never came round and another death could be added to Sobraj's murderous account. He had hooked up with two more Western women, and they all travelled to Delhi where he became involved with a group of French postgraduate students, touring the city. In their hotel, he offered them each a pill to ward off dysentery and many took it, grateful to the handsome, smooth-tongued Frenchman.

The pill was, of course, a sedative and while they were drowsy he intended to rob their rooms. However, immediately after taking the pills, the students began to collapse one by one. Those who had not taken a pill, realised at once what was going on and wrestled Sobraj to the ground.

When the women members of his team were picked up, it all began to unravel. The two new members told the police everything and he was charged with the murder of Jean-Luc Solomon. He was taken to Tihar prison. However, he was well aware of how things worked in the Indian prison system and had concealed 70 carats of precious stones on his body. As ever, he knew that a well-placed bribe would buy him his freedom.

Two years passed before he went on trial and he was found guilty of administering drugs with intent to rob and manslaughter. The penalty for manslaughter was death, but, to everyone's amazement except perhaps Charles Sobraj, the judge sentenced him to a mere seven years. To that sentence was added a further five years for the attempt to drug the French students.

He was actually quite pleased as he knew that there was a Thai warrant for his arrest for murder which was good for 20 years. If he was released before that time, he would be extradited to Thailand and executed.

So he bided his time, practically running the prison. To celebrate his tenth year in jail he threw a party for his friends, prisoners and guards alike. But he had acquired a quantity of sleeping pills and when everyone at the party fell asleep, he simply walked out of prison.

But his plan was not to escape. He wanted to be recaptured and have some more time added to his sentence. It worked and by 17 February 1997, when he walked out of Tihar prison a free man, aged 52, the world had forgotten about him.

He returned to France something of a celebrity, hired an agent and charged journalists large sums of money for interviews. He was reportedly paid upwards of $15 million for a film based on his life

However, a return to his past habits never seemed too far away. He seemed almost to be preparing himself for a return to his old life. 'I have already taken from the past what is best for me,' he said, 'what helps me live in the present and prepare for the future. If I play back a murder, it will be to see what I have learned from the method. I won't even notice the body.'

His penchant for gambling never left him and its tendency to get him into trouble was evident again in September 2003, when he was arrested at the Casino Royale in Kathmandu. He was charged with entering Nepal in 1975 using a fake passport and questioned about the deaths of a couple of backpackers, Californian Connie Jo Bronzich and her Canadian boyfriend Laurent Ormond Carrièrre. Their burnt bodies had been found in a field on the outskirts of Kathmandu in 1975. He denied even being in Nepal at that time but was found guilty of murder in the summer of 2004 and sentenced to life in prison.

As he prepared his appeal Sobraj tried to escape,

using his old technique of drugging the guards, but this time he was foiled.

In December 2007 Nepal's Supreme Court was due to deliver a decision on whether the judge's sentence was correct. If they find it was, Charles Sobraj will spend the rest of his life in prison, although it would be a foolish man who would bet on it.

GERMANY
ADOLF EICHMANN

When an ordinary man commits extraordinary crimes, perhaps it is time for us to stop and consider the question of what each of us is capable of as an individual. Philosophers and psychologists have debated this question for years. Does each of us have the potential to be an Adolf Eichman, to do what he did, to switch off our consciences, ignore morality and abandon compassion? Could we say we were 'just obeying orders', as did this slender man with bow-legs and an all-too-predictable liking for the compositions of Richard Wagner? Eichman claimed to neither agree nor disagree with the tenets of the Nazi doctrine. Rather, he claimed he was just pursuing a career and, given the stops and starts that he made in his civilian career, even after the war, one can certainly understand his decision. But, what a career decision – to accept a role in which he would be responsible for the deaths of millions, making Adolf Eichman, perhaps, the ultimate professional killer.

347

Otto Adolf Eichman was born in Solingen in Germany in March 1906, to an industrialist, Adolf Karl Eichman, and his wife, Maria. He had five brothers, but, in spite of that, as a child he was withdrawn and solitary. When he was eight years old, his family moved to Linz in Austria, but there he still remained something of a problem child. His dark complexion and distinctive facial features led his schoolmates to taunt him with the nickname 'der kleine Jude' – the little Jew – and, neglected by his parents and faring badly at school, he became ever more difficult and moody.

His education suffered as a result and his lack of academic achievement forced him to leave school early to train to be a mechanic. As was to happen so often in his life, this job did not work out and, aged 17, he joined his father's business, a mining company, as a sales clerk. He changed career yet again in 1925 and worked for two years for the Oberösterreichische Elektrobau, before taking a job as a district agent for the Vacuum Oil Company.

Although he had no political ambition, Eichman was seduced by Hitler's idea of a Thousand-Year Reich. In 1932 he joined the National Socialist Party and the SS in Austria, on the advice of a friend, Ernst Kaltenbrunner, who was *Gauredner* (district speaker) and *Rechtsberater* (legal consultant) of SS division VIII.

For Eichman it was an opportunity. He was a nobody, trapped in a life of mediocrity, and the Nazi party offered him a chance to be somebody, which he desired more than anything. It would also provide him with a career after the numerous failures he had so far experienced.

He was accepted as a full member of the SS in November 1932, serving in a mustering formation that was based in Salzburg. Hitler's rise to power in Germany in 1933 persuaded him to return to Germany and he applied for active duty in the SS. In November 1933 he was promoted to the rank of *Scharführer* and was assigned to the administrative staff of Dachau concentration camp. He was responsible for cataloguing items taken from Jewish prisoners and began to learn the basic principles of Naziism, that the state was more important than life itself. As he said at a later date: 'If they had told me that my own father was a traitor and I had to kill him, I'd have done it!'

A year later he applied for a position with the *Sicherheitspolizei*, by this time a powerful force in Hitler's Germany. His application was successful and he went to work in the organisation's Berlin head-quarters. In 1934 he was promoted to the rank of *Hauptsharführer* and later that year, having ascertained that she was of the proscribed racial purity – mandatory for wives of SS members – he married

Veronika Liebl. It was a marriage that produced four sons.

In 1937, now an *SS-Untersturmführer*, Eichman was sent on an important mission with his superior, Herbert Hagen, to the British mandate of Palestine. Their objective was to assess the potential for the forced migration of German Jews to Palestine. Their mission stalled, however, when the British authorities refused them entry into Palestine.

Eichman returned to Austria in 1938, following the Anschluss, the annexation of Austria by Germany. His role was to organise the SS in Vienna, work that earned him another promotion, to *SS-Obersturmführer*. It also led to his being selected to create the Central Office for Jewish Emigration, the department with responsibility for forcibly deporting and expelling Jews from Austria. Eichman threw himself into his work enthusiastically, reportedly becoming a student of Judaism, to the extent that he tried to learn Hebrew. 'I did not greet this assignment with apathy,' he wrote in his memoirs. 'I was fascinated with it.' His assiduousness earned him a reputation as the Nazi who understood the Jewish people.

He impressed his superiors with his effectiveness. In his first eight months in the job, having first stripped them of all lands and possessions, he forced 45,000 Jews out of Austria and by the end of the year, 150,000

Jews had disappeared. He estimated that by the time he ended his assignment, he had removed almost a quarter of a million people, many being sent to the extermination camps and others fleeing the country with nothing more than the clothes they stood up in.

He held the rank of *SS-Hauptsturmführer* – equivalent to captain – at the start of the Second World War, when he returned to Berlin as head of the notorious Section IV B 4 of the *Gestapo*, the department that, with cruel efficiency, would organise the extermination of millions of people in the next few years. Eichman now wielded real power and he used it ruthlessly. By 1941 he had risen to the rank of *Obersturmbannführer*.

He played a crucial role in the Wannsee Conference, held in 1942, which formulated Germany's anti-Semitic measures into an official policy of genocide of the Jews – the 'Final Solution to the Jewish Question'. Richard Heydrich, chief of the Reich Security Main Office which included the *Gestapo, Sicherheitsdienst* and *Kripo* Nazi police agencies, invited Eichman to the conference as recording secretary and he was also given a key role in the genocide process – Transportation Administrator. He would control all the trains that would carry Jews to the concentration camps in occupied Poland.

Camps such as Auschwitz, Dachau, Treblinka and Buchenwald were little more than death factories, killing 24 hours a day, seven days a week. Some of them were capable of killing 10,000 people a day. And like ordinary factories, they were expected to turn a profit. The victims were robbed of all possessions, no matter how small. Human hair was removed to be used in commercial products and tons of gold were ripped from the teeth of the dead to be melted down and reused.

Eichman delivered to these camps the raw materials – millions of innocent and terrified Jews and Gypsies from Austria, Holland, the Baltic countries, France and Yugoslavia. They were 'resettled' in Poland, the Warsaw ghetto becoming a particularly ferocious killing ground with tens of thousands starving to death and others being shot, or gassed in mobile gas chambers. 316,322 Jews were killed in that city alone. Eichman, by now a stranger to reality, wrote later, 'Jewry was grateful for the chance I gave it to learn community life at the ghetto. It made an excellent school for the future in Israel – basically most Jews feel well and happy in their ghetto life.'

The demands on his logistical skills were increasing. He was responsible for delivering people to no fewer than 164 camps in Eastern Europe. He improved efficiency, making the death trains larger, to accommodate more people. They travelled often huge distances without food or water and thousands died on the trains even before arriving at their destinations.

Eichman also used his organisational skills to improve the efficiency of the killing. Vast, windowless rooms disguised as shower rooms, served as gas chambers. He considered the carbon monoxide gas used not cost-effective and advocated the use of the cyanide-based insecticide, Zyklon B.

An incident in France in 1942 shows Eichman's cold efficiency, his absolute abandonment of humanity. He had ordered a round-up of Jews in Paris which yielded a total of 7,000 people, 4,051 of them children, planning to transport them all to the camps in the east. However, the city powers objected and days of negotiation took place while the Jews were held in a cycling stadium, without food or water. After six days of talks, he won the day. The adults were taken to Eichman's trains and shipped to the east. Several days later, the children, too, were put on trains and transported to Auschwitz and the gas chambers. Eichman's response when questioned about the incident later was to deny responsibility. 'Once a shipment was delivered to the designated stations,' he told the Israeli police, ' . . . my powers ceased.'

In 1944, fearful of a Russian invasion, Germany invaded Hungary and Eichman was sent there to organise the deportation of Hungarian Jews. He sent 400,000 to their deaths in the gas chambers.

It was obvious to many in the German leadership by 1945 that the war was lost and they hastily began to cover their tracks. Heinrich Himmler, head of the SS, put a stop to the extermination of the Jews and hastily ordered all traces of the Final Solution to be destroyed. Eichman was appalled by Himmler's orders, deciding arbitrarily to carry on as before, sending tens of thousands of Jews to the camps. He was also terrified that he would be assigned to the last-ditch fighting that was taking place. In 1944 he had been commissioned as a Reserve *Untersturmführer* in the *Waffen-SS* which made him eligible for combat duty.

In 1945 the Russians entered Hungary and, finally, Eichman fled, returning to Austria and trying to solicit help from his old friend Ernst Kaltenbrunner. Kaltenbrunner, now a major figure in the Nazi Party, was trying to save his own skin and would have nothing to do with Eichman. His work in the camps had made him a dangerous man to be associated with.

The US Army captured Eichman around this time, but he gave a false name and escaped from custody in 1946. He went into hiding in Germany, moving from place to place and, although he actually obtained a landing permit for Argentina in 1948, he chose not to use it until later. Instead, he travelled to Italy in 1950. Alois Hudal, a Roman Catholic bishop who had praised Hitler before the war and who helped many Nazi war criminals escape, helped Eichman to obtain a humanitarian passport from the International Committee of the Red Cross and an Argentinian visa made out to 'Riccardo Klement, technician'. He finally sailed for Argentina on 14 July 1950.

Once established in his new country, he brought his family over and for ten years his career followed a similar trajectory to the earlier years of his life. He worked in a number of jobs in the Buenos Aires area, amongst which were factory foreman, water engineer and even rabbit farmer.

Meanwhile, the authorities were fully aware of his presence. The CIA knew that he was living in Argentina, they thought under the name 'Clemens', but took no action as his arrest would represent an embarrassment to both America and Germany by focusing attention on the former Nazis they had recruited at the conclusion of the war, not least of whom was Hans Globke, German President Konrad Adenauer's national security advisor. Globke had worked directly with Eichman on Jewish affairs and, in 1935, had helped draft the Nuremberg Laws, justifying racial discrimination against German Jews. Globke's name was even deleted from Eichman's memoirs which had been sold to *Life* magazine by the Eichman family.

Meanwhile, not even the Israelis could find Eichman, but many other Holocaust victims refused to give up searching for him. Famous Jewish Nazi-hunter, Simon Wiesenthal, suspected that he was in Argentina, a suspicion confirmed by a postcard from a friend who had moved to the Argentinian capital: 'Ich sah jenes Schmutzige Schwein, Eichman,' (I saw that dirty pig, Eichman) he wrote, adding that he was living near Buenos Aires and working for a water company. Wiesenthal and the Israelis used this and other information to build a picture of Eichman's life in exile.

Lothar Hermann, a German of Jewish descent, had been sent to Dachau at the time that Eichman was an administrator at the camp. He had fled to Argentina at the end of the war and had established a family there. Coincidentally, his daughter Sylvia became involved with one of Eichman's sons, Klaus. Klaus foolishly boasted to Sylvia about his father's past, crediting him with responsibility for the Final Solution. When Sylvia informed her father about this, he realised he was onto something.

He wrote to Fritz Bauer, Chief Prosecutor of the German state of Hesse, and also contacted Israeli officials. For several years they worked on a plan to capture Eichman. Finally, in 1960, the Israeli government approved a plan to kidnap him and bring him to Israel where he could be tried as a war criminal.

On 11 May 1960, following intense surveillance of Eichman's every move, four agents of the Israeli secret service agency, Mossad, waited for him to return home from his latest job as a foreman in a Mercedes-Benz factory. One waited for the bus he would be travelling on, while another two pretended to repair a broken down car near the bus stop. The fourth agent travelled on the bus with their target.

Arriving at his destination, Eichman climbed down from the bus, setting out in the direction of his house. As he passed the car, one of the agents asked him for a cigarette. He reached into his pocket, but as he did so was pounced on by the other two. One of them, a black belt in karate, dealt him a sharp blow to the back of the neck, rendering him unconscious. They quickly bundled him into the car and drove him to a safe house they had prepared.

Here, he was stripped naked and examined. Under his armpit they found the absolute proof that he was an SS man – a partially removed tattoo. All members of the SS were tattooed as a form of identification. When they asked him for his name, he replied: 'Ich bin Adolf Eichman!'

On 21 May, heavily sedated, he was smuggled out of Argentina as part of a delegation of Jewish trade union members on a commercial flight to Israel. A few days later, when Israeli prime minister David Ben

Gurion, announced to the Knesset, the Israeli parliament, that Eichman had been captured, he received a standing ovation.

The sensational news that Eichman had been caught created an international incident between Argentina and Israel. The United Nations Security Council was convened, the Argentinians claiming that Eichman's abduction was a 'violation of the sovereign rights of the Argentine Republic'. Israel retorted that Eichman had been captured not by Israeli agents but by private citizens. The Security Council accepted the Argentinian allegation and ordered Israel to make 'appropriate reparation'. However, it also noted that its decision in no way condoned the crimes with which Eichman was charged.

His trial began on 11 April 1961 in the newly built Beth Ha'am (House of the People) where he was indicted on 15 charges. These included crimes against humanity, consisting of the murder of millions of innocents in the death camps; the introduction of the poison gas, Zyklon B; the creation of plans that murdered 80,000 in Lithuania, 30,000 in Latvia, 45,000 in Belorussia, 75,000 in the Ukraine and 33,000 in the city of Kiev. He was further accused of issuing the orders to send hundreds of thousands to Auschwitz, causing the suffering and death inside the Warsaw ghetto in 1939 and 1940, the slaughter of 500,000

Hungarian Jews in just eight months in 1944, enslaving millions across Eastern Europe in forced labour camps, performing forced abortions on pregnant women, forced sterilisation of thousands of Jewish men in Germany and, finally, of being the person in command of the entire Nazi bureaucratic structure that brought starvation, ruin and death to millions of people before and during the Second World War.

The trial was broadcast live around the world and included testimony from many Holocaust survivors. One critical piece of testimony was provided for the court by an American judge, Michael A. Musmanno, who had questioned the defendants at the Nuremberg trials. He said that Hermann Göring, Hitler's second-in-command, had 'made it very clear that Eichman was the man to determine in what order, in what countries, the Jews were to die'.

Eichman did not dispute the facts of the Holocaust. His defence was the same as many other Nazi war criminals – he was only following orders. 'I never did anything, great or small,' he claimed, 'without obtaining in advance express instructions from Adolf Hitler or any of my superiors.'

One witness, Otto Winkelman, who had occupied a senior position in the SS in Budapest in 1944, stated that Eichman 'had the nature of a subaltern, which means a fellow who uses his power recklessly, without moral restraints. He would certainly overstep his authority if he thought he was acting in the spirit of his commander [Adolf Hitler].' Another witness, a former brigadier-general in the German secret service, testified that Eichman had been a total believer in Nazi principles and that he adhered to its most extreme doctrines. He also said that Eichman had more power than other department chiefs.

As for Eichman, during the trial he displayed the mediocrity of his personality and demonstrated neither guilt nor hatred.

After 14 weeks, as expected, he was convicted on all counts and sentenced to death by hanging. He appealed unsuccessfully and then had a plea for mercy turned down by Israeli president Yitzhak Ben-Zvi on 29 May 1962.

Adolph Eichman was hanged just after midnight on 1 June 1962 at Ramla prison in the only execution ever to be carried out in Israel. His body was cremated and the ashes were scattered in international waters in the Mediterranean. He had refused a last meal, opting instead for a bottle of Israeli red wine, of which he drank half. On the gallows he refused to don the customary black hood. He went to his death declaring: 'Long live Germany. Long live Austria. Long live Argentina. These are the countries with which I have been most closely associated and I shall not forget them. I had to obey the rules of war and my flag. I am ready.'

INDIA
PHOOLAN DEVI

The crowd of almost 10,000 people roared their approval above the blaring Hindi film music, as a slip of a girl – no more than five feet in height – climbed up onto a 23-feet-high stage that had been erected in the village of Bindh. She wore a new khaki police superintendant's uniform and a red shawl. On her head was a red bandana, holding back her long dark-brown hair. From her shoulder hung a rifle and a silver bangle, a symbol of her Sikh faith, dangled on her wrist. She grinned and waved to the crowd before kneeling in homage, touching the feet of Arjun Singh, chief minister of the state of Madhya Pradesh in central India. She then slowly turned to face the screaming crowd, raising her rifle above her head, before placing her hands together in the traditional form of Indian greeting and lowering her eyes. The crowd went wild and the hordes of VIPs on the dais turned to shake each other by the hand, as the Bandit

Queen, Phoolan Devi, surrendered to the authorities.

It had been a long and arduous journey to this lavish stage in Bindh from the tiny Utter Pradesh village of Gorha Ka Purwa. A cluster of mud huts with conical thatched roofs, on the banks of the Yamuna River, Gorha Ka Purwa is like the half- million or so other similar villages in India. Sacred cows wander the lanes and tracks between the houses as if they own them and poverty is a way of life for the half-billion peasants who live in them. At best, the peasant family will own less than an acre of land; at worst it will not own any land and will be dependent on its landlord.

In this society, straight-jacketed by the Brahmanical caste system, women have little more value than is allowed by their ability to give birth to sons. They marry young, work long hours in the fields and live the lives of countless generations of poor Indian women, with little chance of escape.

Phoolan Devi was born in August 1963 into a family of the shudra sub-caste of boatmen called *mallah*, but her father Devidin was at least better off than some in the village, owning about an acre of land. Life was still hard, however, and he had to work hard to support his family of one son and four daughters, of whom she was the second eldest. Devidin was, however, in Phoolan's words, 'a simpleton' and lost almost all his inheritance, some 15 acres, to his smarter, older brother and the brother's son, Maiyadin. This was a disaster for the family and an outrage to Phoolan who, even when young, fought to regain the land. Once, when she was ten, she staged a sit-in on the land and Maiyadin beat her with a brick until she was unconscious.

At the age of 11, with the connivance of Maiyadin, she was sent far away from her village to marry a widower 20 years older than her. Her family received a cow in exchange. Her life with the widower was miserable. He beat her and raped her until she could take no more and she escaped not long after her twelfth birthday, walking all the way back to her village – a huge distance.

Her return was a scandal for her family and her mother ordered her to kill herself by jumping down the village well. Naturally she did not, although many would have, and spent her adolescence coming and going from Gorha Ka Purwa. When she was there, she cut the grass on the family land and tended their water buffalo. She married a cousin but the marriage did not last and gradually she began to develop a reputation for promiscuity. She never gave up her war with her cousin, however, even taking the case to the High Court in Allahabad when she was 20. He took revenge a year later when he had her arrested for a robbery he claimed had taken place at his house. She was held in custody for a month and, during that time, she was raped repeatedly by the policemen who had arrested her.

In July of that same year, 1983, Phoolan heard that a band of dacoits were camped near her village. One night they came to her hut and kidnapped her, marching her out of the village and into the ravines in which the dacoit gangs hid out. For three days she was sexually assaulted by the leader of the gang, Babu Gujar, but on the evening of the third day, his second-in-command, a tall good-looking young man called Vikram Mallah, who had always liked Phoolan, shot and killed Gujar. He snatched the leadership and Phoolan became his mistress and partner. As the news spread, the people in villages for miles around made up songs and stories about the low-caste village girl who had restored her honour.

For her part, Phoolan had a rubber stamp made that said: 'Phoolan Devi, dacoit beauty; beloved of Vikram Mallah, Emperor of Dacoits.' Vikram made her cut her hair short and bought her a radio and a cassette recorder on which she could listen to her beloved Indian film music. He taught her the ways of the dacoits; she learned how to handle a gun and became an excellent markswoman.

He also taught her a valuable lesson: 'If you are going to kill, kill 20, not just one. For if you kill 20, your fame will spread; if you kill only one, they will hang you as a murderess.'

The fame of the couple spread as they rampaged through the lands of Utter and Madhya Pradesh, robbing, looting, holding up trains, plundering higher-caste villages and houses, and murdering and kidnapping. They ransacked the village where Phoolan's husband lived. She stabbed him and dragged him in front of the villagers. Then they left him lying close to death with a note pinned to him warning old men not to marry young girls.

All the while, Phoolan interpreted omens and took signs from the goddess Durga. Once, she said, she was wakened in the middle of the night by a snake slithering across her legs. She woke Vikram and their men and ordered them to flee. Minutes after they had left, the police arrived at their empty campsite.

Another time, in August 1980, they were not so lucky, however. She claims to have seen a crow perched on a dead tree at the edge of their camp and pleaded with Vikram to leave the place in which they were preparing to spend the night. He refused and a short while later when she heard noises, she thought they were surrounded by police. When Vikram sat up, he was felled by two bullets and died, his head cradled in her lap.

The killers were two brothers, Sri Ram and Lala

Ram, who had returned to the gang after being released from prison. They were avenging the murder of the former leader, Babu Gujar, and because they were of the opinion that Vikram was too low caste to be leader. There had been a great deal of tension between Shri Ram and Vikram, especially after Shri had made advances to Phoolan.

The brothers abducted Phoolan, sailing downriver to the village of Bahmai. There, she was locked in a filthy hut and subjected to terrible sexual abuse for three weeks. She was raped repeatedly every night by the turbaned Thakur men of the village. Eventually, Santosh Pandit, a priest from a neighbouring village, freed her, carrying her to safety.

Back in the ravines, she formed her own band of dacoits with Man Singh and they carried out a series of violent robberies, targeting upper-caste homes and villages. Seventeen months after her escape from Bahmai, she finally returned to wreak revenge on the men who had assaulted her.

The gang, dressed in police uniforms, entered the village and gathered to pray at its shrine. Then, when they had sealed off all the exits from the village, she spoke to the terrified villagers through a megaphone, telling them to bring out all their gold and valuables and to hand over the Ram brothers who she thought were hiding in the village. When the Rams were not forthcoming, she ordered 30 young men to be brought out. She again asked them where the Rams were, spitting in their faces and striking them in the genitals with her rifle butt as they pleaded for their lives, saying they did not know where the brothers were. The men were then lined up beside the river, ordered onto their knees and shot. Twenty-two of them died in what was the largest dacoit massacre in Indian criminal history and most of them had not been involved in the sexual assaults she had endured. Later, she claimed she had not carried out any killings, blaming her gang instead.

There was outrage, and for the Indian government it was an atrocity too far. Prime Minister Indira Gandhi was afraid that a caste war could break out as a result and ordered a massive police search. The chief minister of Uttar Pradesh was forced to resign, and dolls depicting Phoolan as the Bandit Queen, as she was now being called, dressed in a blue police uniform and with a bandolier of bullets around her body, were being sold in Uttar Pradesh markets.

For two years the police failed to locate her, in spite of a reward of 412,620 rupees (£5,300) being offered, and the government finally announced that it would negotiate a surrender. She was happy to give up the dacoit life, as she was in poor health and the majority of her gang had now been killed. She said she would only surrender on her own terms and only to the

Madhya Pradesh authorities; she did not trust the Uttar Pradesh police. Her conditions were numerous: she and her gang would not be hung; they would serve no more than eight years in prison; her 14-year-old brother would be given a government job; her father should have the land stolen by her cousin returned to him; her family would be settled in Madhya Pradesh on government land and they would be accompanied by her goat and cow.

She walked into Bindh where 300 police waited to arrest her and the remnants of her gang. After surrendering herself onstage, she was charged with 48 crimes and went to prison for 11 years, slightly more than her negotiated demands had stipulated. In prison, she suffered from cancer and had an involuntary hysterectomy.

She was finally released in 1994, launching *Eklavya Sena*, an organisation that aimed to teach lower-caste Indians the art of self-defence. She met and married Umaid Singh, a New Delhi business contractor.

Her fame was huge. They made a film about her life, *Bandit Queen*, but she hated it and tried to get it banned. She sued the film's producers and won $60,000 from them. Although illiterate, she put together an autobiography and travelled abroad, publicising it.

In 1996 she caused astonishment and outrage in equal measure when she announced that she would be standing in the forthcoming election. She was heavily criticised by a group formed of the widows of the Behmai massacre who had formed an organisation to campaign against her. Nonetheless, she was duly elected as a member of the Indian parliament. Her political career was not a successful one, however, and scandal and trouble seemed to follow wherever she went. When she had a train halted at an unscheduled stop so that she could meet some friends there was outrage, and when she tried to visit the inmates of her former prison to be told that it was not visiting time, she abused the staff terribly.

On 25 July 2001, as she was climbing out of her car at the gate of her house in New Delhi, Phoolan Devi was shot dead by two men who escaped in an auto rickshaw. Her killer, Sher Singh Rana, surrendered later, confessing to her murder and informing police that he was avenging the 22 deaths at Behmai.

The Bandit Queen could not, in the end, escape from her terrible past. She was 37 years old.

VEERAPPAN

A group of women stood wailing at the burial place as people bent to pick up handfuls of mud as souvenirs, wrapping them lovingly in bits of cloth. Women, rearranging the flowers on the mound of mud, sobbed and placed pieces of coconut and burning incense sticks on it. They whispered about the man they had just buried, Koose Muniswamy Veerappan, known all over India simply as Veerappan. He was a Tamil bandit commonly thought of by the poor people who worshipped him and followed his every exploit as a sort of Robin Hood figure whose battles were all with the police and officialdom and never the poor. They talked of how the police had never intended to take him alive after his last encounter with them, insinuating that they had always meant to kill him.

His charge sheet, if the police had taken him alive that October night instead of shooting him, would, indeed, have been prodigious. He was wanted for murdering roughly 124 people, including many senior police officers and forest officials, killing about 2,000 elephants, and smuggling ivory worth almost £2 million and an entire forest of sandalwood worth close to £11 million. They had put a price of 50 million rupees (£600,000) on his head, but still he managed to evade arrest for 30 years until he was finally gunned down in 2004.

Veerappan was born into a family of poor cattle grazers in 1952, in the village of Gopinatham in Tamil Nadu, a state at the southern tip of India. Desperate to escape the mundane existence in his village and follow the example of Malayur Mammattiyan, a notorious bandit of the 1950s and 1960s who had been born and brought up in a village close to his, at the age of 18 he joined a gang of elephant poachers. Over the next few years he eliminated all rival gangs and achieved control of the entire forest belt, gaining a monopoly on the smuggling of sandalwood and ivory.

He also led his gang of around 40 men in other activities such as killing and kidnapping, most of his victims being forestry officials, police officers and informers. His kidnappings and killings sometimes featured prominent people, senior officials or high-ranking policemen, the first being a senior forest official whom he kidnapped in 1987 and hacked to death shortly after. That same year he killed five members of a rival gang.

Veerappan married four times, the first to a shepherdess, Muthulakshmi, in 1991. He had three daughters with her. However, he displayed the same calm ruthlessness towards his family as he did towards everyone else. Once, when he and his gang were hiding from some police officers who were nearby, he was afraid the crying of one of his daughters would alert them to his whereabouts. Chillingly, he strangled her.

In spite of such horror, Veerappan was a surprisingly cultured man, with a deep love and knowledge of Carnatic music, a form of Indian classical music. He was religious and attended the Bannari Amman temple regularly, listened avidly to the BBC and adored the film *The Godfather*, which he watched more than 100 times, probably while tending to his fantastically extravagant handlebar moustache. He watched, fascinated, as the reformed bandit Phoolan Devi became a member of the Indian parliament, expressing a desire to one day do the same.

Amongst the peasants of the Biligirirangana Betta and Male Mahadeshwara Betta Hills and the Sathyamangalam and Gundiyal forests, some 6,000 square kilometres of territory in the states of Karnataka, Kerala and Tamil Nadu, he was a hero. They saw him as someone who fought the many injustices that they faced at the hands of the hated police and the authorities. They provided the gang with food and clothing and protected them when necessary, although this may simply have been done out of fear or because he actually paid them to help him. It goes without saying that there were dire consequences for anyone who refused to help or gave the police information about his activities.

In 1986 it looked like Veerappan's days were numbered when he was finally arrested, the only time he was ever taken into custody. However, a payment of just over £1,000 to a corrupt police officer soon won him his freedom. Just a year later he rose to prominence with the killing of a forest officer called Chidambaram who was trying to bring a halt to the smuggling of sandalwood. In 1989 he kidnapped three forest personnel in the Begur forest. Their mutilated bodies were discovered 19 days later.

By 1990 the state and national government were frustrated. They had thrown everything they could at him – extra resources and weaponry – and had still failed to capture Veerappan and his gang. Even more irritating was the near-mythical status that he had achieved in the region and this increased as the media began to show a greater interest in his activities and, particularly, in Veerappan the man. There were profiles of him, photographs and even interviews.

On 10 November 1991 he killed the Karnataka Deputy Conservator of Forests, Pandillapalli Srinivas, whom he blamed for the suicide of his sister Mari. Srinivas was a popular man who had instituted a number of welfare measures in the region. He was trying to bring Veerappan to heel by persuading local villagers to boycott him and refrain from giving him any help. Therefore, when Veerappan sent word through his brother Arjunan that he would meet Srinivas at a farmhouse in Gopinatham to discuss surrendering, Srinivas believed him. Veerappan, of course, had no intention of surrendering and when the official arrived at the rendezvous, the bandit shot him and then beheaded him. In a gruesome warning to others who might try to interfere in his activities, Veerappan left the official's severed head on a rock where it was discovered several days later.

This atrocity was the last straw for the authorities. It was decided to constitute a Special Task Force (STF) of some 2,000 troops specifically to comb the forests and hills for Veerappan's gang. The omens initially looked good when they actually succeeded in capturing some gang members.

Then, in February 1992, still more progress was achieved when they caught up with and killed Veerappan's second-in-command, Gurunathan. A huge man, over six feet tall and with a luxuriant moustache, Gurunathan was arrested by Shakeel Ahmed, Sub-Inspector of Police, and later killed by

Police Superintendent Harikrishna in the Mysore district.

Veerappan plotted his revenge. Firstly, he staged an attack on the Ramapura police station in the Chamarajanagar district, killing five officers and capturing a quantity of arms and ammunition. The STF killed four members of his gang in retaliation. Then in August 1992 he laid a trap for the two men responsible for Gurunathan's death and, attacking them with hand grenades and bombs, killed them and four other policemen. Further bad news came the following year, however, when his wife Muthulaksmi was arrested by the task force.

His killing now escalated. He used a landmine to blow up a bus, killing 22 passengers including police and civilians. That year he also killed another six policemen. However, the Border Security Force and the Special Task Force, working together, succeeded in capturing 19 gang members and killing six in an action in which three police officers also lost their lives.

Veerappan, at this point, requested an amnesty, but the authorities bent to the wishes of the relatives of the victims and the request was ignored. So the abductions and ransom demands continued. On 12 July 1993 he kidnapped nine forestry officials and issued demands for their release which again included an amnesty for himself and his men. His request was rejected, but he still released the men at the end of August.

In December 1994 he kidnapped a deputy super-intendent of police in the Coimbatore district of Chidambaranathan. Amongst his ransom demands was yet another amnesty request, but the main aim of this action was to try to get urgent medical aid for his brother Arjunan, who had been wounded in a previous action. The authorities complied with the request for medical help and Arjunan emerged from the forest to receive treatment. However, he and two other gang members accompanying him, were killed as they were being transported to Mysore. The police version said that they had committed suicide by taking cyanide. Veerappan, needless to say, thought otherwise.

In 1996 he took plentiful revenge, killing another 11 policemen.

After a gap of a year, Veerappan demonstrated that his killing was not just limited to policemen and forest officials when the bullet-riddled body of his heir apparent – known as 'Baby' Veerappan – was discovered in the forest. Just for good measure, though, he kidnapped another nine forest officials that year, as well as a couple of wildlife photographers.

One of his most notorious kidnappings, and the one that was to bring him national as well as international notoriety, involved the abduction of the hugely popular film star, Dr Rajkumar. The 72-year-old Dr

Raj, also known as 'Natasarvabhouma' or 'Annavru' (Big Brother) by his millions of fans, was the John Wayne of south Indian cinema. On 30 July 2000 Veerappan abducted him, his son-in-law Govindaraju and two others, from his ancestral home at Gajanur in Tamil Nadu. For the actor's safe return Veerappan demanded the release of a number of his men who had been arrested under what he described as a defunct terrorism law.

The Karnataka state government was thrown into deep crisis and arguments raged as to whether the army should be sent in to release the men. But they decided against it, and, after 108 days' captivity, Dr Raj was finally released, unharmed, by Veerappan. It is unclear what the conditions of his release were, but one story has it that a ransom of 500,000 rupees or just over £6,000 was handed over.

Then, in August 2002, he carried out another audacious kidnapping. It was the turn of the former state minister, H. Nagappa. Three months later, the ransom had not been paid and Nagappa was found dead in the forest. The authorities were now becoming alarmed by the fact that Veerappan was now working closely with Tamil extremist groups, demanding the release of their men who had been captured, and the reward for the capture of the bandit was increased to a massive 50 million rupees, about £600,000.

They finally caught up with him in October 2004, although the circumstances of his death are even now shrouded in mystery and intrigue. Veerappan and two gang members were apprehended near the village of Paparapatti in Tamil Nadu by the Special Task Force, headed by Director-General of Police K. Vijay Kumar, Suprintendent Sentamarai Kannan and Suprintendent F. M. Hussain.

The official statement said that men of the Special Task Force ambushed an ambulance in which Veerappan and his men were travelling. When they ordered the bandits to surrender, someone from inside the vehicle opened fire and the police officers responded in kind, killing all the occupants, including Veerappan. Press reports, featuring photographs of the bandit leader with a bullet hole above his left eye, seemed to contradict the police version, suggesting a straight-forward execution. Veerappan's widow claimed that they had actually been arrested several days pre-viously, interrogated and then executed. She claimed that Veerappan had threatened that if he were arrested, he would blow the whistle on every police-man and official he had bribed during his 30-year criminal career.

He was buried in the village of Moolakadu in Tamil Nadu, permission having been refused for a burial in his home village as the authorities feared what might happen with the large crowds that had gathered there. The police had wanted him to be cremated, but his family insisted on a burial and on an October day in 2004, tens of thousands fought their way through lines of police security to be at the graveside of their hero.

Veerappan may be dead but his legend lives on.

RUSSIA
ALEKSANDR SOLONIK

Contract killing has become a way of death for contemporary Russians. A crime expert at the Russian Interior Ministry's Scientific Research Institute has suggested that there may be anything between 500 and 700 contract killings a year. So, in recent years, as the country has stumbled from communism towards a market economy, the hitman has become commonplace. You can order a death like you can order a pizza, they say, and the going rate is anywhere between a $100 and hundreds of thousands of dollars. It depends who the victim is. Sometimes it is cheaper, not to say easier, to pay to have someone killed than to settle a dispute in court. If you live in a communal apartment, for example, with an elderly relative who seems to be living forever, it is easy and inexpensive – around $300 – to hire a drug addict to kill him or her. In one case, in the town of Zhukovsky, two Ukranians were arrested and charged with the stabbing to death of a 23-year-old man. The victim's mother had paid them $300 to kill him. Another police official claims that for the price of a bottle of vodka, it is possible to get a homeless man to kill someone for you. Life is, indeed, cheap.

Consequently, it comes as no surprise that an entire contract killing industry has grown up and the last 15 years have seen a wave of killings of prominent people. In 1995 TV anchorman Vladislav Listyev was gunned down in Moscow; in 1998 it was the turn of Liberal member of parliament Galina Starovoitova; in 2002 Valentin Tsvetkov, governor of the Magadan region, was killed in Moscow; 2004 brought the shooting of Paul Klebnikov, US editor of *Forbes* Russian edition, killed outside his office; in 2005 Aleksandr Slesarev, a former bank head, died; in 2006 Andrei Koslov, first deputy chairman of Russia's Central Bank, and campaigning journalist Anna Polikovskaya, were both shot dead. For most of these crimes, no one has been brought to justice.

One hitman stands head and shoulders above the rest, the 'Superkiller' as he is known, Aleksandr Solonik, who was born in the Russian city of Kurgan in 1960. As a boy, Solonik showed great interest in martial arts and guns and it seemed inevitable that, when he left school, he would go into the army. He joined the militia, a special internal security commando unit, and started training at the Gorkovskaya Institute. Stories suggest that the unit to which he was attached may have been trained in the assassination of senior officials of NATO countries. This is disputed by his lawyer who says that he served in Germany, but not as a special intelligence officer. Whatever the truth of his military service, it did not work out and after six months he was expelled from the institute, returning home to work as a gravedigger. He married a local girl and had a daughter but, like his military training, the marriage was short-lived and ended in divorce. Another marriage resulted in a son, but Solonik was a difficult man to live with.

He tried to become a policeman, but again it did not work out for him and he had to leave the service. Then, in autumn 1987, he faced his first criminal charge when he was arrested for rape. Although the victim failed to prove his guilt and had, in fact, only gone to the police some months after the incident, he was treated harshly and sentenced to eight months in a correctional facility in the Gulag. But Solonik was not the type of man to stay locked up for very long. The day that he was due to leave for prison, he was allowed some time to say goodbye to his wife, but Solonik used the opportunity to smash a window and leap from the second-floor room in which he was meeting her and escape. After several months of freedom, he reached the city of Tyumen and was in the process of having all of his distinguishing marks removed – a mole on his face and a crown-shaped tattoo on his hand – when he was arrested in the room in which they were carrying out the work. This time they did not take their eyes off him.

Normally, when a prisoner had been a soldier, he was sent to a special facility or kept in isolation from other prisoners due to a fear of repercussions. However, in Solonik's case this did not happen and when it became common knowledge that not only had he been a soldier, but had also been a member of the militia, he was in serious danger. The other prisoners attacked him, but Solonik was a tough individual and is said to have outfought groups of men, sometimes as many as 12 at a time. After a while, he gained the respect of his fellow inmates and they left him alone.

In prison, he was a loner. He did not smoke, did not do drugs and was not interested in tattoos. He spent his time working out and stayed away from difficult prisoners. It paid off because he was soon sent to the industrial part of the prison where prisoners had more freedom of movement. He was merely biding his time, however. In April 1990, having served two of his eight years, he escaped again, squeezing through a small air vent. He headed back to Kurgan where he joined the local Kurgan crime organisation as a hitman and disappeared from view for four and a half years.

His first target was the leader of a rival criminal outfit whom he killed in Tyumen in July 1990, just six weeks after escaping from prison. Having proved he was capable of killing, and having earned some money, he and some others from Kurgan travelled to Moscow where there were numerous opportunities for an ambitious contract killer. There, he earned the nickname 'Aleksandr the Great' due to his ability to shoot in the Macedonian way – with both hands.

His first hit in the capital was Russian criminal Viktor Nikiforov, and six months later he shot dead Russian gang boss Valeri Dlugatsj in a crowded disco. This hit was all the more impressive because Dlugatsj was surrounded, at the time, by heavily armed bodyguards. Vladislav Vinner, who replaced Dlugatsj, did not last long. Solonik killed him in 1994.

Around that time, Solonik was attempting to extort money from a Russian gangster who was refusing to play ball. When the man placed a phone call and put the phone on speaker, Solonik realised he was listening to the voice of Otari Kvantrishvili. Kvantrishvili was a sportsman, philanthropist, businessman and politician – loved and admired by many for his support of war veterans, orphans and elderly athletes. He was also, as everyone was aware, one of the most powerful criminal bosses in Russia. Solonik would not be getting his money.

Some weeks later, however, as Kvantrishvili emerged from the Krasnopresnenskie bathhouse, surrounded by bodyguards, he was shot dead by a sniper using a rifle with telescopic sights. The shooter had taken aim from the attic of the building that housed Kindergarten No. 392, from which there was a clear line of fire to the car park of the baths, 200 yards away. Alexey Kuzmin led the group which included other members of the murderous Orekhovo– Medvedkovo Criminal Group, one of whom was Solonik.

By this time, Solonik had attained legendary status in the Russian underworld as well as amongst Russian law enforcement officers. Naturally, they were keen to send him back to the Gulag and when he was arrested, along with an associate, in a bar, it looked as if it was all over for him. They escorted him to the police station on Moscow's Petrovsky market place, but foolishly failed to search him properly, unaccountably ignoring the fact that he was carrying a raincoat over his arm. The raincoat hid a gun. In the police station mayhem broke out when he produced the gun and, firing indiscriminately, shot dead four policemen. Fleeing from the building, out into Moscow's Petrovsky market place, he shot dead another two officers. He climbed over a fence and headed for some railway lines, but was hit by a police bullet in the kidney before being cornered. After holding out for a while, he realised the situation was futile and surrendered.

The police were impressed with Solonik's accuracy with a gun. At one point as he was running away, he had turned and fired three times at an officer hiding behind a pole. Each bullet hit exactly the same spot on the pole.

This time he was sent to the notorious Matrosskaya Tishina prison in northern Moscow from which no one had ever escaped . . . until Solonik arrived there, that is. Initially he spent his time, after the operation to remove the bullet from his kidney, learning foreign languages and studying literature. Eight months after his arrest, however, in July 1995, he did what he always did when they locked him up. He escaped. A prison guard provided him with climbing equipment and a pistol and the two men climbed onto the prison roof before lowering themselves to the ground and fleeing in a waiting BMW.

Solonik again seemed to vanish into thin air. There were sightings in Spain, Italy and Cyprus, but he had in fact travelled to Greece on a fake passport that he had obtained from the Greek consulate in Moscow. There, he set himself up, assembling a team of some 50 men and dealing in drugs and contract killings.

His legend had grown in his absence, especially when he made it on to Russia's ten 'Most Wanted' list. But it all came to a violent end in February 1997 when a phone call to Greek police reported the discovery of a body about 20 kilometres outside Athens. Next day, the Greek newspapers carried reports of a Russian mob boss being found dead. He had been strangled with a cord and wrapped with plastic bags. Although there was nothing on the body to identify him, it was soon confirmed that the body was Aleksandr Solonik. A few months later, a suitcase was found containing the dismembered body of Solonik's girlfriend, Russian model Svetlana Kotova, near the villa the two had shared. When they had raided this villa as well as his other properties, police had discovered an arsenal of weapons and had learned that Solonik was about to carry out a hit in Italy.

Rumours suggested that he had been killed by a Moscow gang and before too long, five men, believed to be members of the Orekhovskaya criminal organisation, were charged with the two murders. Amongst those charged was another infamous Russian contract killer, Aleksandr Pustovalov, also known as 'Sasha the Soldier'.

However, there are those who believe Aleksandr Solonik is still out there, plying his murderous trade. After all, they were unable to completely identify the body – the prints on file for Solonik were fake. Furthermore, no one knew exactly what he looked like any more as he had had plastic surgery to change his appearance.

Even death may not have been able to hold Aleksandr Solonik for very long.

PART SEVEN

KILLER
GANGS

THUGGEE

Arguments still rage about the Thuggee. Did they really exist or were they just a scare story dreamed up by the British colonial powers? Were they a religious cult or sect, or just a bunch of murderous robbers dressing up their acts with religious respectability? Did they come into being back in the mists of time, or were they a response to the British East India Company's annexation of the subcontinent?

What is for sure is that in India there was a network of secret fraternities of professional assassins, supported by zamindars (landowners), Indian princes, law-enforcement officials, merchants, and even ordinary people. They strangled and then robbed travellers – although never the English – from at least the 17th century onwards, but arguably from as far back as the 13th. Through the efforts of a remarkable man called William Sleeman, who approached his task with almost messianic zeal, the British colonial authorities managed to eradicate the Thuggee during the 19th century. All that remains of them is the word 'thug', appropriated by the English language as a description for a violent person.

The Thuggee were well organised, subtle and sophisticated in their methods. Disregarding religious divides – gangs were made up of Muslims, Sikhs and Hindus – they would travel around India in groups ranging from 10 to 200 men, befriending unsuspecting wealthy travellers, winning their trust and even travelling with them, sometimes for hundreds of miles, before killing them. These professional killers had a respectable air about them and were very mindful of family, social and religious obligations. The very aspects of their personalities that made them so plausible as con-artists – social and rhetorical skills – ensured that they were treated with great respect by their equals.

For the British colonial authorities the most frightening thing about the Thuggee was its invisibility, its skill in the art of hiding itself and its victims, and the difficulty of getting people to accept that it contravened the law. There was no blood, no weapon and the murders were mostly carried out a long way from the victim's home. Great care was exercised in the disposal of the bodies. Corpses were buried immediately after the strangling, with heavy rocks piled on top of them to prevent animals from getting to them and exposing the remains. Landowners, police and rulers tended to ignore the killings, either because they were superstitious or because they, themselves, stood to benefit from the deaths. The peasants simply turned a blind eye to the bodies that would regularly turn up in wells or in their fields.

Each group had its own function – some pretended to serve as guardians or protectors of travellers; others would flatter and compliment their victims, winning their trust that way. They were patient in the extreme, only killing their victims when the time and place were such that they could do it unobserved and then efficiently dispose of the body.

The killing was done, sometimes by two or three men trained in the art of strangulation since child-hood, according to ancient and rigidly prescribed forms and rituals. It was carried out only after a number of complex omens had been observed, and afterwards sacred rites were performed in the goddess Kali's honour and a proportion of Thuggee spoils would always be set aside for Kali. Thuggee strangled their victims most often using a yellow silk scarf, or *rumal*, a symbol of Kali, the Hindu god they worshipped and whom they called Bhowanee. But not all followers of Kali were Thuggee. Indeed, there were many who did not hold with the religious views of the cult, but who still worshipped Kali. Their method of dispatch led them to be known also as Phansigars, literally noose-operators, although it is reported that various other methods, such as swords and poison, were also used. After the killing, they would rob their victims before disposing of the bodies in inaccessible places – often throwing them down wells or burying them in remote spots. The locations they selected for their murders were special places, known as *bhils*, that they often knew well. The killings would take place, more often than not, in darkness and, while two or three men carried them out, the remainder of the group would make music and dance to cover the noise and pretend that nothing untoward was happening.

Thuggee spoke their own dialect or cant known as *Ramasee*, and a series of secret signs enabled them to recognise each other as they travelled the country. Old and infirm members of the cult still associated with it, even though they were no longer able to take part in the stranglings. They would prepare food and cook meals or they sometimes served as lookouts or spies.

The Thuggee first appear in literature in around 1356, in the *History of Firoz Shah* written by historian Ziaud din Barni. It recounts the story of the rule of the Muslim leader of the North Indian Tughlaq Dynasty: 'In the reign of that sultan, some Thugs were taken in Delhi, and a man belonging to that fraternity was the means of about 1,000 being captured. But not one of these did the sultan have killed. He gave orders for them to be put into boats and to be conveyed into the lower country, to the neighbourhood of Lakhnauti, where they were to be set free. The Thugs would thus have to dwell about Lakhnauti and would not trouble the neighbourhood of Delhi any more.'

But some writers trace the origins of the Thuggee cult back even further, to the Arab, Afghan and Mughal conquests of India that took place several centuries before Firoz Sha's rule; there have even been suggestions that their existence can be traced as far back as the Greek historian Herodotus, who lived in the fifth century BC.

According to the Thuggee, their sect had an ancient and divine origin. They believed that when the three Hindu gods, Brahma, Vishnu and Shiva, became Creator, Preserver and Destroyer, respectively, there was an initial balance between creation and destruction. However, Brahma, the Creator, was too successful and the earth became overcrowded. At this point, Shiva asked his consorts, Devi, Bhawani and Kali for help in decreasing the population. Bhawani created a band of ferocious men and ordered them to go out and destroy. She assured them that they would be immune from all earthly retribution and had only one purpose on earth – to kill. They need not worry about disposal of the bodies, as she would take care of that.

So, this band of Thugs began their task, killing many

people, the bodies being disposed of by Bhawani. However, one band of men wanted to see the god and waited, hidden, near the bodies of some of their victims for her to appear. She spotted them waiting and became angry, telling them that from now on she would withdraw her help and they would have to dispose of the bodies themselves. Furthermore, their protection from earthly retribution was removed. If they were caught in the act of killing or somehow implicated, she would not protect them and they would have to face earthly justice. Consequently, Thuggee had to take great care in their choice of location for the murders and the disposal of the bodies afterwards.

The secrecy and security of their organisation, coupled with the fact that killing for gain was a religious duty to the Thuggee, made it, to Indian minds at any rate, an entirely honourable occupation. Being a Thuggee was recognised as a proper profession and some even paid taxes on their ill-gotten gains.

Being a Thuggee was mostly a hereditary right, passed from father to son and from generation to generation, and leaders – known as *jamaadaar* – were certainly hereditary. Sometimes, Thuggee were the children of victims who had been taken and trained in the ways of the cult. Other Thuggee were men whose fathers had not been members, but who embraced the Thuggee creed in order to escape a poverty-stricken existence. Women in a household in which Thuggee lived, were entirely ignorant of their husbands' or sons' profession and this was encouraged by the fact that when not killing, Thuggee were often engaged in normal, peaceable occupations and were pillars of their local society.

It is very difficult to arrive at an estimate of exactly how many perished at the hand of the Thuggee. The *Guinness Book of Records* claims approximately 2,000,000 deaths, but British historian Dr Mike Dash provides a more conservative estimate of 50,000, although he bases his figure on an assumption they only started killing about 130 years before they were rendered extinct.

Thuggee gang leader Behram is calculated to be the world's most prolific killer. He is said to have been involved in some 931 killings between 1790 and 1830, although he seems to have been inconsistent in statements he made at the time about how many could actually be attributed to him. In one manuscript he says that he had 'been present at' more than 930 carried out by his particular gang. In other sources he claims to have personally strangled about 125 people. Behram turned King's Evidence, informing on his associates, and never stood trial, and as a result his claims have not been tested in a court of law.

The end of the murderous road arrived for the

Thuggee in the 1830s with the appointment of a remarkable civil servant, Captain William H. Sleeman. In 1809 Sleeman had joined the Bengal army and served in the Nepal War from 1814 to 1816. Then in 1820 he became assistant to the Governor-General's agent in the Saugor and Nerbudda territories. Previously, the lack of evidence, bodies and witnesses had made it almost impossible to prosecute the Thuggee and, if captured, Thuggee never confessed. However, the unexpected confession of one cult-member, a man called Feringheea, provided vital information on the cult's modus operandi. Following that, Sleeman launched an extensive campaign. Using profiling, confessions and local intelligence, he created detailed Thuggee family trees containing details of each man's crimes, his place of origin, his place in the caste hierarchy, and all personal and professional antecedents. Sleeman also mapped out all the *bhils* – places of slaughter and burial – in central India. Every thug could then be located on a gigantic grid, and information and operations were centralised. One Thuggee, Ameer Ali, writing in Confessions of a Thug, shows just how debilitating this was for the cult members: 'The man unfolded a roll of paper written in Persian, and read a catalogue of crime, of murders, every one of which I knew to be true; a faithful record it was of my past life, with but few omissions.' At the same time, Sleeman compiled a dictionary of Ramasee, the secret language of the Thuggee. There was no escape.

The police set up a Thuggee and Dacoity Department to deal with the problem, and appointed Sleeman as its superintendent. It remained in existence until 1904 when the Central Criminal Intelligence Department took its place, even though the Thuggee cult was extinct by the 1870s. Captured Thuggee were encouraged to inform on their groups and were offered protection if they did so. As a result, thousands of Thuggee were arrested and executed, imprisoned or exiled.

Although the Thuggee cult was no more, the concept of criminal tribes and criminal castes still remains in existence in India today.

EGAN'S RATS

From 1890 until 1924 the Irish-American street gang, Egan's Rats, was amongst the most powerful organised crime operations in St Louis. Although its members and its leadership were mainly Irish-American, it also included in its ranks a number of Italian-Americans and Jewish mobsters, immigrants from Eastern Europe.

Thomas Egan was born and brought up in St Louis's Irish ghetto, the Kerry Patch, the son of a tough saloon-keeper. The Kerry Patch was a harsh environment in which to grow up, a violent and dangerous place in which vicious gangs formed and fought for control of what little ill-gotten gains there were. Tenement slums housed hundreds of people, entire families living in a single room. Sewage was non-existent and washing consisted of a monthly visit to the public bathhouse. Violence was a way of life and one city guidebook of 1878 said that 'the chief amusements of Kerry Patchers consist of punching out each other's eyes'.

Like many youngsters in the Patch, Tom Egan began running with a local gang, a bunch of thugs known as the Ashley Street Gang who picked pockets, burgled properties and carried out armed robberies. Soon, Egan had graduated to leadership of the gang whose activities, by this time, included breaking up strikes and other union activities including political fixing. He was friends with another hard man, Thomas 'Snake' Kinney, who also happened to be a Democratic Party politician. On election-day, the Ashley Street boys would hang around the polling booths intimidating voters to vote Democrat. It worked for Kinney who became a delegate to the Missouri House of Delegates and later served in the Missouri State Senate.

By 1904 the Rats were the pre-eminent gang in St Louis, now a thriving metropolis and the fourth largest city in the United States. Their activities now encompassed bootlegging and labour rackets as well as murder. They would kill anyone for money, regardless of the consequences. On one infamous occasion, in 1909, they killed a man on trial in the city court-house for murdering several Rats.

By 1912 Egan's Rats numbered 300 or 400 men, and with the death of Tom Kinney from tuberculosis that year, they began to move into new rackets, especially bootlegging. The union activity would become less profitable and Egan correctly surmised that alcohol prohibition would be introduced some time in the near future and, with that in mind, set up a sophisticated booze-smuggling network. He did not live long enough, however, to see the fruits of his labour, dying of kidney disease the same year as his vision became reality with the passing of the Volstead Act – the Act that introduced Prohibition – on 28 October 1919.

Tom's younger brother Willie took control of the gang, but he was not the man that Tom had been and he soon fell out with the other gang members. He wanted to establish the bootlegging side of their activities as a long-term business. However, the younger members, known as 'red hots', were not prepared to wait for the money to come rolling in. They preferred the fast and easy money that armed robbery provided and rebelled against the boss, carrying out numerous attacks on banks, armoured cars and bank messengers.

Max 'Big Maxie' Greenberg was an unhappy senior member of the gang and when he double-crossed Willie Egan in a whiskey deal, Egan tried to kill him but failed. This was small thanks for the time when Big Maxie was imprisoned on federal charges of interstate theft. Then, Willie Egan had used his influence, reportedly all the way up to President Woodrow

Wilson, to have Greenberg's sentence reduced. He served a mere six months of a five-year sentence. Greenberg went off to New York for a while, setting up a successful rum-running operation with bootlegger Waxey Gordon and New York crime boss Arnold Rothstein, before returning to St Louis in 1921.

By now Egan had enemies on all fronts and a new rival gang was beginning to muscle in on his rackets. The Hogan Gang had been founded by Edward 'Jellyroll' Hogan and his brother, James. Jellyroll was one of six sons of a St Louis police officer and was also involved in city politics. In 1916 he was elected to the legislature as a state representative. He also happened to be the Missouri State Beverage Inspector. When Greenberg returned to town, he was working with the Hogans against the hated Egans.

Willie Egan incurred the Hogans' anger when, in March 1921, his men took some potshots at Max Greenberg while he was standing in a group of men in the middle of town. Greenberg was only wounded in the incident, but political lobbyist John P. Sweeney was killed. Six months later the Hogans took their revenge when they shot Egan to death outside his saloon on Franklin Avenue. Jellyroll Hogan and his gang were the main suspects and the story went that $30,000 was the price of the hit. Egan died in City Hospital, refusing to the last to name his killers. 'I'm a good sport,' were reported to be his last words on the subject. A week later Greenberg walked into a police station and provided a watertight alibi for the day of the murder, accompanied by Jacob H. Mackler, the Hogan Gang's lawyer.

The Rats' next leader was the aggressive former plumber and First World War infantryman, William 'Dint' Colbeck. Colbeck struck back hard at the Hogan boys, and violence stalked the city streets with both mobsters and passers-by being gunned down. Colbeck knew that Greenberg had planned the murder of Egan, that the lawyer Macklin had been involved in the payments for the hit, that James Hogan had been one of the shooters and that Hogan hitmen John Doyle and Luke Kennedy had also been involved.

They killed John Doyle first, in January 1922. Then they failed to injure Macklen, Kennedy or James Hogan when they opened fire on their car in town. A short while later, however, Macklen's luck ran out when 15 bullets were pumped into his car on Twelfth Street. He died instantly. The Hogans replied with a hit on Rat, George Kurloff, in a restaurant and the Rats responded in this tit-for-tat war by leaving the bodies of three Hogan Gang members, Joseph Cammarata, Joseph Cipolla and Everett Summers, in ditches beside remote country roads. Then it was Luke Kennedy's turn. His car was peppered with bullets in May 1922. When Dint Colbeck's plumbing store was shot up, the Egan boys retaliated by doing the same to Jellyroll Hogan's house.

The public and the media were outraged. In one incident, a young boy had been hit by a car driven by gunmen trying to escape. The anger was such that Colbeck was forced to move his headquarters out of the city. They converted an 11-roomed mansion into a club they called the Maxwelton Club and they commandeered an old, abandoned horse and motor-cycle track where they would drive round at speed shooting at tin cans and empty bottles.

There had now been 24 deaths in the war between the Hogan Gang and the Egan Rats, but the Rats still wanted to take care of their nemesis, Greenberg. It was getting too hot for Big Maxie and he took off for New York, picking up where he had left off with Waxey Gordon. Although he did not die in St Louis, someone caught up with him eventually. He was found murdered in a New Jersey hotel room in 1933.

In March 1923 the Rats messed up an attempt to assassinate Jellyroll Hogan and his sidekick, Hogan Gang enforcer Humberto Costello, as they drove down Grand Boulevard in St Louis. Two of the shooters were arrested – Elmer Runge and Isadore Londe – and Hogan was invited to the police station to identify his assailants. 'I'll identify them, alright,' he is reported to have growled. 'I'll identify them with a shotgun.'

Next, the two mobs staged a Wild West-type shoot-out on a St Louis street, Lindell Boulevard, scattering passers-by, but, fortunately, injuring no one. Colbeck, speaking to reporters, denied his boys' involvement and railed at them for fingering his team for any bit of violence that happened in the city.

The city had had enough and rushed to bring the shooting to an end. In April 1923 Philip Brockman, president of the Board of Police Commissioners, and a Catholic priest, Father Timothy Dempsey, brokered a peace between the two gangs. It lasted just two months. Some Rats spied James Hogan in a crowd of people. They opened fire, missed him and killed two innocent men, one of whom was a state representative. Colbeck attributed the atrocity to 'boyish high spirits'. 'I know three of the boys were full of moonshine and were riding around in a big touring car,' he is reported as saying. 'They might have seen Hogan in the crowd at Jefferson and Cass and maybe took a few shots at him for fun.'

In the meantime, Colbeck was maintaining the Rats' income with a stream of spectacular armed robberies, netting, it is estimated, some $4.5 million in a five-year period. In one robbery alone, in April 1923, they stole

$2.4 million in cash and negotiable bonds from a mail van, with the help of another St Louis gang, the Cuckoos.

Things were going well and the Hogan Gang had just about had enough. The Rats got them to agree to a peace treaty but a tidal wave of robbery and killing followed. The Rats were ruthless, killing anyone who got in their way, even their own gang members.

By now Dint Colbeck thought he was untouchable. He was famous for his flamboyance and liked nothing more than to pull out a wad of cash and go up to a uniformed policeman and say to him: 'Want a bribe, officer?'

In 1924, however, the bubble burst when captured Rat, Ray Renard, started to cooperate with state prosecutors. On the back of his information, a hoste of Rats were arrested and charged with armed robbery – Dint Colbeck, Louis 'Red' Smith, Steve Ryan, David 'Chippy' Robinson, Oliver Dougherty, Frank Hackenthal, Charles 'Red' Lanham, Gus Dietmeyer and Frank 'Cotton' Epplesheimer. They went to prison for 25 years each.

The imprisonment of the gang's leadership led to the break-up of Egan's Rats but those who had not gone to jail started causing havoc in other parts of the country. One team, led by Frankie 'Killer' Burke, surfaced in the Midwest where they carried out numerous contract killings, robberies and abductions. They are also believed to have been part of the team that Jack 'Machine Gun' McGurk used in the St Valentine's Day Massacre in Chicago in 1929.

Ex-Rat, Leo Vincent Brothers gained underworld notoriety when he gunned down *Chicago Tribune* reporter, Jake Lingle. Lingle was slain, gangland-style, at the Illinois Central Station underpass, during rush hour on 9 June 1930, in full view of crowds of people. The Mob were horrified as they insisted they only killed their own. It transpired later, however, that Lingle did, in fact, have racketeering connections.

Pete and Thomas 'Yonnie' Licavoli set up on their own with the River Gang which became the main bootlegging operation in Detroit as well as in Toledo, Ohio, while another former Rat, Elmer Macklin, was the murderer of Detroit crime boss Chester LaMare in February 1931.

When the Rats were released from prison in the early 1940s, most of them went to work for the organised crime boss Frank 'Buster' Wortman, while Colbeck tried to regain his former power. However, driving home one night in February 1943, at around 10.30 p.m., a car drew up alongside his vehicle, at Ninth and Destrehan Streets. There was a burst of sub-machine-gun fire and Dint Colbeck died with half a dozen bullets in him. He was 58 years old.

Meanwhile, Jellyroll Hogan remained in Democratic Party politics for 50 years. He served five terms in the Missouri state house and four in the state senate, retiring in 1960 when he lost his seat to Theodore McNeal, the first black man to be elected to the Missouri state senate. Hogan died in 1963, aged 77, after a short illness.

THE BONNOT GANG

In France before the First World War, conditions for workers were bad. Wages were low and if anyone dared to demand an improvement in pay or conditions he was branded a militant and sacked or, worse still, arrested. Jules Bonnot was such a man. In 1911 out of work and largely unemployable because of his political beliefs, Bonnot decided to follow what seemed to him at the time, to be the only path available – a criminal one.

Born in 1876 in Pont-de-Roide, a town in eastern France, Bonnot's mother had died when he was five, leaving him to be brought up by his father, a factory worker, and his grandmother. His childhood was, needless to say, difficult. He was a handful, being sent to prison twice as a teenager – on one occasion for assaulting a police officer. To cap it all, he was sacked from a factory job for allegedly stealing copper shavings.

Eventually, aged 21, he was conscripted into the French army, serving for three years as a car mechanic. He learned to shoot a rifle, becoming an excellent shot, and left the army with the rank of corporal.

In 1901 he married, but soon began to experience problems with employers who were wary of his political views and suspicious of his connections with anarchists. Consequently, he was blacklisted as an agitator. Moving to Geneva he managed to find employment, but lost his job when he struck his boss with an iron bar. By 1907 his wife had had enough and left him, taking their child with her.

In 1908 Bonnot was working with a gang of Italian anarcho-individualists who were involved in counterfeiting. In addition to counterfeiting, he was also involved in small-time theft and burglary which progressed to the theft of luxury cars in France and Switzerland, the knowledge he had picked up about cars in the army being put to good use. By 1910 he was in Lyon, robbing the houses of rich lawyers. He would pose as a businessman and case their properties while apparently visiting on business.

In order to avoid arrest, Bonnot moved to Paris in 1911 where he hooked up with an anarchist group led by Octave Garnier. Garnier had come from a long line of trouble-makers. His father had been a militant syndicalist who had refused to do military service and consequently had spent his life on the run. His son, known as 'Poil Du Carotte' due to his red hair, had followed suit.

The group aired their views through *L'Anarchie*, an anarchist newspaper, and consisted of a disparate band of people sharing similar political views. They had all been unemployed for some time and, given their politics, it was unlikely that anyone would give them a job. Most of the gang had associations with the syndicalist movement which, put simply, wanted to run society for the greater good of the majority. Almost inevitably, they gravitated towards criminality to achieve their ends. As far as they were concerned, there was no alternative apart from starvation or joining the army.

There were around 20 of them, and they were people of all sorts, from Victor Kibalchich, a Russian revolutionary who took the name Victor Serge, to André Soudy, a young grocer who suffered from tuberculosis. Soudy had been sacked from a number of jobs because of his political activities and had also contracted tuberculosis following several terms in prison. Nonetheless, illness had failed to dampen his rebelliousness. Other members included the Belgian Eduard Carouy, a huge man with a massive physique, who brought added muscle, and Raymond Callemin, known as 'La Science', a lover of the theatre and music who came to the gang with a dislike of violence which did not last long. The gang's first robbery was a historic one – the first time in history that a motor car was used to escape from the scene of a crime. They snatched a satchel from the shoulders of a bank courier as he left the Societé Générale Bank in the Rue Ordener in Paris on 21 December 1911, fleeing in a Delaunay-Bonneville that they had stolen the previous week and firing at anyone who got in their way. Bonnot, Octave Garnier, Raymond Callemin and Eugéne Dieudonné, an anti-militarist from Nancy, got away with 5,126 francs.

A week after the bank robbery, the gang broke into the Foury Armoury in Rue Lafayette, just as it was closing down for the Christmas holiday. They would later add to their armoury in the New Year when they raided the American Armaments Factory in Boulevard Haussmann, stealing pistols and rifles. Then on 2 January 1912 they entered the home of a Monsieur Moreau, brutally murdering both him and his maid and escaping with loot valued at 30,000 francs.

In February, now known as the Bonnot Gang and after Bonnot gave an interview in the *Petit Parisien* newspaper, they moved their activities to the south, stealing a car from an industrialist in Beziers, in the Languedoc, and robbing the Nimes Mining Company because one of them had been sacked from a job there due to his trade union activity. Throughout February they carried out a wave of robberies and their name became famous throughout France for their daring and their use of modern technology – cars and firearms – that left the forces of the law in their wake. Hysterical headlines in the papers screamed: 'Where will they strike next?'

A political and philosophical debate also raged as to whether this activity was aimed against political repression or was just plain criminality with the objective of enriching the perpetrators. But the public were drawn to this gang whose actions seemed to them to be charmingly amateurish. Ordinary people cared little for banks losing money and less for a police force not known for its sensitivity. They liked the fact that the gang was an assortment of types, from the suave good-looking characters from good backgrounds, to the honest labourer; from the huge, physical presence of a man like Carouy, to the small, intellectual form of the arts-loving Callemin. There were intellectuals and trade union militants and the gang even had women members who supported their men no matter what. The members talked ceaselessly of revolution and placed articles in the anarchist press defending their actions. They made little effort to disguise themselves; their photographs were circulated by the newspapers, which described the authorities' efforts to capture the gang as laughable. In fact, when the press made a mistake in its coverage of the gang's activities, they would be sure to receive a letter from a gang member, putting them right.

They even communicated with the police through the pages of newspapers. In March 1912, in an open letter to Sûreté Chief Xavier Guichard, Octave Garnier wrote: 'I assure you that all this hue and cry doesn't prevent me from having a peaceful existence. As you've been frank enough to admit, the fact that I've been traced has not been due to your perspicacity, but to the fact that there was a stool pigeon amongst us. You can be sure he's had his come-uppance since. Your reward of 10,000 francs to my girlfriend to turn me in, must have troubled you, N.L. Guichard . . . you really shouldn't be so lavish with State funds. A bit more, and I'll hand myself over, with guns thrown in. You know something, Guichard, you're so bad at your lousy profession I feel like turning up and putting you right myself. Oh, I know you'll win in the finish all right. You have a formidable arsenal at your disposal, and what have we got? Nothing. We'll be beaten because you're the stronger and we're the weaker, but, in the meantime, we hope that you'll have to pay for your victory. Looking forward to seeing you (?) – Garnier.'

In the face of a huge public outcry and an outraged and sarcastic press, the Sûreté Nationale launched a huge manhunt. Using the registry of anarchist organisations they succeeded in making one arrest, but by this time the gang had escaped to Belgium where they disposed of the stolen car they had been using. While attempting to steal another, they shot dead a Belgian policemen.

The car thefts and robberies continued and another two policemen were shot. But by 1912 the police had begun to make inroads, arresting a number of people connected to the gang. On 25 March 1925, in a forest south of Paris, the gang shot a driver in the head and stole his car, a De Dion-Bouton. They drove it to the north of Chantilly and robbed a branch of the Societé Générale Bank. In the process, they shot three of the bank's cashiers, escaping in the stolen car and pursued somewhat ridiculously by two gendarmes, one on a bicycle and one on horseback.

Now, the authorities were becoming very irritated. The gang seemed to do as it pleased. Sûreté Chief Guichard, who later appeared in Georges Simenon's *Maigret* books as the eponymous detective's superior, became personally involved in the hunt. Meanwhile, politicians were becoming concerned and an extra 800,000 francs was made available to police funds. Banks increased their security and cashiers began turning up for work carrying guns. The Société Générale Bank offered a reward of 100,000 francs for information leading to the arrest of gang members.

Eventually things began to unravel and a number of gang members were picked up. On 30 March 1912, a few days after they had shot dead a man as they were stealing a car, André Soudy was arrested at Berck-sur-Mer on the Channel Coast. Soudy's tuberculosis was at an advanced stage and he said that he no longer cared whether he died from his illness or by guillotine. Eduard Carouy was arrested four days later and Raymond Callemin four days after that. An angry mob gathered when news of Callemin's arrest began to spread and police had to hold them at bay to prevent them from lynching him on the spot. Another, Antoine Monnier, was arrested in Paris on 24 April. By now 28 gang members and their supporters were locked up. But still the gang's three founder members, Garnier, René Valet and Jules Bonnot himself, remained at large.

Bonnot had almost been taken on 24 April when they had surprised him at an apartment belonging to a well-known fence. In the resulting gunfight he killed one gendarme and wounded another before escaping over the rooftops.

Four days later he was tracked to a garage in the Paris suburb of Choisy-le-Roi, owned by a Bonnot Gang sympathiser, Jean Dubois. Five hundred police officers, soldiers, firemen, military engineers and armed private individuals besieged the house and Dubois was shot dead when officers charged the garage. Then, after shots had been exchanged by Bonnot and the soldiers and police officers outside, Police Chief Lépines ordered three of his men to place an explosive charge beneath the house, the resulting explosion completely demolishing the front of the building. When police entered what remained they found Bonnot hiding in a rolled-up mattress. He opened fire on them, but was hit in the head by a bullet said to be from the police chief's gun. The shot, however, did not kill him immediately.

Outside, the crowd that had gathered went mad and police again feared that a lynching might take place. They calmed the situation by declaring that Bonnot had already died and had been buried in a secret grave. He did die shortly afterwards on the way to the police station but had taken care to leave behind a note acquitting the others of responsibility, placing all of the blame on himself.

Garnier and Valet remained at large until 14 May when they were discovered in a house in Nogent-Sur-Marne, in Paris's eastern suburbs. Once again, a huge force assembled – 300 policemen and 800 soldiers – with Sûreté Chief Guichard taking personal control of the operation. An intense gunfight raged for some time before Guichard decided enough was enough. At two in the morning he ordered that the building be blown up. Garnier died in the explosion, but Valet, seriously wounded, continued firing for some time until he, too, was silenced. Like Bonnot, Garnier left a confession, implicating himself and exonerating all the others.

At the trial of the surviving members of the Bonnot Gang which began on 3 February 1913, Victor Serge was sentenced to five years for robbery, Eugéne Dieudonné got life, and Carouy and Marius Metge were given life with hard labour. Raymond Callemin, Antoine Monnier and André Soudy refused to plead for clemency, preferring to be executed on the guillotine.

THE WEST END GANG

The West End Gang has been active in the Canadian city of Montreal's west side and beyond since the early years of the 20th century, consisting mostly, though not exclusively, of members of Irish descent. Originally known simply as the Irish Gang, it focused, during its formative years on truck hijacking, kidnapping and armed robbery.

Like numerous other criminal organisations, the West Enders branched out into the world of drugs in the 1970s, importing hashish and cocaine into Canada for sale in the United States and forging alliances with the Montreal Mafia, Cosa Nostra and the Hell's Angels. The three groups together make up what is known as the 'Consortium' and work together to fix drug prices. Police estimates place a value of $80 billion on the ten tons of cocaine and 300 tons of hashish they smuggled into Canada from the 1970s to the 1990s.

Frank Peter 'Dunie' Ryan was perhaps the most successful leader the West End Gang ever had. He was known as 'Mother' to his employees because he really did seem to look after them, if they played the game.

Born in 1942, his father abandoned the family when Ryan was just three years old. By his mid-teens, he had dropped out of school and launched himself on a life of crime, forming a gang and leading them in acts of petty theft, truck hijacks and burglary. This continued until the mid-1960s when he was arrested in America for armed robbery after he, four other Montrealers and a Boston gangster carried out a Massachusetts bank robbery. Aged just 24, he was sentenced to 15 years in prison. After being paroled, he is reported to have returned to Montreal with $100,000 in cash, the spoils of a string of robberies in the States. He invested the cash in loan sharking, but claimed to have lost the lot. It was at this point that he moved into the racket that would bring him real riches – drugs.

Soon his drug-smuggling was being carried out on a grand scale and he had set up a network that covered Quebec, Ontario and the provinces on Canada's east coast. By now he was the dominant criminal force in Montreal, more powerful than other criminal organisations, principal among which were the Hell's Angels and the Cotroni family. He could ask them for favours such as when he felt he had been ripped off by one of his own men, Hughie McGurnaghan. All Ryan had to do was contact the Hell's Angels North Chapter and they sent one of their members, Yves 'Apache' Trudeau, to sort out the problem. A bomb in McGurnahgan's Mercedes took care of him and delivered an important message to anyone who thought he could get one over on Dunie Ryan.

He had a near-monopoly on all the hashish coming into Canada and reputedly carried $500,000 around with him in a briefcase to invest in the various schemes he came across in his day-to-day business.

Despite doing him favours, Ryan was disliked by Montreal's other criminal elements such as the Hell's Angels and the Mafia, because they wanted a share of his drugs business. Ryan, however, was unwilling to let them in, and resentment grew. He boasted of connections with the IRA that were more powerful than any to be found in Montreal. 'Mafia, pafia,' he would say. 'If there's a war, we've got the IRA.'

Ryan was not a believer in the banking system and refused to entrust any of his vast fortune to them. Once, when testifying before the Quebec Police Commission's inquiry into organised crime, he was asked where he kept his money. Ryan replied that he buried it in the ground. The Crime Commission lawyer suggested that he was joking, but Ryan replied:

'I don't believe in the banks. I know that the police can go to banks and see the safety deposit boxes and check them.'

This led to a couple of maverick Hell's Angels planning to kidnap his children and hold them hostage until he told them where these holes containing his money were located. Ryan was passed information about what was going to happen and once again called in his Angel of no mercy, Apache Trudeau. The two Angels died before they could put their plan into action.

Ryan's reign as the king of Montreal finally came to an end on 13 November 1984. He was working in his office at the Nittolo's Garden Motel when he was interrupted by a West End Gang member, Paul April. April told him that there was a woman waiting to have sex with him in one of the motel's rooms. Ryan went to the room and discovered waiting for him April, a small-time Montreal crook by the name of Robert Lelièvre, and two other men. They all had guns and planned, like the two Hell's Angels, to find out from him where he had stashed the $50–100 million he was believed to be worth. As they tried to restrain Ryan, he struggled and was felled by a blast in the chest from a shotgun. A slug from a .45 through his right cheek finished him off. At least his stash was safe. He was only 42 but would be remembered fondly for many years after his death by those who worked with him. One, William 'Billy' McAllister, had nothing but kind words to say about Ryan: 'Mother [Ryan] was a criminal genius and a nice person. He wasn't ruthless, but you couldn't put your hand in his pocket to steal from him. But that's the law on the street. He was very kind-hearted and generous. He was an honourable man.'

Allan 'The Weasel' Ross picked up where Ryan left off. He had been a loyal sidekick of Ryan's since the early 1960s when the West End Gang was still known as 'the Irish Gang'. By the early 1980s he was an enormously powerful and wealthy man, reputed to be the fifth biggest cocaine-trafficker in North America.

Paul April decided the time was right to make a leadership bid, but Ross, called in the ever-reliable Apache Trudeau, offering him $200,000 and the chance to have his sizeable drug debt wiped out if he took on a contract for April and the others who had been in the Nittolo's Garden Motel room with Dunie Ryan.

Twelve days later an explosion destroyed the entire apartment block in which April and his associates were holed up. April, Lelièvre and two other gang members died and eight other people were injured.

Ross consolidated his position when Edward Philips, one of his associates, was murdered in a restaurant car park in March 1985. Ross found out that his murderer was a drug dealer called David Singer and decided to make an example of him. He sent his henchmen Raymond Desfossés and Allan Strong, a.k.a. Jean-Guy Trépanier, to Florida where Singer was hiding out.

On 10 May Singer got into a car with Ross's men. While Desfossés drove the car, Strong covered a struggling Singer's face with a pillow and fired several shots into it. They dumped the body at the side of the road and sped off. In their haste, however, Desfossés was seen jumping a red light by a Highway Patrolman. He was pulled over, but as the cop approached the car, Desfossés pulled out his gun and fired at him, hitting the officer in the leg. They took off once again, managing to escape.

They thought they were in the clear, but police officers discovered the phone number of Allan Ross's wife in the dead Singer's pocket. The trail led straight back to Desfossés, Strong and Ross. It took a while to build up the case, but finally, in October 1991, Ross was arrested in Fort Lauderdale, Florida, on the evidence of an informer and attempt to bribe the federal agent arresting him with $200,000. The officer, however, was having none of it. He was charged with murder and cocaine-trafficking, the evidence against him was overwhelming. No fewer than 15 informants were willing to testify against Ross. One, however, a

Montreal drug dealer named Gaétan Lafond, missed his day in court. He was murdered a month before while eating in a restaurant in Medillin, Colombia's drug capital. His killers walked up to his table and calmly pumped eight bullets into him. No one has ever been arrested, but the killing proved that Ross's power reached far beyond the bars of his prison cell.

In November 1997 Allan Ross was sentenced to life in prison, the judge telling him he would have to serve at least 45 years before being eligible for parole.

Defossés was arrested in 1992 and fought extradition to Florida from Canada. Eventually, however, in 1997, he was extradited for the murder of David Singer and the attempted murder of the policeman he shot.

Strong, meanwhile, had gone on the run, only being apprehended in February 1994, in Amsterdam in the Netherlands. Extradited to Florida on the murder rap and charges of drug smuggling, his case was lost when a member of his crew, Jean-Francois Leboeuf, testified against him. He went to prison for 25 years.

While Ross had been under arrest, it came to light that Sidney Leithman, lawyer to Frank 'Dunie' Ryan and another leading Montreal underworld figure, Frank Cotroni, had been a police informer since 1985 when he had informed on a client who was involved in a drugs case. Once the news was out, it was obvious that he would not be doing too much more informing.

He was shot dead at the wheel of his black Saab convertible at 6.48 a.m. on 13 May 1991. Leaving his home, he had been cut off by a car at a set of traffic lights. A man waiting in a nearby telephone kiosk walked over to his car and fired four bullets into him from a .45 pistol. A bag of smoked meat was then thrown on the body, to add insult to injury.

Leithman had traces of cocaine in his blood and was known to have had an escalating habit. When he was killed, he was under investigation as a co-conspirator in Ross's case, Ross being another of his clients. He was being further investigated for obstructing the course of justice following reports that he had been bribing drug dealers not to talk to the police. However, there is little doubt that if he had been charged, he would have been in a position to get a lot of people into trouble.

One of them was senior police officer Claude Savoie, who was head of the drug squad. He shot himself in his office just before he was going to be interviewed by internal affairs officers about his dealings with Leithman. When Leithman was shot, he had Savoie's telephone number in his pocket and Savoie had had several meetings with Leithman and Allan Ross, unaccompanied by any other police officer. These meetings had taken place while Ross was being investigated by the American Drug Enforcement Administration.

Following Ross's arrest, Daniel Serero, known as 'The Arab' as he had been born in Casablanca, took care of business for a while. Serero described himself as a florist and had declared only $21,959 in salary since 1989. However, he seemed to be able to make his money go a long way because when the authorities investigated his finances, he was discovered to be spending more than $45,000 a month. He dressed in the finest designer clothes, dined in expensive restaurants, lived in a plush penthouse in the affluent city of Westmount, at one time the richest community in Canada, and drove a Rolls Royce. In September 1996 he went to jail for 11 years.

The only members of the leadership left on the streets were the Matticks brothers, Gerry and Richard. They maintained the gang's hijacking and drug-trafficking activities and allegedly ran things at the Port of Montreal.

At present, the West End Gang consists of around 125 to 150 members according to Montreal police estimates. Serero is back on the streets again and can only be presumed to be carrying on with his previous activities, but the gang's current leader is unknown since Gerry Matticks, too, was jailed in 2003.

PART EIGHT

BRITISH KILLERS

JIMMY MOODY

He was known to the staff of the Royal Hotel in Hackney simply as Mick. He would come in now and then for a couple of drinks, speak to no one, finish his drink and leave. Always polite and always quiet.

On 1 June 1993 it was no different. He sat on a stool at the bar minding his own business, making his pint last and staring at the bottles hanging from the optics behind the bar. A man in his early forties, wearing a leather jacket, came through the door and went to the Gents, presumably caught short out in the street. Just moments later he emerged, a .38 revolver in his hand. He stopped, took aim and fired three bullets from his Saturday Night Special into the chest of the man known as Mick. Mick slumped to the floor and as he did so, the man in the leather jacket fired another round into his back, just to make absolutely certain. He then calmly turned and walked out the door, climbed into a waiting Ford Fiesta XR2 and was driven off, never to be seen again.

The dead man – Mick – turned out to be a gangster called Jimmy Moody who had once been a member of the gang run by Charlie and Eddie Richardson that terrorised South London in the 1960s. At the height of their power, the Richardsons had had a reputation for employing some of London's most infamous and sadistic gangsters. They were also known as the 'Torture Gang', which tells you all you need to know – their 'speciality' was pinning victims to the floor with six-inch nails and/or removing their toes with bolt cutters. They had legitimate businesses – Charlie was into scrap metal and Eddie was into fruit machines – but these enterprises were merely fronts for their more lucrative criminal activities – fraud, theft and fencing stolen goods.

Their business methods were unorthodox. If Eddie wanted you to install one of his fruit machines in your pub, it was not wise to refuse, unless you wanted to have to pay for repairs to the damage his heavies would do. Their principal mode of operation was the use of 'Long Firms'. These were companies that would be set up by someone they knew. The business would operate legally for a while, establishing a credit rating. This achieved, they would then place a large order for goods, often washing machines, fridges or televisions, and would sell them. Instead of using the proceeds to pay their supplier, however, they would simply pocket the money and the company would vanish into thin air. Nonetheless, the Richardsons managed to stay out of prison. It was amazing the difference a tidy donation to the Police Benevolent Fund could make to a case.

Jimmy Moody had been the number one enforcer for the Richardsons in a criminal career that spanned four decades and in which his associates included some of the most infamous British criminal names – Jack Spot, Billy Hill, Mad Frankie Fraser and the Krays, to name but a few. He was a powerfully built man, a devoted body-builder, extraordinarily fit and strong. However, 13 years before his leather-jacketed assassin had strode into the Royal Hotel, he had seemed to disappear off the face of the earth. He had been locked in his cell in Brixton Prison one night while awaiting trial. Next morning, he, along with a couple of cellmates, was gone.

His short stay in Brixton followed an armed robbery that had gone awry. In the late 1970s he was working with an accomplished armed robber named Billy Tobin. Tobin had assembled a crew known as the Chainsaw Gang, or sometimes the Thursday Gang. They became the most successful armed robbers of the 1970s. Their game was hijacking security vans, often using extreme violence, cutting them open and making off with the contents – usually very large sums of money. They were nothing if not innovative in their methods and they planned their robberies in meticulous detail, carrying them out with military precision.

Moody is reported to have once dressed up as a policeman and forced a security van to stop in the Blackwall Tunnel, collecting the keys of the cars that had stopped behind the van to delay the raising of the alarm. It was when they rammed a security van in Dulwich with a mobile crane that Tobin was finally caught. But Moody got away and hid out in a lock-up garage that he kept ready for just such an eventuality. It contained books, food, body-building equipment and even a chemical toilet. He made the mistake of visiting his son, however, and was arrested and charged with robberies with estimated takings of £930,000. Awaiting trial in Brixton, he enjoyed what his brother Richard brought in for him – in those days a prisoner's family could provide him with food and little luxuries. Unfortunately for the authorities, Richard's steak and kidney pies also hid drill bits, hacksaws and other tools useful in a prison breakout.

Moody and his cellmates, Provisional IRA bomb-maker Gerard Tuite and an armed robber called Stanley Thompson, worked away at the bricks that made up the cell wall; it was just like a World War Two prisoner-of-war film as they got rid of the bits of rubble in their chamber pots at slopping-out every morning. On 16 December 1980 they removed the bricks they had loosened and squeezed out on to the flat roof beyond the wall. A ladder had been left there by a gang of roofers and that was all they needed.

Moody disappeared. His fingerprints were discovered in a raid on a flat in West London, but that was all they ever found of him.

Strangely, given his associates, he had not been a regular in court. His only conviction was in 1967, when he and his brother Richard were convicted of the manslaughter of a young ship's steward named William Day at a party in South London. They were each sentenced to six years in prison.

It wasn't that he had not already been involved in criminal activity, however. In March 1966 he was working with the Richardsons and was present on the night that a crook called Dickie Hart was killed in a fight at Mr Smith's club. He drove the badly injured hood, Harry Rawlings, to Dulwich Hospital in Eddie Richardson's Jaguar, dumping him there and disappearing. He was arrested and charged with affray as a result of that night, but the jury failed to agree on a verdict and he was acquitted. He was acquitted again when he was charged along with the Richardson brothers and Mad Frankie Fraser in the so-called 'torture trial' in 1967 in which Charlie was sentenced to 25 years and Eddie had ten years added to an existing five-year stretch. The Richardson gang was finished.

There were various theories as to why someone wanted to take out a contract on Jimmy Moody. One suggested that he had been having a fling with a married woman and the husband had found out and paid someone to kill him. It is true that Moody had a reputation as a bit of a ladies' man. They said that he required the services of a different woman every night.

Frankie Fraser believes, however, that he was hit in revenge for his killing of a man called David Brindle in the Bell public house in Walworth in 1991. The Brindles had been engaged in a war with another family, the Dalys, and Moody was working behind the bar of a pub owned by the Dalys. He had reportedly beaten Brindle with a baseball bat and later shot him to prevent reprisals for the beating.

What is certain is that during those 13 years in which he was a fugitive from the law, he worked as a hitman and a number of deaths have been allocated to him.

Gwenda and Peter Jackson, who disappeared during a walking tour in Pembrokeshire in 1989, for instance, and 32-year-old Maxine Arnold and her boyfriend Terry Gooderham. Gooderham worked as a stock-taker for a number of pubs and clubs in London and Hertfordshire. He is believed, in the course of his work, to have 'redirected' not inconsiderable sums of money and, understandably, made enemies. Or, as another theory puts it, he was involved in the monies from the Brinks-Mat robbery at Heathrow in 1983 when robbers got away with £26 million of gold bullion. Or perhaps, as the press suggested, he had been trying to become a player in the lucrative Spanish ice cream market and had upset a few people. Or maybe it was a crime of passion? Gooderham had several women on the go, apart from the unfortunate Maxine; one of them could have organised the hit, having found out about his two- or three-timing.

Whatever the reason, he and Maxine, who was probably just in the wrong place at the wrong time, and certainly with the wrong person, were gunned down in their black Mercedes in Epping Forest in December 1989.

Moody is also thought to have been involved in the killing of a 47-year-old dealer in antiques and cocaine. Peter Raisini was shot dead in the garden of his home in Palmers Green in London in March 1991 when a gunman approached him from behind and pumped four bullets into his back.

Attractive 42-year-old Patricia Parsons was found dead in her Volkswagen Cabriolet in Epping Forest on 24 June 1990. Parsons owned a sauna in Camden Town and, on 23 June, was due to help in the restaurant owned by her Turkish boyfriend in Harlow, north of London. She failed to arrive at the restaurant, and next day the car containing her body was discovered in the forest. At first police thought she had been killed by a spear-gun, but it turned out to be a bolt from a crossbow. She had been made to drive, it was presumed, from her home to Epping where she was killed. Why was she killed? Perhaps because she possessed a little black book that contained the names of over 200 men who had made use of the services at her sauna parlour. The list was thought to contain at least one judge, as well as the names of barristers and celebrities. It was never found and her death brought a sudden end to a deal she had done with a British Sunday newspaper to name names.

It is alleged that all of these hits, and more, were the work of Jimmy Moody.

Gerard Tuite, Moody's cellmate in Brixton, had shared many stories of British brutality and torture in Northern Ireland with Moody and, it is reported, Moody had come to sympathise with the aims of the terrorists. It is alleged by some sources that his particular skills were very much in demand in the Province and that he was recruited on a freelance basis by the Provisionals to put them to use. He became notorious for his hits which sent shudders through the government and the security services; victims were referred to as having been awarded an O.B.E. – One

Behind the Ear. A three-man hit squad, made up of elite SAS men, is said to have been assembled, specifically to find Moody and eliminate him.

By that time, though, he was gone, living in a flat in South London, with a completely new identity. But London was a different place to the one he had left a few years previously. Criminals were now far more interested in drugs – cocaine and ecstasy – than in the armed robberies of his day. Huge drug deals financed extravagant and lavish lifestyles; the stakes were higher, but then so were the profits.

Moody had also, by this time, built a list of enemies as long as his arm – other criminals, the RUC, the Met, the British security services, they were all after him.

It was only a matter of time before Jimmy Moody would be awarded his very own OBE.

THE CURSE OF THE BRINKS MAT MILLIONS

They say that anyone wearing gold jewellery bought after 1983 is probably wearing the proceeds of the massive heist from the Brinks Mat warehouse at Heathrow on 26 November of that year.

That night, at around 6.40 p.m., six armed South London men wearing balaclavas, broke into the warehouse, and beat up the security guards, hitting one over the head with a pistol and then pouring petrol over them, threatening to set them alight if they did not reveal the combinations to the locks. They had a man on the inside, security guard Anthony Black, brother-in-law of Brian Robinson whose idea the raid was. Black had provided them with a key to the main door and information about the security systems at the warehouse which, with his information, they were able to switch off.

The robbers had been expecting to find £3 million in cash, a sizeable sum for any self-respecting thief. What they did find, however, staggered them. 6,800 gold bars – ten tonnes of the stuff – packed into 76 cardboard boxes. There were also two boxes of diamonds for good measure. The total value of their unexpected haul was £26 million, amounting to the biggest sum ever stolen in a robbery in Britain. The van they had arrived in was too small and they had to go and get a bigger one in which to haul the gold away. After the robbery, a £2 million reward was offered for information leading to their capture.

Cash would have been easy to handle. They knew what to do with that and could dispose of it quickly without too much fuss. But this was gold, loads of it. They knew nothing about gold and how to turn it into cash. So they called in experts, men such as Kenneth Noye, who had the ideal contact in a man called John Palmer who owned a Bristol-based gold dealership called Scadlyn where the bullion could be melted down and recast so that it could be sold on. They were meticulous, even mixing less pure gold coins with the gold to reduce its purity and disguise its origins. However, before too long, large movements of cash through a Bristol bank came to the notice of the police. More than £10 million was deposited by Palmer, Noye and a man called Brian Perry, and £3 million was withdrawn at one point, requiring the Bank of England to supply the notes and the Treasury to be informed.

Their suspicions raised, the police placed Noye under surveillance and in 1985 he discovered a police officer, John Fordham, in his garden and stabbed him to death. He was sensationally found not guilty of murder at the subsequent trial on the grounds of self-defence.

In 1986, however, 11 gold bars were discovered at his house – the only gold ever retrieved from the robbery – and he was convicted of conspiracy to handle the proceeds of the robbery. He was fined £700,000 and sentenced to 14 years in prison, of which he served eight.

Others were also imprisoned. Micky McAvoy and Brian Robertson were picked up soon after the robbery and went to jail for 25 years each. McAvoy tried to do a deal in return for the return of some of the proceeds, but his share, given to friends to look after for him, was gone. McAvoy and Robertson had behaved particularly stupidly, moving from their council houses into huge mansions in Kent and paying for them with cash. McAvoy even bought two rottweilers, calling one Brink and the other, Mat. Anthony Black, the man on the inside, whose family connection to Robertson emerged after the raid and Robertson's arrest, got six years.

Although a few of the robbers received jail sentences, most of those who played some part in the robbery got away with it and some three tonnes of gold, valued at around £10 million, was never recovered despite two decades of relentless police investigation. Some, such as

Kenneth Noye, lived the high life. He was living in a luxury villa in Spain when he was arrested for a road rage murder in England in 1996, being jailed for that in 1998.

But what has become known as 'the Curse of Brinks Mat' has accounted for a number of the participants. There have been some nine murders, many of them by hitmen. There has been no honour among these thieves.

Brian Perry ran a minicab company in the East End of London. He was the one who had suggested bringing in Kenneth Noye. But, three years after the robbery, the authorities came after him for money-laundering in connection with it and he was arrested and sentenced to nine years. It emerged during his trial that he had received a threatening letter, but he probably felt safe as he had employed 'Mad' Frankie Fraser as his bodyguard. Mickey McAvoy believed that Perry had stolen his share of the robbery cash, but Perry seems to have managed to convince McAvoy while he was in jail that this was not true. He did his time and when he came out of prison, worked at building up his cab business and making a few property investments. He seemed to be in the clear and did not feel the need for protection of any kind.

On 16 November 2001, now 63 years old, he was climbing out of his car which he had parked outside the offices of his Blue Car cab firm. He had a bag of shopping in his hand.

Suddenly, a man, his face hidden by a mask, appeared out of nowhere and fired three rapid shots into the back of Brian Perry's head. Perry was dead before his bag of shopping spilled onto the pavement.

It is presumed that Perry had been unable to account for large sums of money he had been given to look after. There was still a lingering doubt that he had not been completely honest about McAvoy's money, something which no doubt irritated McAvoy as he had needed the money for the deal he wanted to cut with the authorities for a lesser sentence. An appearance on television by Perry, talking about McAvoy, had not helped.

Two men, Joseph Pitkin and Bilal Akhtar, were arrested and charged with the murder. It was alleged in their Old Bailey trial that Pitkin was the gunman while Akhtar was the 'quartermaster' supplying the gun, the ammunition and the getaway car. However, the pair were cleared after the judge declared that the evidence was purely circumstantial.

Then there was Saul 'Solly' Nahome. Solly was a jeweller who had emigrated to Britain from Burma in 1961 and had run a business in London's Hatton Garden district. But he had got into some bad company and had done work for the north London crime syndicate, the Adams Family, laundering their profits from drug-dealing. He was an ideal choice to help sell on the smelted-down gold.

Again, however, the curse of the Brinks Mat millions struck. On 27 November 1998, as he walked from his car to his home in Finchley, he was shot four times by a gunman who then sped off on a motorcycle. Solly's money-laundering days were at an end.

And we should not forget George Francis. Francis was a former associate of the Krays who is linked to at least 20 killings. He was a career criminal who rose to prominence in 1979 when he became a member of a drug-smuggling gang. Huge quantities of cannabis were imported in containers from a shoe factory in Pakistan, hidden by legitimate goods. All went well for a while and the gang members began to enjoy the fruits of their work with an ostentatious show of their new-found wealth, even down to lighting cigars with £20 notes in south London pubs.

But the authorities were on to them and when one of the gang, Lennie 'Teddy bear' Watkins, spotted the team that was carrying out a surveillance operation on them, he panicked, shooting dead one of the customs officers. Watkins got life, and the others were also arrested. Francis is said to have offered £100,000 to anyone who could nobble the jury. The north London Adams Family picked up the contract and, following a trial in which the jury had failed to reach a verdict, Francis was acquitted in the retrial. Like Perry, he had been charged with the safekeeping of some of the money and he also laundered hundreds of thousands of pounds for the gang. However, also like Perry, he had not been terribly careful with the money and the robbers believed that a lot of it had gone into his own pocket.

Added to that, Francis had, over the years, rubbed a lot of people up the wrong way. He once sold a London crook a Rolls-Royce which turned out, in reality, to be a hire car. So it was no surprise when, in 1985, a hitman tried to shoot him at the pub he owned in Kent. Francis was lucky, turning away at the vital moment and the bullet hitting him in the shoulder. Some said that he was shot for not paying a chunk of the £100,000 jury-nobbling money.

In August 1990 Francis was found guilty of smuggling cocaine with a value of a million pounds aboard a private yacht. He was sentenced to 16 years. When he was released, he started a courier firm and moved into a large house in Bromley. He did not, at that time, seem to have been involved in any criminal activity.

But Francis lived by the sword and was pretty sure he would also die by it. Speaking to the *Daily Mirror* a few weeks before he was actually killed, he told the reporter that his old man had been a villain and he hoped that his kids would grow up to be villains. He talked about how he had lived by violence and was pretty sure he would also die by it. How right he was.

Early in the morning of 14 May 2003 he was shot four times in the face, back, arm and finger as he opened the gates of his haulage company, Signed, Sealed and Delivered. The gunmen hit him as he leaned back into the car to pick up a newspaper. He was found behind the wheel of his brand-new Rover 75 in Bermondsey in East London and the CCTV camera that normally covered the spot where the shooting took place had been moved so that it pointed away from the gates. Witnesses reported seeing four men driving away from the scene.

The following September, three men – Harold Richardson, John O'Flynn and Terence Conaghan – were arrested after it was claimed that Richardson had taken out a contract on Francis to avoid repaying a £70,000 debt that he owed him. O'Flynn and Conaghan, men with more than 60 convictions each, had carried it out, O'Flynn getting £30,000 and Conaghan £9,000. However, the jury rejected this theory, preferring the notion that Francis was killed purely and simply because he had not returned the £5 million from the Brinks Mat robbery that he had been given to look after. O'Flynn and Conaghan were sentenced to life and Richardson was acquitted.

The Brinks Mat curse was not finished yet. In March 1994 Colin Hickman, a 55-year-old solicitor specialising in civil litigation, answered a particularly persistent ringing of his doorbell. On opening the door, he was viciously attacked by a man wielding a knife. Hickman was stabbed 16 times in the head and chest and died as his attacker ran off, covered in Hickman's blood.

At the time, no one considered any connection with the Brinks Mat robbery. However, when, a year later, one of his business associates, Tim Caines, was charged with the murder, it emerged that Hickman had been about to go to the police to tell them about a series of fraudulent deals.

Caines admitted being at the house on the night that Hickman had been killed, but said that he had been forced to go there at knifepoint by a mystery man. Curiously, Hickman's partner Vera Phillips-Griffiths, who had run downstairs on hearing the commotion, described the attacker as six feet tall, blonde and white, while Tim Caines is five feet ten, dark-haired and black. Nonetheless, Caines was given life. In 2003 it emerged that Hickman and Caines had been involved in the laundering of large sums of money. That money had come from the Brinks Mat heist.

There have been nine murders so far, but police are not convinced we have seen the last of them. The curse of the Brinks Mat millions looks set to continue.

DESMOND NOONAN AND THE NOONAN FAMILY

'They [the police] reckon I am behind most of the murders in Manchester. I've got a bigger army than the police. We've got more guns than the police. Silly bastards. I am down for 25 murders. What a load of bollocks.'

Desmond Noonan is sipping at a bottle of beer in a pub in Manchester. He is a huge lad, six feet tall and weighing 20 stones, with a large round face and short, dark hair. The bottle seems tiny in his large hands. He is talking to film-maker and investigative journalist Donal Macintyre who is making a programme called *The Trials of Mr Lattlay Fottfoy*. Asked by Macintyre if he was indeed responsible for 25 killings, Noonan smiles, covers his mouth and says, 'No.' His brother Dominic – the Lattlay Fottfoy of the programme's title – then says it is actually 24 before Desmond Noonan holds up seven fingers and thumbs, indicating 27.

His brother Dominic adds: 'He's a good Catholic.' And Desmond says: 'I am a Catholic. I don't believe in a life for a life. I don't believe in taking life.'

Then the convicted armed robber laughs, adding with mock sincerity: 'I'm sorry. I want to say sorry to everyone.'

In the programme, Noonan goes on to boast chillingly about how he prevents witnesses from testifying against him. 'The police pressurise key witnesses to tell lies about us. In the end they see sense and don't come to court. Some can't go to court because they haven't got the bus fare. Some are deranged and delusioned because they are in the back of a trunk tied up! . . . That's a joke, by the way,' he adds. 'No one wants to hurt us at the end of the day. And if they did, by God there would be some fireworks.'

The programme would be aired four days later, but Desmond Noonan would not live long enough to see it. By the time his 15 minutes of fame arrived he was lying on a coroner's slab, dead of stab wounds.

Desmond Noonan, known to his friends as Dessie, was born in 1959 into a family where there would be 14 children in all, each bearing a name that began with the letter 'D'. Home was the infamous Manchester suburb Moss Side, one of the city's poorest areas, made up of row upon row of terrace housing and home to a large black community. In the 1980s and 1990s it was renowned for the large amount of crime and gang warfare that took place there and for serious rioting that would break out now and then. A lot of the crime involved Dessie Noonan and his two brothers, Dominic and Damian.

Dessie began his criminal career as a bouncer on the doors of Manchester clubs in the early 1980s. His immense size and strength made him a good one, too, and he started to gain a reputation as a hard man. Before long, he was putting his own men on doors across the city and by the late 1980s, 80 per cent of the security of Manchester's clubs and bars was under Noonan family control. Unfortunately, a 15-year stretch for taking part in a bank robbery put brother Dominic out of the picture for a while.

Damian Noonan and another brother, Derek, started to forge links with other notable Manchester gangs such as the Cheetham Hill Crew, and in Moss Side Dessie was supplying the black gangs with guns and other weapons. He fancied spreading his wings a little, however, and began to forge strong links with gangs in other British cities, London, Newcastle and Liverpool. He was also involved with the IRA in Northern Ireland and the AFA, a militant anti-fascist organisation.

In May 1988 he was convicted of perverting the course of justice and wounding. One charge involved 'making threats of violence and death toward prosecution witnesses and relatives in an attempt to stop evidence being given at court'. The witnesses were, in fact, police officers.

In 1991, the Noonans took control of organised crime in Manchester when rival gang leader Anthony Johnson, was murdered after taking part in a botched security van robbery. Known as White Tony because he was, bizarrely, the leader of a black drugs gang, he and three other men took around £360,000 from the van, but had to leave behind another million because they did not have sufficient transport to carry it away. It took police only a few hours to round up Johnson and his accomplices who took part in identity parades and were then released.

All that was found of the stolen money was £120, discovered in the Wendy House of a relative of a man called Craig Bulger. Bulger was charged with dishonestly handling the cash, but was furious that he was not going to be paid what he was due. He went to Desmond Noonan demanding his share, £80,000. Noonan informed him that there was only £40,000 left. Bulger told Noonan he was going to complain to White Tony. This did not please Dessie at all, as White Tony had previously threatened some Noonan men with a shotgun in 1991 while they were working on the door of the Hacienda Club.

A week later, Noonan was out driving one night with a man called Paul Flannery when he spied Anthony Johnstone, accompanied by an associate, Tony McKie, driving a white Ford Cosworth close to a pub called the Penny Black which Dessie part-owned. A gun was fired from Noonan's car and Johnstone took off, trying to escape over a wall. He was shot in the back and fell backwards before being finished off on the ground.

At the 1992 trial for Johnstone's murder, Damien Noonan was cleared of any involvement in the killing and, following a retrial, in February 1993, Dessie and Derek were acquitted after the jury failed to reach a verdict. Interestingly, over the next few years Desmond Noonan faced a number of convictions over jury-tampering and witness-nobbling.

By the mid-1990s Noonan was king of all he surveyed, a feared enforcer, with extensive links with the main players in Britain's underworld and, naturally, he wanted it to remain that way. However, in 1995 he was convicted of brutally beating twin brothers who turned out to be London gangland figures trying to elbow their way into the lucrative Manchester guns and drugs scene. Noonan was described as behaving psychotically during the attack and pleaded guilty to violent disorder and causing grievous bodily harm. He was sentenced to two years and nine months in jail.

By 2000 police estimated that the Noonans were connected to at least 25 gangland murders and countless robberies. They controlled security in cities the length and breadth of the United Kingdom and their criminal efforts were reckoned to have brought them earnings of at least eight million pounds.

One-time Kray associate Curtis Warren, London gangster Dave Courtney and Newcastle's crime supremo Paddy Conroy, all became involved with the Noonans in some way or another, showing the respect that they had accumulated and lending them even greater credibility. Dessie was connected to many leading IRA figures, especially Paddy Logan, a violent individual who once bit off the ear of an Ulster Loyalist at a press conference and who was later shot dead. It is rumoured, although it has never been proved, that, through those contacts, Dessie Noonan was involved in the bombing of Manchester city centre in 1996.

Nothing is forever, however, and Dessie was an alcoholic by the time Dominic was released from prison in 2002 to assume leadership of the family's activities. Then he was devastated when brother Damian was killed in a motorbike accident while on holiday in the Dominican Republic. As many as 18,000 people turned out for the funeral, one of the biggest gangland funerals ever staged in this country.

Dessie fell to pieces, became addicted to crack cocaine and went into a deadly spiral.

On the night of Friday, 18 March 2005, he had been drinking in the Parkside pub in the Wythenshawe area of Manchester. Around 11.30 p.m., his wife Sandra answered the phone. It was Dessie and he told her he had been stabbed and was in Merseybank Avenue in Chorlton. He asked her to get in the car and come and pick him up. When she got there, he was unconscious and she immediately dialled 999. It was too late, however. Dessie Noonan died of his wounds in the ambulance.

His funeral was not quite as big as that of his brother Damian, but more than 5,000 local people turned up to watch his body arrive at Chorlton Church in a horse-drawn hearse. There were 40 limousines, 30 security men and a 25-piece, kilted pipe band. Out of 'respect' and for safety, motorways, businesses and two Manchester high schools were closed. As the priest spoke and the top-of-the-range 'pieta' coffin was lowered into the ground, Dominic's mobile phone went off. It had also gone off while he was having a meeting with the undertaker; it was a death threat.

Derek 'Yardie' McDuffus was sentenced to life imprisonment at Preston Crown Court for the murder of Desmond Noonan. It is believed that Noonan had been using his violent reputation and family connections to force local drug dealers to supply him with free drugs and McDuffus had objected. A fight ensued and he had stabbed Dessie and thrown him out into the street where he bled to death.

Dominic said of his brother's death: 'Dessie was drunk at the time so we believe that someone took advantage of him. It was certainly not a robbery. He was a good lad. He helped a lot of people out. Everyone always turned to the Noonans to solve their problems. His death could be connected to a problem that he was involved in. Sandra is shocked. If people do not want to talk to the police then they can talk to us. He was a very funny guy and everyone is terribly upset. He was very well known and very well liked.'

McDuffus languishes in solitary confinement for fear of retribution by the Noonan family.

NICHOLAS VAN HOOGSTRATEN

Nicholas Marcel Hoogstraten, aka Nicholas van Hoogstraten, was born in 1945 in the seaside town of Shoreham-by-Sea, on England's south coast between Brighton and Worthing. He has been called by judges of various cases he has been involved in as a 'bully' and even a 'self-styled emissary of Beelzebub'.

His father was a shipping agent and he was educated at the local Jesuit school, leaving it at the age of 16 in 1962 to join the Royal Navy. Leaving the Navy after a year he launched his phenomenally successful business career as a property developer and landlord by selling his stamp collection for £1,000 and buying property in the Bahamas. He remains to this day an important philatelist. His own personal property portfolio, bought with some of his £500 million fortune, now boasts homes in Florida, St Lucia, Barbados, Cannes and Zimbabwe, a country he adores. In fact, he has described Zimbabwean

President Robert Mugabe as '100 per cent decent and incorruptible', a view not held by very many people around the world. He is less happy with Mugabe these days as the President has seized his estates in Zimbabwe as part of his land distribution programme.

Returning to Britain from his travels in the 1960s, van Hoogstraten began buying properties in Brighton and freeholds with sitting tenants in London's Notting Hill Gate. He was able to evict these tenants and refurbish the properties, making a fortune in the process. By 1968 he was being lauded as Britain's youngest millionaire, having built up a portfolio of some 300 properties. Nonetheless, controversy was never far away and he perhaps signalled what was to come when, aged 23, he spent four years in Wormwood Scrubs prison for ordering a grenade attack on the home of a Jewish clergyman, Reverend Braunstein, whose son owed him £2,000. In an interview in the *Sunday Times*, van Hoogstraten said: 'He wasn't a rabbi, he was only a cantor'.

He went to jail again for handling stolen goods and was rearrested as he left Wormwood Scrubs and sentenced to another 15 months for bribing prison officers to bring him in luxuries. Freed on appeal, he was, later that year, fined for forcible entry and conspiracy to cause damage.

By 1980 he was the owner and landlord of more

than 2,000 properties. However, the property boom of the 1990s, coupled with a battle with the Inland Revenue – he went into the *Guinness Book of Records* for owing more money to the Inland Revenue, £5 million, than anyone in British history – persuaded him to sell the majority of his houses and put his money into other areas, including mining in Nigeria and Zimbabwe.

In 1985 van Hoogstraten began the construction of Hamilton Palace, near Uckfield in East Sussex. This enormous neo-classical mansion was planned to be half a mile long and would be the biggest private house built in the 20th century. It was going to contain his collection of art and, in the east wing, a mausoleum for himself. The floors would be solid marble and the doors would be oak. Intricate detailing would add to the overblown extravagance of it all. Up to 2006 he had spent around £40 million and it was still a long way from completion.

Van Hoogstraten has been engaged in a long-running feud with the Ramblers Association – he describes ramblers as 'perverts' and 'the absolute scum of the earth' – over a footpath that crosses Hamilton Palace's land. For ten years he has padlocked gates, installed barbed wire and built across the path. He once snapped at a barrister representing the ramblers: 'You dirty bastard, in due course, you are going to have it.' He has never backed out of a fight, even at school, where he grabbed a chair-leg a nun was using to beat him and hit her with it. 'She never tried again,' he said.

Meanwhile, work stopped on Hamilton Palace several years ago and it now stands, something of a ruin, with rain pouring through its copper-domed roof. Instead of being the greatest country house project of the 20th century, it has deteriorated into, as one of the builders employed on the site described it as, 'the 20th century's greatest folly'.

Van Hoogstraten has always had a robust approach to doing business. A great fan of Margaret Thatcher – she made him 'proud to be English' – he believes in the survival of the fittest. He has been known to use dogs and enforcers to clear tenants out of his properties. He has even had staircases removed to chase them away. When a fire destroyed one of his houses, killing five people, he showed an especially callous disregard for them, describing them as 'lowlife, drug dealers, drug takers and queers – scum'.

Sixty-two-year-old father of six, Mohammed Raja was a slum landlord with a reputation for bad maintenance of his properties and more than 100 convictions against him for breaching regulations. He was born in Pakistan and moved to Brighton as a young man.

Van Hoogstraten claimed that the feud between them had begun 16 years previously when he had loaned Raja more than a million pounds to buy properties. However, van Hoogstraten held on to the deeds. The slump in property prices in the early nineties rendered Raja unable to repay the loans and van Hoogstraten threatened to change the locks on the properties. He wrote to tenants claiming that Raja had been declared bankrupt and that rent should from now on be paid to him.

In 1994 Raja began a civil action against van Hoogstraten, alleging that he had forged his signature on legal documents and accusing him of a breach of contract. In 1999 Raja escalated things, changing his case to one of alleged fraud. If the case was successful, van Hoogstraten would then face criminal proceedings and almost certainly go to prison for quite some time.

Van Hoogstraten decided he wanted to teach the man he called 'the Maggot' a lesson. He had met a man called Robert Knapp in Gloucester Prison a number of years before. Knapp had become an associate of van Hoogstraten who called him 'Uncle Bob', and he was delegated to take care of Raja. Knapp took on another ex-con, David Croke, to help.

Raja was well aware what he was dealing with, realising the danger of beginning proceedings against van Hoogstraten. Therefore, when his doorbell rang on the evening of 2 July at his home in Sutton, south London, he is likely to have picked up a knife on his way to answer it.

Raja's grandsons, upstairs at the time, reported later that they heard raised voices and then a loud bang. Running downstairs, they were horrified to find their grandfather covered in blood and in pain, clutching his chest. He shouted: 'They are Hoogstraten's men and they have hit me.' In his delirious state he then addressed his mother, who had died 14 years earlier, saying: 'Mum, they have hit me!' He had been stabbed five times and shot in the face at very close range with a sawn-off shotgun by Knapp and Croke who had first appeared in Raja's street disguised as gardeners.

It did not take a genius to work out that van Hoogstraten might be behind the killing. He had, after all, allegedly told Raja's son, Amjad: 'Your dad is a maggot. He does not know what I am. We pick thorns who are a pain and we break them.'

At the Old Bailey in July 2002, van Hoogstraten – in his words, 'the richest man ever to be tried at the Old Bailey' – claimed that, although he admitted he had wanted Raja harmed, he had not wanted Knapp and Croke to kill him; they had gone too far.

The two men were found guilty of murder and, as he sentenced them to life, Mr Justice Newman said that they were 'plainly very dangerous men indeed. It is the place of everyone to consider what brings men to take a sawn-off shotgun and a knife to an elderly man and, having stabbed him fatally, to shoot him in the head at a range of 6–12 inches. In this case, no remorse between the stabbing and the shooting, no hesitation, simply delay, simply to reload the shotgun. No holding back in the presence in the house of the grandsons, no apparent concern for the horror they had to witness, no remorse in this court, no motive to the killing, save one, greed, greed for some money or the receipt of favours.'

In the case of van Hoogstraten, there were some strange goings-on. Firstly, another associate of his, Michael Hamdan, who was due to give evidence in the trial, fled to Lebanon, apparently in fear of his life. It had been Hamdan who had implicated van Hoogstraten in the murder but he claimed that van Hoogstraten had made it clear to him that he would never be able to give his evidence and, if he did, and van Hoogstraten did go to jail, Hamdan and his family would die. Naturally, van Hoogstraten denied it all.

Then, Tanika Sali, van Hoogstraten's girlfriend, refused to testify for the prosecution after saying she would. She retracted her police statements and, in spite of warnings about the consequences, would not say why she no longer wanted to go into the witness box. It was noticed when she arrived at the court, however, that she was wearing an expensive new outfit. She claimed friends had purchased it for her.

Van Hoogstraten, dressed in expensive casual clothes, gave evidence for several days, during which he denied paying Knapp £7,000 to carry out the hit. He alleged that Hamdan was, himself, in dispute with Raja and was attempting to frame him for the killing. He admitted that he had a terrible temper and had threatened violence and even death in the past to people who had crossed him. He reminded the court that 'there have been no dead bodies'. It emerged during the trial that, although he was a multi-millionaire, when police searched his home they found teabags drying on a draining board ready to be used again and testament to van Hoogstraten's legendary meanness.

It took the jury of six men and six women 37 hours and 49 minutes to reach a verdict, not of murder but of manslaughter, and by a verdict of 11 to one. He was sentenced to ten years in prison. In July 2003, however, he was given leave to appeal and his sentence was sensationally overturned due to a flaw in instructions to the jury during the trial.

As soon as he emerged from prison, the Raja family mounted a civil action in which they were awarded £6 million. Naturally, he counter-sued and refused to divulge his assets. Anyway, by this time, he had set up trust funds for his five children who had basically become walking banks for him.

The judge found 'that the recruitment of the two thugs was for the purpose of murdering Mr Raja and not merely frightening or hurting him' when he awarded the six million to the Rajas. High Court judges ordered him to pay £500,000 interim costs, but he refused and stated defiantly that the Rajas would 'never get a penny'.

The man who says that people who live in council houses are 'worthless and lazy' and who believes that 'the only purpose in creating great wealth like mine is to separate oneself from the riff-raff' continues to manage his business affairs, training his son Rhett to take over from him one day. In a recent interview he said: 'It's a difficult task because I keep everything close to my chest, nothing's in writing, there are no records of anything.' Hardly surprising, really.

THE CLERKENWELL CRIME SYNDICATE

The target walks down the street, perhaps stopping at a flower stall to buy a bouquet for his wife, or at a news-stand to grab a copy of the evening paper. The noise of city traffic echoes all around him. But, above that sound, there is a persistent, high-pitched engine noise, coming ever closer. Curious, he turns around, just as a high-performance trail bike skids to a stop just behind him. There are two men on it, the driver and a pillion rider, bodies swathed in dark leathers and large crash helmets, visors down, covering their heads and faces. The passenger quickly, but carefully, swings his leg over the seat and dismounts. His hands are by his side. One of them holds a gun. The target does not even have time to think. The leather-clad man takes two steps towards him, raises the gun and fires several times into the target's temple at almost point-blank range. Before the target's body has even hit the ground, the pillion rider is back on the bike and it is speeding away down the street, engine screaming as it climbs rapidly up through the gears.

The Adams Family has struck again.

In the days before 10 Downing Street became his home, Tony Blair could be regularly seen skipping down the path of his Islington home, through a scrum of newsmen and photographers into a waiting limo. However, if you had stepped out of Richmond Crescent, where the Blair house was situated, skirted the eastern perimeter of Barnard Park and crossed Barnsbury Road, you would have arrived just a short distance away from the future Prime Minister's house, on the Barnard Estate, home of another famous family – possibly Britain's most notorious crime family since the war – the Adams Family.

Islington is now one of London's premier residential areas, an easy journey away from the bustle of the City or the West End. Houses shift for exorbitant sums and you have to have a very healthy bank balance to consider moving there. It has not always been thus, however. The area has traditionally been the patch of heavyweight London criminals like the Nashes, the Regans and the Smiths, gangs that were so tough even the Krays and the Richardsons gave them a wide berth in the 1960s.

The Adams parents, Florence and George, live there

still, in a council flat, with walls festooned with pictures of their 11 children. The family, not all of whom are involved in criminal activities, have mostly moved away, the dodgier elements to Spain or to prison. However, during the 1980s and 1990s they ruled a drug empire that brought them wealth beyond their wildest dreams. It also brought violence and death.

In the beginning, Terry, the oldest, and his brothers, Patsy, born in 1955 and Tommy, born in 1958, were just local Catholic lads involved in petty, small-time crime. They were as far removed from the big league as it is possible to be. They extorted money from traders and stall-holders working street markets in Clerkenwell, gradually moving into armed robbery for which Patrick Adams went to prison for seven years. Their fortunes changed, however, when they took on a local gangster and won, grabbing control of a number of his drinking dens. As money began to roll in, they expanded their interests into clubs and bars, places where drugs could be sold. At the time, cocaine and cannabis were the drugs of choice of London's clubbers. Later they would move on to ecstasy.

The vast sums of money they earned presented problems. They had to find new and innovative ways to launder it, surrounding themselves with corrupt financiers, accountants, lawyers and other professionals to help them clean their cash before it could be invested in property and legitimate businesses. They also used Hatton Garden, London's jewellery quarter, working in particular with the diamond merchant Solly Nahome.

Glasgow hitman Paul Ferris once explained how the Adams Family worked. There was no one boss, although Terry Adams, as the oldest, often seemed to hold more power than the others. One detective described it as being run like a business, the leaders acting like a board of directors, making decisions for the entire team.

The secret of their success was undoubtedly the air of violence that hovered over them and attached itself to their name. The Adams name was so potent that they were known to have franchised it out to other criminals who used it in difficult situations. Just the mention of a connection to the hardest team in London had a habit of making problems go away.

They were responsible for numerous hits – some say 25 – and are credited with the dubious honour of inventing the notorious 'two-on-a-bike hit', although Griselda Blanco, the notorious Colombian criminal, is also credited with its invention. A bike pulls up; the passenger dismounts, pulls out gun and shoots the victim who has no idea where they have come from. The perpetrators cannot be recognised because, of course, they are wearing motorcycle helmets and they make their getaway at speed, almost before anyone realises what has happened. It is reckoned that the Adams Family killed at least 20 people using this method.

Amongst the killings with which they have been linked are pub accountant Terry Gooderham, suspected of stealing £250,000 from the Family. He went to meet Adams Family members in Epping Forest in 1989 with his girlfriend, Maxine Arnold. Their bodies were later found in his Mercedes. Contract killer Jimmy Moody may have been brought in to help out. The story goes that Gooderham begged them not to shoot him in front of his girlfriend. The killer obliged by shooting her dead first.

Then there was Irishman Tommy Roche. Roche had offered to act as a go-between in a drug deal, but the Adams brothers feared that he had given information to their rivals in the deal. He was shot through the heart by a motorcycle hitman in 1993 while working for a road repair firm near Heathrow.

After Terry Adams was finally sent to prison, one former henchman described the extent of the Adams brothers' capacity for violence. 'If they liked you,' he said, 'life was good. If you fell out with them, your life was over pretty quick.' He described how he went with the brothers to a club they owned, called Ra Ras, in north London. As another villain entered the club, one of the brothers nodded in the man's direction and said he had to go. No more was said, but the man never made it home that night. He was stabbed to death en route.

On another occasion, David Mackenzie, a money-launderer for the Family, made some bad investments and lost them £1.5 million. In April 1997 Terry Adams' brother-in-law John Potter summoned him to a meeting at his house. As soon as Mackenzie came through the front door, an Adams enforcer grabbed him. For 20 minutes he was kicked, beaten and slashed with a Stanley knife. By the end, the room was soaked in blood and Mackenzie's left ear and nose were hanging off. But he survived and two years later faced his attacker in court, Christopher McCormick. However, in spite of the fact that Mackenzie's blood was found on his jacket, McCormick walked free from court, laughing and inviting the jurors to the pub across the road for a drink.

The Adams brothers are no strangers to firearms, either. Mickey, the youngest, was convicted of possession of a firearm in the mid-1980s, and a number of years ago, a dispute with another crime family, the Rileys, escalated into an all-out gunfight in Finsbury Square in London. Fortunately, there were no casualties.

Unlike the Krays and some others, the Adams boys shun the limelight. No West End clubs for them . . .

unless they own them of course and, even then, it is strictly business. Former armed robber, turned journalist, John McVicar, wrote about them in an article in 1987 and,not long afterwards received a 'friendly' warning from the Family not to do it again. He failed to listen, however, and put pen to paper in 1992 in a piece that described the shooting of East End enforcer 'Mad' Frankie Fraser in Clerkenwell the previous year, a shooting long thought to have been carried out by the Adams Family. He received another visit from an Adams associate, but when he apologised he was informed that it might be wise to get some insurance and avoid any trail bikes that might be in his vicinity.

Patrick Adams is the muscle of the gang and is considered to be one of the most violent criminals in Britain. It was Patrick who dreamed up the motor-bike method of hitting people and he is suspected of at least 25 crime-related deaths over a period of just three years. It is also Patrick who is thought to have tried to eliminate Frankie Fraser in 1991. His violence appears to know no boundaries. In the late 1990s he is said to have sliced off a part of his own son's ear in the course of a drug deal. Behaviour like Patrick's does not earn you many friends and his villa in Spain, just south of the resort of Torremolinos, is surrounded by a high wall and bristles with security cameras.

Each brother has his role. Tommy acts as financier.

Cleared in 1985 of laundering gold bullion from the infamous Brinks Mat robbery, he now lives in Spain. Tommy is a fixer and has established connections with other criminal organisations such as the Yardies, as well as gaining a reported $80 million credit line from the Colombian drug cartels. He went to jail in 1998 for smuggling £8 million of hashish.

Terry Adams is said to be a man of sophisticated tastes. He is a collector of antiques, wine and classic cars, and lives in a large house in Finchley in north London. However, he claimed to have retired from criminal activity in 1990. This was confirmed several times on tapes recorded by bugs planted by MI5 in a number of rooms in Terry's home. Having less to do at the end of the Cold War, the spooks had turned their attention to organised crime and a secret squad was assembled to work on the downfall of the Adams Family. What they heard was Terry telling his adviser, Solly Nahome, that he was legitimate these days.

His income tax was not legitimate, however. When the Inland Revenue started asking questions about the £2 million house in which he was living and the antiques and classic cars he owned, he provided them with a list of occupations, including jeweller and PR executive. When he was eventually arrested in 2003, he was in possession of art and antiques with a value of more than £500,000 and jewellery worth tens of thousands of pounds. He had £59,000 in cash in the house. In March 2007 he was sentenced to seven years in prison and ordered to pay £4.7 million in legal fees to three law firms – it made up for the free legal aid he had received during his trial.

Several of the Adams Family's associates came to sticky ends. Gilbert Wynter, who walked with a limp following a collision with a police car in 1992, was a much-feared individual who worked for them as an enforcer. He claimed to be the son of an African princess and used African oils to ward off evil. He is thought to have been responsible for a long line of murders sponsored by the Adams brothers. One was the former British high-jump champion Claude Moseley, who got into trouble in 1994 over a drugs deal. Wynter stabbed him with a samurai sword, almost cutting his body in half. When a witness withdrew his statement, Wynter walked free.

Wynter disappeared in 1999, about the same time that Adams Family financial adviser Solly Nahome was gunned down by a man on a motorbike outside his Finchley home. One theory suggests that Nahome and Wynter were double-crossing the Adamses and were punished for it. Others say that Wynter was Nahome's assassin and he staged his own disappearance immediately after the shooting. Another story has it that Wynter had been asked to collect a van in

Islington. It was raining and he did not want the expensive suit he was wearing to get wet. He climbed into the van backwards, closing the umbrella, not noticing that there was someone waiting for him, ready to kill him. It is said that his body lies buried in the foundations of the Millennium Dome.

The Adams Family once seemed invulnerable, immune to police investigations. They were said to have senior police officers in their pay and seemed able to tamper with juries at will. In recent years, however, they have been in disarray. As well as Terry's incarceration, Tommy was sent down for seven years for supplying cannabis and cocaine and for possession of a revolver. After being sentenced he was led, laughing, from the dock. During the trial, when the judge had ordered him to surrender some of his profits or face spending a further five years in prison, his wife had twice arrived in court with a case filled with £500,000.

Are the Adams Family finished? It's unlikely.

PART NINE

WOMEN KILLERS

BELLE GUNNESS

At close to six feet tall and weighing in at more than 14 stone, Belle Gunness was a big woman, a big woman who killed at least 20 people and is estimated by some commentators to have actually dispatched close to 100, a number of them – in particular her own immediate family – killed for insurance policies.

Although, like most details of her life, knowledge about Belle's birth is sketchy, most agree that she was born as Brynhild Paulsdatter Størseth, in Selbu in Norway in 1859. While still a young woman in Selbu, an incident is said to have occurred that was to change her personality, and her life, forever. It seems she got pregnant, although we do not know who the father was. Attending a dance, she was attacked and kicked in the stomach, losing her baby. Belle was never the same again and resolved to go to America to seek her fortune, as her sister Nellie had done some years previously. She worked for three years as a servant and saved enough to pay her passage to the New World.

She left Norway in 1881 and, at this point, changed

her name to the more American-friendly 'Belle'. In the beginning she worked, as she had in Norway, as a servant, but she was very ambitious and always wanted more.

In 1884 she married a man called Mads Albert Sorenson in Chicago. They opened a confectionery store, but it proved a flop. A year after it opened it mysteriously burned down. According to Belle a kerosene lamp exploded, but no evidence was found to support that claim. Nonetheless, the insurance money was paid out.

They used the insurance money to buy another house, in the suburb of Austin, but in 1898 that, too, burned down. Once again, the insurance money for that went towards the purchase of another house.

Insurance was proving pretty lucrative to the money-hungry Belle and she picked up even more when her husband Mads died suddenly in July 1900, coincidentally the day that two insurance policies overlapped. The doctor initially suspected that his death was due to strychnine poisoning, but he had been treating Mads for an enlarged heart and eventually concluded that he had died of heart failure. Luckily for Belle, there was no autopsy.

Belle's in-laws were both appalled and suspicious when she applied for the insurance money just one day after Mads' funeral. It was $8,500, a tidy sum in those days. Whispers began that she had poisoned him and they started to agitate for the body to be exhumed and an inquest to be carried out. It is unclear whether this actually happened, but what is known is that the insurance companies coughed up yet again and Belle bought a farm just outside the town of La Porte in Indiana into which she moved with her children in 1901. Some researchers assert that the couple actually had four children but two, Caroline and Axel, had died in infancy of acute colitis. Interestingly, the symptoms of that illness match perfectly the symptoms of many forms of poisoning. Needless to say, both children had been insured.

Shortly after she moved in, there was the customary fire. The boat and carriage houses were destroyed and Belle collected more insurance money.

She met Peter Gunness and married him in April 1902, but tragedy struck when his young daughter died of unknown causes just one week after the wedding. When she died, she had been alone in the house with Belle. And then, before too long, it was time for Peter Gunness to take his leave. His demise was extremely suspicious, especially to the neighbours who began a whispering campaign against Belle. According to her, he was working in the shed when a heavy part of a sausage-grinding machine fell off a shelf above him onto his head, splitting his skull open, killing him and earning Belle $3,000 in insurance. The neighbours found it hard to believe that Gunness could have made such a mistake and the district coroner who reviewed the case announced that he thought Gunness had been murdered. An inquest was convened to investigate the death. Matters were made worse when Jennie, one of Belle's children told a friend at school that her mummy had 'killed her poppa with a cleaver'.

The child denied having said this when she was brought before the inquest and Belle swayed the jurors herself with a bravura performance in the dock, playing the role of a woman left all alone to bring up her family. It helped that she was heavily pregnant and she was released.

Rather than remarry immediately, she now hired a series of men to help run the farm, and by 1906 a man called Ray Lamphere was installed as her handyman. Around this time, Jennie, the child who had given evidence at the inquest, disappeared, Belle explaining that she had gone to a Lutheran college in Los Angeles. Needless to say, Jennie had actually been killed.

Belle decided that she was now ready for marriage again and placed an advert in a number of newspapers, saying:

PERSONAL – comely widow who owns a large farm in one of the finest districts in La Porte County, Indiana,

*desires to make the acquaintance of a gentleman equally
well provided, with view of joining fortunes. No replies by
letter considered unless sender is willing to follow answer
with personal visit. Triflers need not apply.*

It should probably have read: 'Anyone wanting to
survive need not apply.'

Well-off suitors started to arrive at the farm and
almost as quickly disappear. John Moo came from
Elkhart Lake, Wisconsin, willing to pay off Belle's
mortgage in exchange for wedded bliss. He disappeared a week after arriving. George Anderson,
another Norwegian immigrant, from Tarkio, Missouri,
wisely did not bring his money with him, but, although Belle had turned out to be not quite as
attractive as he had hoped, he agreed that he would
pay off her mortgage if they married. He would return
to Tarkio, get the money and come back and marry
her. That night, he awoke in the farm's guesthouse to
see Belle standing by his bed with a strange, sinister
expression on his face. He let out a yell and she fled
from the room, almost dropping the candle she was
carrying. Anderson leapt out of bed, put his clothes
on as quickly as he could and ran for his life down the
country road that led to La Porte, all the while expecting her to come after him. In La Porte, he jumped on
the first train to Missouri.

Nevertheless, they kept flooding to the farm, lonely, middle-aged and older men with sizeable wallets. But none of them ever left. A widower from Iola, Wisconsin, Ole B. Budsburg was seen at the La Porte Savings Bank on 6 April 1907. There, he signed over the deed to his land in Wisconsin and walked out with several thousand dollars in his wallet. When his sons found out where he had gone, they wrote to Belle, enquiring about his whereabouts. She wrote back saying she had never seen him.

Puzzlingly, Belle began to have large trunks delivered to the farm which she manhandled herself. The shutters of the house were shut all day and night, and at night Belle could be seen digging away in the pig-pen. Passers-by noticed that there was a lot of digging at the farm, some of it done by Lamphere.

The suitors kept arriving . . . and disappearing. Andrew Helgelien turned up after an amorous correspondence with the widow Gunness. He brought with him his total savings of $2,900. A few days later, Gunness began to visit the bank to make deposits, firstly of $500 and then $700.

But things were starting to go wrong. Ray Lamphere was in thrall to Belle, deeply in love with her. He would do anything for her and was insanely jealous of the men who came with the intention of marrying her. Things became fraught between them and she fired Lamphere.

Then, possibly worried that he would go to the authorities and tell them what she had been up to, she made an appointment at the courthouse in La Porte. There, she declared that Lamphere was not right in the head and represented a danger to the public. They summoned Lamphere to a hearing but found him to be of sane mind. Unperturbed, Belle had him arrested a few days later for trespassing.

Lamphere began to threaten Belle with exposure, even confiding in one farmer that Helgelien would not be a problem; 'We fixed him for keeps,' he said.

They may have 'fixed' Helgelien, but his family were troubled by his disappearance and his brother, Asle, wrote to Belle. When she replied, saying that he had probably gone to Norway to visit family, Asle did not believe her. He said that he believed his brother was actually still in the La Porte area. She persuaded him that if he came to La Porte and instigated a manhunt, it could be expensive for him. He delayed his visit for some months.

Belle began to panic. There were now two people who could, conceivably, expose her and send her to the gallows. She took steps to neutralise one of them, informing a lawyer – not the police – that Lamphere had threatened to kill her and burn her house down. She told him she wanted to make a will and left everything to her children. She then went to the bank and paid off her mortgage, having withdrawn all her money.

A man called Maxon, who had replaced Lamphere at the farm, awoke on the morning of 28 April with the smell of smoke in his nostrils. The house was on fire. He screamed Belle's and her children's names, but there was no response. Flames blocking his escape down the stairs, he jumped from the window of his room which was on the second floor and ran to town to get help. But by the time they arrived at the farmhouse it was little more than a smouldering ruin. They searched the property and found four bodies in the cellar. One, that of a woman, was headless and so could not be positively identified as Belle, although it was presumed to be her. The bodies of her children were lying next to her.

Lamphere was, of course, suspected and was picked up immediately. Unfortunately for him, a witness was found who said that he had seen Lamphere running down the road from the farm just before the fire broke out. He was charged with murder and arson. Meanwhile, the sheriff and his deputies began a careful search of the ruins, looking for evidence.

Was it the body of Belle Gunness that was found? When the remains were measured, it strangely proved to be the corpse of a woman only five feet three inches tall, eight or nine inches shorter than Belle. Further complicating matters was the fact that she weighed just under eleven stones, some three stones lighter than Belle. Either being burnt to death is very slimming or this was not Belle Gunness. Her friends certainly did not think it was her. Several neighbouring farmers looked at the corpse and said it was not her. Some friends who arrived from Chicago said it could not be her. The La Porte clothiers who made her dresses and other garments categorically stated that it was not her.

Then the case was thrown wide open when the doctor examining the dead woman's internal organs found that she had died of strychnine poisoning.

However, on 19 May, Louis 'Klondyke' Schultz, who had been detailed to sift through the debris to try to find some dental evidence from the headless corpse, that would link it to Belle, discovered two human teeth. They were identified as two porcelain teeth and a gold crown on some bridgework that had belonged to Belle. That was enough proof for the coroner and at a subsequent inquest it was declared that the body found in the ruins was, indeed, that of Belle Gunness.

Meanwhile, Asle Helgelien had arrived on the scene, insisting that a search be carried out for his brother. On 3 May the first of a series of grisly finds was made – the body of Belle's daughter Jennie. Then, one after another, the bodies began to be pulled from the earth in the pig-pen – Ole B. Budsberg, Thomas Lindboe of Chicago, who had been one of Belle's handymen, Henry Gurholdt of Scandinavia, Wisconsin, who had brought $1,500 to Belle with the intention of marrying her, Olaf Svenherud of Chicago, John Moo, Olaf Lindbloom from Iowa and many more whose remains could not be identified. More than 40 men and children were discovered buried in shallow graves around the farm.

Ray Lamphere admitted to arson, but denied the murder of Belle and her children. He was found guilty of arson, but acquitted on the charge of murder and was sent to jail for 20 years, dying in prison in 1909.

He made a deathbed confession, claiming that, although he helped Belle to bury a number of her victims, he had not taken part in their murders. He explained her method. She would welcome her guest with a hearty meal and a cup of drugged coffee. When the man had fallen asleep she would come up behind him and split his head with a meat cleaver. Or sometimes she would chloroform her victim when he was in bed asleep before carrying the body to the basement where she would dissect it. The remains were buried around the farm or sometimes they were fed to the pigs.

He also shed some light on the headless woman, explaining that she had been lured to the farm believing she was going to be Belle's housekeeper. But Belle, of course, had other plans for her. She had drugged her, killed her and cut her head off, throwing it into a nearby swamp. Then she chloroformed her children, suffocated them and put them in the basement. She dressed the woman in her clothing, set fire to the house and fled, leaving her false teeth behind. Lamphere had been part of the plan, but she had evaded him after the fire and disappeared.

He said that by this time she was rich. He estimated she had murdered 42 men and each of them had brought with him at least $2,000. By the time she disappeared, he reckoned that she had saved around $250,000.

Belle Gunness became an American Lord Lucan. Sightings were reported for decades. She was seen in Chicago, San Francisco, New York. She was reported to be living in Mississippi as a wealthy landowner. Nothing was proved, however.

Interest grew in her case once again, in 1931, when a woman named Esther Carlson was arrested in Los Angeles for poisoning a suitor, August Lindstrom, for money. Some said she looked like Belle, but before they could confirm whether or not it was her, up to her old tricks, she died while awaiting trial.

In November 2007 the body of Belle Gunness was exhumed. Tests are being undertaken to prove once and for all whether it was her body that was found without a head in the basement in Indiana all those years ago.

GRISELDA BLANCO, THE BLACK WIDOW

'If she owed you money, she'd kill ya. If you owed her money, she'd kill ya.' So said a retired Miami homicide detective of the woman who is possibly the most notorious and ruthless female criminal of all time – Griselda Blanco. Blanco can be said to have been the world's first female drug-trafficker and at the height of her success was estimated to be worth around half a billion dollars, money earned from the importation of vast quantities of cocaine into the United States. She was a drug-trafficking visionary, being the first to realise the vast potential of using a drug-smuggling bridge from Colombia to Miami and then New York. Even amongst the drug-traffickers of Medellin, probably the most dangerous criminals who ever lived, she stood out, a psychopath who took pleasure in killing and who introduced her sons into the business of drug smuggling. Not for nothing was she known as the 'Godmother of cocaine', but she also enjoyed another nickname, the 'Black Widow', as her husbands and lovers had a nasty habit of turning up dead in the morning.

One policeman involved in her case said that she may have been the most prolific killer of all time, having had hits carried out regularly in New York, Miami and Colombia. Her ruthlessness showed in the methods that were used. One man, arriving at Miami International Airport, was stabbed by one of her hitmen 19 times with a bayonet as he came through Customs. He survived but, probably wisely, refused to press charges.

Griselda Blanco was born in 1943 into abject poverty in the area of Santa Marta, in northern Colombia, on the Magdalena estate which belonged to a man called Blanco. The estate is close to the Guajiro Peninsula, home of the Wayuu tribe, an ethnic group so fierce that the authorities found it almost impossible to police the area. Senor Blanco was, himself, half Wayuu.

Griselda's mother worked as a servant on his estate and, as was often the case, she became pregnant by her boss. When the baby, Griselda, was born, Blanco gave her a few pesos, threw her off the estate, and they trudged off in the direction of the north Colombian seaport Cartagena. In the absence of work, Griselda's mother took to begging in the streets, using the baby as a means of tugging at people's heartstrings. Griselda's life consisted of begging and being beaten by her mother for the slightest thing as the pair wandered through the towns and cities of the north of the country, living in the worst slums and barely finding the means to survive. Men came and went and children inevitably followed.

At the age of 13, Griselda, a street urchin, but an expert beggar, made the friendship of a gangster by the name of Carlos Trujillo. Trujillo made his money from forging the requisite documentation to help illegal immigrants obtain entry to the United States. He worked mainly in Queens in New York where there was a burgeoning Colombian community, flying back and forth between there and Medellin in Colombia. Griselda moved in with him and before long she had taken advantage of his skill with forged documentation and had relocated to Queens.

By her early 20s Griselda had been working for a number of years as a pickpocket and forger. She had learned from Trujillo the tricks of the trade and was now adept at creating visas, green cards and passports. They had three sons – Dixon, Uber and Osvaldo, all of whom were born in Medellin. Suddenly, however, Carlos was taken ill. He was admitted to hospital in Queens with cirrhosis of the liver and hepatitis, dying not long after and leaving Griselda to run the business and bring up her boys alone. Needless to say, she was up for it.

She flew immediately to Medellin, hardly taking any time to mourn the father of her children. She planned to run the forgery business herself, but was keen to add another activity to her portfolio – cocaine-trafficking. It was a trafficker from Medellin, Alberto Bravo, who introduced her to the world of narcotics smuggling. But he lived to regret helping her when, after he had said something that annoyed her, she stuck the barrel of a loaded pistol in his mouth and pulled the trigger. It was one of the first of her many murders.

It was now 1971 and she was running her own drug-trafficking network, buying the drugs from any number of different sources and using mainly female mules to carry them into the United States. They are said to have worn lingerie designed by Blanco that was on sale in a boutique she owned in Medellin. The versions the mules wore, of course, were tailored slightly differently. There were pockets sewn into them in which could be secreted two kilos of cocaine. Before long, her lucrative business was pulling in some $8 million a month.

She was flying backwards and forwards from Medellin to Miami, but finally set up home in Miami in 1978. There she assembled a crew of ruthless assassins known as 'the Pistoleros'. To become a member was simple. You just had to kill someone and cut off a part of your victim's body as proof.

In Queens, around this time, homicide detectives were bemused by a string of corpses that all had one thing in common. They were bloodless. This was the handiwork of one of Griselda Blanco's Pistoleros, Roy Sepulveda, who became the father of her fourth son. He would render his victims senseless, hang them upside down, cut their throats and let the blood drain out of their bodies. It made sense – a body folds much better if it does not contain any blood. So, Sepulveda's victims could easily be folded over and stuffed into boxes that were dumped on the street to be discovered by horrified passers-by.

One of Griselda's most notorious actions was the Dade County Shopping Mall Massacre which was carried out on her orders in 1979. She had arranged to meet two drug suppliers to whom she owed a great deal of money at a liquor store. Of course she never had the slightest intention of paying the debt, sending instead two of her hitmen who arrived in a van advertising party supplies. Armed with automatic weapons the hitmen entered the store and shot dead their targets. But there were also two shop assistants present who had witnessed the murders. The hitmen pursued the two men through the shopping mall, spraying bullets in every direction and only succeeding in wounding the shop assistants. The police immediately identified Griselda Blanco as the number one suspect and a group was assembled called CENTAC, Central Tactical Unit. Its members were detectives from both New York and Miami and its sole objective was to nail Griselda Blanco.

By this time, however, the Black Widow had returned to Colombia where she owned vast tracts of land. They were aware that she still travelled back and forward between Colombia and Miami and became increasingly aware of the number of murders being committed by her Pistoleros in both Miami and New York.

In 1982, for instance, she ordered the death of one of her former enforcers, Chucho Castro, who had made the disastrous mistake of kicking one of her sons on the backside. Tragically, however, when her assassins pulled up alongside Castro's vehicle and opened fire, they missed their target, hitting instead his two-year-old son Johnny twice in the head and killing him. As one of the hitmen said later, Blanco was angry at first that they had missed Castro, but when she heard that they had killed the son, she was delighted and declared that they were even now. The same year as the child was killed, she ordered the execution of Alfredo and Grizel Lorenzo in their south Miami house. They owed her money for a drug transaction and were killed while their children were watching television in an adjoining room. When her men returned, informing her that they had killed the couple but left their three children alive, she was furious.

In the early 1980s Griselda succumbed to her own product and became a heavy cocaine user, reportedly spending $7 million on her growing habit. She used a powerful, smokable version of the drug known as bazooka, and began to behave more and more erratically. She spent a fortune on Eva Peron's diamonds and purchased a tea set once owned by the Queen. And now she was killing for fun, innocent strippers and topless dancers numbering amongst her victims. She once even shot a pregnant woman in the stomach. Her capacity for violence knew no limits. She ripped off her best friend for almost two million dollars and had her tortured and beaten before shooting her and having her thrown into a canal. She indulged in orgies – both lesbian and bisexual. She was known to cut the throat of her lovers after they had slept with her and she sported an emerald and gold-encrusted MAC-10 sub-machine gun.

She had a great many enemies, especially in Medellin where she had ripped off many of the people with whom she had done business. At one point, to put the numerous hitmen who pursued her off the scent, she had a coffin shipped back home, purportedly containing her remains.

As she got older and put on weight through her use of cocaine, she was reduced to forcing men to have sex with her at gunpoint. One of her hitman, Jorge Ayala, known as Riverito, was understandably hesitant when she asked him to be her lover. 'Everyone who fucks you winds up dead,' he candidly said to her. She began to develop a painkiller and tranquilliser habit and passed control of the day-to-day running of the business to her sons, although she still supervised them. She moved to the town of Irvine in Orange County, California and she lived there like an ordinary housewife with her fourth and youngest son who enjoyed the bizarre name of Michael Corleone Sepulveda, named after the character in *The Godfather*, a film she adored.

DEA agent Bob Palumbo had been on Griselda's case for years and he was the man who finally got to arrest her in February 1985. For months he had been trailing a team of Colombian hitmen who were pursuing her. When apprehended, they were found to be carrying a semi-automatic assault rifle equipped with a silencer and high-powered 9mm weapons. Shortly after that, she was arrested and extradited to Florida to face murder charges. Her former associate Riverito had connected her to 12 murders in Queens, 12 in Miami and everyone knew that there were also an unknown number in Colombia with which she would probably never be charged. Police estimates were higher, though. They thought that at least 40 murders had been committed by her or on her orders in the United States alone.

She was to be represented in court by one of America's highest-profile attorneys, Roy Black, famous for gaining an acquittal for Kennedy family scion William Kennedy Smith on a rape charge and for representing right-wing radio broadcaster Rush Limbaugh. However, to the disappointment of the case detectives, who had hoped that Blanco would receive the death penalty, the trial was postponed in extraordinary circumstances. It emerged that the principal witness for the prosecution, Jorge Ayala, aka Riverito, had been paying for phone sex, from a Witness Protection prison, with some secretaries at Miami-Dade State Attorney's office. There were understandable fears that the case was irredeemably compromised. Finally, in October 1998, state prosecutors were left with little option but to agree to negotiate a plea with Blanco's lawyers. She pleaded guilty to the murders of the Lorenzos and the killing of Chucho Castro's son in return for a sentence of 20 years in prison. She was 56 years old and had already suffered a heart attack while incarcerated awaiting trial and although prosecutors and police were disappointed, they thought that perhaps those 20 years would, indeed, be a life sentence. It was not to be, however. In June 2004, now weighing 196 pounds and no longer the good-looking woman of her youth, she completed her 20-year prison sentence and was deported to Colombia, a chilling prospect as three of her sons had been murdered on their return to their homeland after serving prison sentences and being deported.

There were rumours that Griselda Blanco's immense wealth had been salted away in structured money-laundering accounts in Panama, but after legal fees and the wreckless spending of her sons, no one knows how much was left when she climbed on board her flight to Colombia in 2004.

What became of her is also a mystery. Did she return to the business of narcotics-trafficking, or was she killed by someone with a long memory? As one website says, Griselda Blanco's current status is unknown.

Te Rangimaria Ngarimu

The name of Britain's first hitwoman rolls with some difficulty off the tongue – Te Rangimaria Ngarimu. In 1992, this 24-year-old New Zealander of Maori origin was living in Britain and working in a pub in north London. She was a bright, well-educated girl. A double first in chemistry from a university back home in New Zealand was testament to that. She had played hockey to a high standard, was a decent surfer and could speak fluent Japanese. And her confident, bubbly personality made her popular. Sparky, as they called her, was enjoying life to the full and planned to spend the next five years in the UK. Hopefully, she would save enough money to be able to return to New Zealand and buy her own mobile home.

In the course of her work she made the acquaintance of a couple of the pub's customers, 34-year-old Paul Tubbs from Enfield in north London and 21-year-old New Zealand-born Keith Bridges who lived in Camden. Sparky needed a place to stay and Bridges rented her a room in his flat where the two became good friends.

Tubbs and Bridges were co-owners of a roofing business with a man called Graeme Woodhatch. Strange things had been happening, however, and they were convinced that Woodhatch was fiddling them, stealing thousands of pounds from the business. When police later investigated Woodhatch and his business dealings, they discovered that he owed almost £1 million to a variety of creditors. You cannot owe that amount of money, still drive a Porsche and enjoy expensive foreign holidays without making a few enemies and Woodhatch had his share of people who would have liked something nasty to happen to him. Bridges and Tubbs got there first, however.

When Sparky told Bridges during a conversation at the flat that she had been a good shot with a gun back in New Zealand, he realised that she could be the answer to their prayers, a way of stopping Woodhatch from wasting all their hard work of the past few years.

When he talked about 'knocking off' Woodhatch, she readily agreed to do it for £7,000 – the total fee was £10,000, but Bridges was skimming off a three grand commission – and began to plan the hit.

Armed with a photo provided by Bridges, she followed her victim as he went about his daily business, getting to know what he looked like. When she found out that he did not have children, it made her feel easier about carrying out the hit.

Bridges also provided her with the murder weapon – a .22-calibre pistol. Sparky knew her guns and decided that hollow-tipped bullets would cause maximum damage to the intended victim. A hollow point, also known as a hollow tip, is a bullet that has a pit, or hollowed-out shape, in its tip, which causes the bullet to expand upon entering its target, thus decreasing penetration and disrupting more tissue as it travels through the target. Additionally, hollow-point bullets offer improved accuracy by shifting the centre of gravity towards the rear of the bullet.

So she now knew what the hit looked like and had the weapon with which she would carry it out. Only one question remained: where would be the best place to do it? Bridges gave her the ideal solution. Woodhatch was going into the Royal Free Hospital the following week for an operation for piles. What more anonymous location could there be for a hit than a hospital? People constantly coming and going with no questions being asked, lots of exits, everyone focused on their own problems. It couldn't be better.

Sparky bought the clothing that would form her disguise – a baseball cap, sunglasses, gloves and tracksuit bottoms. Her face would be hidden and her shape would be covered up. No one need even know she was a woman.

The first time she went to the Royal Free, in Pond Street in north-west London, she had to abandon the hit as she was unable to find the correct ward. When Bridges heard he was none too pleased and reminded Sparky that the only way she was going to get the money for the mobile home quickly was if she killed Woodhatch. She said later: 'I had always wanted one [a mobile home]. It cost about $30,000 (£10,000) back home. I thought about it all the time. It was the goal of my life.'

She returned to the hospital with this in mind and, on this occasion, asked a nurse for directions to the main male ward where Woodhatch was situated. She got into a lift with a mother and her child and two elderly women and pressed the button for the third floor. The doors slid shut and the lift began to climb. Arriving at her floor, she exited the lift, leaving the others in it, and entered the corridor leading to the ward. All of a sudden she realised she was enjoying a massive stroke of luck. There, in front of her, was the man she had come looking for. Woodhatch was leaning against a wall, speaking quietly into a telephone. As she approached him, he turned his back to her and she strolled past, nonchalantly. She felt in her handbag for the gun, turned and started to walk back in Woodhatch's direction. But just at that moment she could not go through with it. Her hand still in her handbag as if she was looking for something, she walked back to the lift and pushed the button to descend. Woodhatch was at this point no more than three feet away from her. She felt in her bag and flicked off the safety catch on the .22.

Quickly, in one movement, she pulled the gun from her bag and aimed it at her target. At that exact moment, Woodhatch noticed her but it was too late. As she squeezed the trigger he tried to protect his face with his hands, but the first bullet hit him smack in the middle of his forehead; the second ricocheted off his backbone and the third shattered his nose. A fourth hit him in the shoulder.

Sparky later described how she felt. 'Something just snapped inside and I did it. There were four shots, but I remember pulling the trigger only once. That first shot hit him in the face – he was facing towards me. I do not remember firing the other shots, although I heard four. I remember seeing him rolling around on the floor screaming. He had his hands on his face.'

Woodhatch did not roll around for long. By the time the fourth bullet entered his body he was well and truly dead.

As a man entered the corridor from the other end, the lift doors slid closed and Sparky was gone. She calmly strode out of the hospital entrance, ensuring she did not look as if she was in a hurry, thus drawing attention to herself. Just minutes after the hit, as people gathered round the body of Graeme Woodhatch on the third floor of the Royal Free, she was seated in the back of a taxi, adrenaline pumping through her body, on her way back to the Camden flat. At the flat, she wiped the gun of fingerprints and then removed all her clothes, stuffed them into a plastic bag and barked at Bridges to get rid of them.

There were no witnesses to the killing and .22 bullets are very small. So it took some four hours for the medical staff at the hospital to work out that Graeme Woodhatch had, in actual fact, been shot. They had tried to resuscitate him and his girlfriend had spent four hours with the body before it was taken away to be prepared for the mortuary. At this point they became suspicious about his facial injuries and, examining him closely, spotted the tiny bullet wounds. As was pointed out at the time, medical staff working in British hospitals were not accustomed to dealing with bullet wounds and they can be difficult to identify as they may not even bleed. However, the police did admit that had they known earlier that Woodhatch had been shot, they would have been able to launch their investigation earlier.

And it was going to be a difficult one. Twelve lifts near the scene of the hit, two fire escapes and three different public exits would complicate things for the police. But they did describe the hit as 'criminally professional', an opinion confirmed by a firearms expert examining the modus operandi and the type of weapon used – 'It is easily available, it fits in the palm of your hand, it is no louder than a cap gun and it does the job.'

Sparky's plan was to get out of the country as soon as she had carried out the hit and within only a few hours of the shooting she was at Gatwick, about to board a flight to New Zealand. Putting her hand in her pocket, as she waited to check in, she realised that she still had in her possession the photograph of Graeme Woodhatch that she had used to identify him. She found the nearest toilet, tore it up and flushed it away down the toilet. Then, panic, fear and paranoia set in. She stripped off all her clothing and changed into a fresh outfit.

Meanwhile, Paul Tubbs arranged for the disposal of the murder weapon, the bullets and the clothes Sparky had worn for the kill. A friend of his chucked it all into a lake. The murder was big news in Britain, the papers covering it on their front pages and the tabloids were having a ball investigating Woodhatch's shady dealings. Bridges sent the cuttings to Sparky who, by this time, was staying with a friend in New Zealand. He included a money order for £1,500. The cuttings brought her one brief moment of remorse when it was reported that Woodhatch's girlfriend was in fact pregnant. She must have felt better, however, on reading that Woodhatch had been due to appear in court a couple of days after he was killed, accused of threatening to kill a 22-year-old secretary employed by his company.

Although it was obvious that any number of people had the motive to kill Graeme Woodhatch, police immediately put Paul Tubbs and Keith Bridges at the top of their list of suspects. It was when they realised that the Maori woman with whom Bridges had been sharing a flat had flown back to the southern hemisphere on the day of the hit, that they began to really sit up. The information that she could handle a gun served to prick their interest more.

Metropolitan police officers left for New Zealand to have a word with Sparky.

Of course, she denied everything when they confronted her. She had the nerve to say that it could not possibly have been her who did it because she was a vegetarian and 'could not even kill a chicken'. They were unable to break her story in three interviews with her and flew home disappointed.

Sparky was a complex woman, however, and as it happens not as cold-hearted as contract killers have to be. In the next few weeks she seems to have 'found the Lord', as she announced it to friends, after reading a Bible given to her by her sister.

Back in London, police had arrested Bridges and Tubbs and charged them with the murder of Graeme

Woodhatch. For Sparky, it all suddenly became too much. Her guilt, made all the more concrete by her new-found religious feelings, overwhelmed her and she called the police, agreeing to return to Britain to face the music.

She was arrested as she left the plane at Gatwick and charged with the murder of Graeme Woodhatch. There was a tabloid feeding frenzy and she was labelled 'Britain's First Female Contract Killer'. She made her first appearance in court at Hampstead Magistrates' Court in north London and was stricken with remorse as she was remanded in custody. She turned Queen's Evidence against her co-conspirators, Tubbs and Bridges.

At her trial, her QC made much of her conversion to Christianity and the fact that she attended Bible classes and went to church on Sunday in Holloway Prison where she was being held. He also told the jury that she was teaching autistic children in prison. None of it made much difference, though. She was sentenced to life in prison.

Before Bridges and Tubbs could be brought to trial, Keith Bridges was mysteriously shot in the chest while out on bail. But the trial went ahead in December 1994 and they were found guilty of conspiracy to murder, also receiving life sentences.

MARY ANN COTTON

Mary Ann Cotton never made it down the aisle to marry her fifth sucker. Suspicions in the village were rife, there had been just too many deaths and too many insurance claims and this time there was the evidence of arsenic in Charlie's stomach. Fortunately for her latest lover the police decided to act and they arrested Mary Ann on suspicion of murder.

She was born Mary Ann Robson in 1832 in Murton, County Durham. The daughter of a miner, Mary Ann was devastated when her father was killed during her 14th year. She filled her life with the church and school, and stayed with her mother until she was 16, at which time she left home to become apprentice to a dressmaker.

By the age of 19 she was married to William Mowbray and expecting her first baby. Mowbray was a timekeeper whose employment involved the family moving home many times. Mowbray had four children by a previous marriage and together they had another four. However, by the time the family moved back to County Durham just five years later, four of their children were dead and a fifth one died soon after.

From County Durham the family moved to Sunderland, where two more of her children died, all reportedly of 'gastric fever'. Then her husband was struck down with the same symptoms and died a few days later. Luckily for Mary Ann, William Mowbray and all the children were insured with the Prudential and, as a result, she collected the handsome sum of £35.

Because the family had lived in so many different places and particularly as infant mortality in the 19th century was commonplace, no one was really suspicious. Left a widow with only one surviving child out of the eight, Mary Ann took up employment as a nurse. She started to flirt with one of her patients, a man by the name of George Ward, and they wasted no time in becoming man and wife.

The honeymoon was brief because George, at the age of 33 years, was struck down with gastric fever and Mary Ann pocketed another nice insurance payout.

Not one to let grass grow under her feet, Mary Ann set her eyes on a shipyard foreman by the name of James Robinson. James was a widower with five children and was flattered by the attention. She took the position as his housekeeper and six months later they were married, but not before three of his children had succumbed to the mysterious gastric fever. Mary

Ann comforted him and then became pregnant. Things were starting to look up, that was until her mother fell ill and asked Mary Ann to return home to look after her one remaining daughter. However, instead of helping the situation, Mary Ann bought some arsenic and killed her mother, returning to her husband with her nine-year-old daughter. This little girl met the same fate as her other siblings, writhing in agony – the official diagnosis was the same, gastric fever.

Mary Ann gave birth to her new baby, but within two weeks it was dead. Meanwhile, she nagged her husband to get himself insured, but James was not fooled and became suspicious of his new wife. When he found out that she had attempted to take out an insurance on his life behind his back, and that she had bled his accounts dry, he kicked her out. Luckily she left one child behind with James who had been fortunate enough to survive the attempts on its life. Foolishly, though, James failed to report his suspicions to the police, leaving Mary Ann Cotton to continue her murderous habits.

For a while Mary Ann earned a living by prostituting herself, that was until she met another widower called Frederick Cotton who had been left to raise two young boys. Mary Ann quickly seduced the lonely widower, and promptly got rid of his sister, who incidently had been kind enough to introduce them.

It wasn't long before Mary Ann found herself pregnant again but, instead of marrying Frederick, she went to work for Dr Heffernan feeling that he had better prospects. However, this relationship was brief because she had to leave in a hurry – but not without taking a few of his valuables – when he found out she was trying to feed him arsenic.

She ran back to Frederick Cotton and, still pregnant with his child, he agreed to marry her. What he didn't know was that the marriage wasn't legal because she had never divorced Robinson. She made sure that her new husband and all his children were insured and, as soon as a new suitor caught her eye, Frederick met the same fate as all the others – gastric fever!

Over the course of the next 20 years Mary Ann managed to kill indiscriminately despite the suspicions of her fellow villagers and physician. However, her last murder, her one remaining son, Charlie, raised enough suspicion for a doctor to carry out an autopsy and sure enough he found arsenic – plenty of it.

On 24 March 1873, Mary Ann Cotton had a hood placed over her head and a noose wrapped around her neck. As the trap door opened and she dropped, the fall failed to break her neck and she struggled and choked for a full three minutes before she finally fell still. Perhaps, some would say, fair punishment for all the suffering she dished out.